CW00497219

Autodesk® Revit® 2018.1
for Landscape Architecture

Learning Guide
Imperial - 1st Edition

Authorized Publisher

ASCENT - Center for Technical Knowledge®
Autodesk® Revit® 2018.1
for Landscape Architecture
Imperial - 1st Edition

ASCENT
CENTER FOR TECHNICAL KNOWLEDGE

Prepared and produced by:

ASCENT Center for Technical Knowledge
630 Peter Jefferson Parkway, Suite 175
Charlottesville, VA 22911

866-527-2368
www.ASCENTed.com

Lead Contributor: Martha Hollowell

ASCENT - Center for Technical Knowledge is a division of Rand Worldwide, Inc., providing custom developed knowledge products and services for leading engineering software applications. ASCENT is focused on specializing in the creation of education programs that incorporate the best of classroom learning and technology-based training offerings.

We welcome any comments you may have regarding this learning guide, or any of our products. To contact us please email: feedback@ASCENTed.com.

Contents

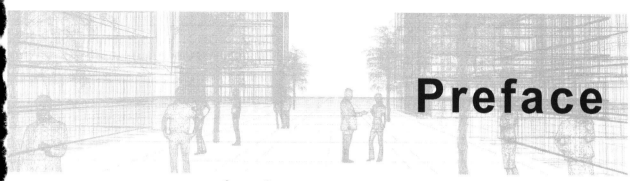

Preface

The Autodesk® Revit® software is a powerful Building Information Modeling (BIM) program that has allowed countless firms to incorporate the BIM workflow into their designs. As a key component of this workflow, Autodesk Revit allows landscape architecture firms to produce powerfully intelligent designs.

This second edition of the *Autodesk® Revit® 2018.1 for Landscape Architecture* learning guide is designed to teach you how to use the Autodesk Revit software, with a focus on creating and documenting full 3D project models for an urban environment, as well as how to use the internal topography tools and the Site Designer add-in extension. You begin by learning about the user interface and basic drawing, editing, and viewing tools. Then you learn how to create topographical surfaces and modify the topography using Autodesk Revit tools and Site Designer tools. From there, you move into modeling hardscapes using walls, floors, and stairs, and adding components such as trees, site furniture and planting areas. Finally, you learn the processes that take the model to the construction documentation phase.

Topics Covered

- Understanding the purpose of Building Information Management (BIM) and how it is applied in the Autodesk Revit software.
- Navigating the Autodesk Revit workspace and interface.
- Working with the basic drawing and editing tools.
- Starting a project based on Autodesk Revit models.
- Creating and modifying basic topography.
- Using Site Designer tools to modify topography with soft terrain features, sidewalks and curbs.
- Adding retaining walls, hardscape, stairs and other building elements.
- Placing components for plantings, furniture, and lighting.
- Setting up sheets for plotting with text, dimensions, details, tags, and schedules.
- Creating details.

Note on Software Setup

This learning Guide assumes a standard installation of the software using the default preferences during installation. Lectures and practices use the standard software templates and default options for the Content Libraries.

Students and Educators can Access Free Autodesk Software and Resources

Autodesk challenges you to get started with free educational licenses for professional software and creativity apps used by millions of architects, engineers, designers, and hobbyists today. Bring Autodesk software into your classroom, studio, or workshop to learn, teach, and explore real-world design challenges the way professionals do.

Get started today - register at the Autodesk Education Community and download one of the many Autodesk software applications available.

Visit www.autodesk.com/joinedu/

Note: Free products are subject to the terms and conditions of the end-user license and services agreement that accompanies the software. The software is for personal use for education purposes and is not intended for classroom or lab use.

Lead Contributor: Martha Hollowell

Martha incorporates her passion for architecture and education into all her projects, including the training guides she creates on Autodesk Revit for Architecture, MEP, and Structure. She started working with AutoCAD in the early 1990's, adding AutoCAD Architecture and Autodesk Revit as they came along.

After receiving a B.Sc. in Architecture from the University of Virginia, she worked in the architectural department of the Colonial Williamsburg Foundation and later in private practice, consulting with firms setting up AutoCAD in their offices.

Martha has over 20 years' experience as a trainer and instructional designer. She is skilled in leading individuals and small groups to understand and build on their potential. Martha is trained in Instructional Design and has achieved the Autodesk Certified Instructor (ACI) and Autodesk Certified Professional designations for Revit Architecture.

Martha Hollowell has been the Lead Contributor for *Autodesk Revit for Landscape Architecture* since its initial 2017 software release.

In this Guide

The following images highlight some of the features that can be found in this Learning Guide.

Link to the practice files

Practice Files

The Practice Files page tells you how to download and install the practice files that are provided with this guide.

Learning Objectives for the chapter

Chapters

Each chapter begins with a brief introduction and a list of the chapter's Learning Objectives.

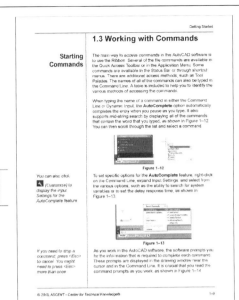

Instructional Content

Each chapter is split into a series of sections of instructional content on specific topics. These lectures include the descriptions, step-by-step procedures, figures, hints, and information you need to achieve the chapter's Learning Objectives.

Side notes

Side notes are hints or additional information for the current topic.

Practice Objectives

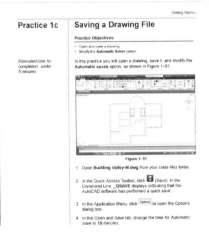

Practices

Practices enable you to use the software to perform a hands-on review of a topic.

Some practices require you to use prepared practice files, which can be downloaded from the link found on the Practice Files page.

Chapter Review Questions

Chapter review questions, located at the end of each chapter, enable you to review the key concepts and learning objectives of the chapter.

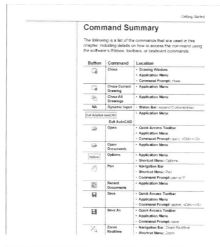

Command Summary

The Command Summary is located at the end of each chapter. It contains a list of the software commands that are used throughout the chapter, and provides information on where the command is found in the software.

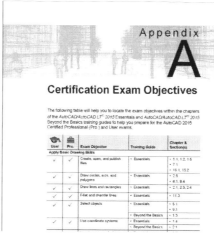

Autodesk Certification Exam Appendix

This appendix includes a list of the topics and objectives for the Autodesk Certification exams, and the chapter and section in which the relevant content can be found.

Icons in this Learning Guide

The following icons are used to help you quickly and easily find helpful information.

Indicates items that are new in the Autodesk Revit 2018.1 software.

Indicates items that have been enhanced in the Autodesk Revit 2018.1 software.

Practice Files

To download the practice files for this learning Guide, use the following steps:

1. Type the URL shown below into the address bar of your Internet browser. The URL must be typed **exactly as shown**. If you are using an ASCENT ebook, you can click on the link to download the file.

Address bar

http://www.ASCENTed.com/getfile?id=pilosus

File   Edit   View   Favorites   Tools   Help

2. Press <Enter> to download the .ZIP file that contains the Practice Files.

3. Once the download is complete, unzip the file to a local folder. The unzipped file contains an .EXE file.

4. Double-click on the .EXE file and follow the instructions to automatically install the Practice Files on the C:\ drive of your computer.

   Do not change the location in which the Practice Files folder is installed. Doing so can cause errors when completing the practices in this learning Guide.

http://www.ASCENTed.com/getfile?id=pilosus

Stay Informed!

Interested in receiving information about upcoming promotional offers, educational events, invitations to complimentary webcasts, and discounts? If so, please visit:

www.ASCENTed.com/updates/

Help us improve our product by completing the following survey:

www.ASCENTed.com/feedback

You can also contact us at: *feedback@ASCENTed.com*

Chapter

1

Introduction to BIM and Autodesk Revit

Building Information Modeling (BIM) and the Autodesk® Revit® software work hand in hand to help you create smart, 3D models that are useful at all stages in the building process. Understanding the software interface and terminology enhances your ability to create powerful models and move around in the various views of the model.

Learning Objectives in this Chapter

- Describe the concept and workflow of Building Information Modeling in relation to the Autodesk Revit software.
- Navigate the graphic user interface, including the ribbon (where most of the tools are found), the Properties palette (where you can make modifications to element information), and the Project Browser (where you can open various views of the model).
- Open existing projects and start new projects using templates.
- Use viewing commands to move around the model in 2D and 3D views.

1.1 BIM and Autodesk Revit

Building Information Modeling (BIM) is an approach to the entire building life cycle, including design, construction, and facilities management. The BIM process supports the ability to coordinate, update, and share design data with team members across disciplines.

The Autodesk Revit software is a true BIM product. It enables you to create complete 3D building models (as shown in Figure 1–1) that provide considerable information that is reported through construction documents, and to share these models with other programs for more extensive analysis.

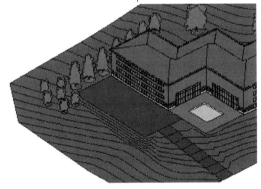

Figure 1–1

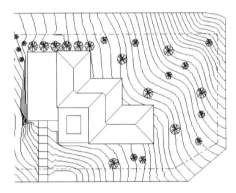

Figure 1–2

The Autodesk Revit software is considered a *Parametric Building Modeler:*

- *Parametric:* A relationship is established between building elements; when one element changes other related elements change as well. For example, if you add an element in a plan view, it displays in all of the other views as well.

- *Building:* The software is designed for working with buildings and the surrounding landscape, as opposed to gears or highways.

- *Modeler:* A project is built in a single file around the 3D building model, as shown in Figure 1–1. All views, such as plans (shown in Figure 1–2), elevations, sections, details, construction documents, and reports such as schedules are generated based on the model.

- It is important that everyone who is collaborating on a project works in the same version and build of the software.

Workflow and BIM

BIM has changed the process of how a building project is planned, budgeted, designed, constructed, and (in some cases) operated and maintained.

In the traditional design process, construction documents made of plans, sections, elevations, details, and notes are created independently. Sometimes, a separate 3D model is created as well. Changes made in one document, such as the addition of a light fixture in a plan, have to be coordinated with the rest of the documents in the set including updating the schedules, as shown in Figure 1–3.

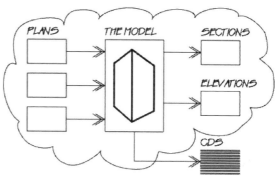

Figure 1–3

In BIM, the design process revolves around the model, as shown in Figure 1–4. Plans, elevations, and sections are simply 2D versions of the 3D model and schedules are a report of information stored in the model. Changes made in one view automatically update in all views and in all related schedules. Even Construction Documents update automatically with callout tags in sync with the sheet numbers. This is called bidirectional associativity.

By creating complete models and associated views of those models, the Autodesk Revit software takes much of the tediousness out of producing a building design.

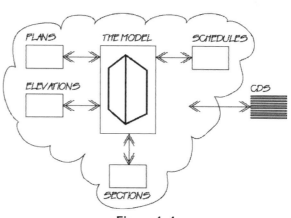

Figure 1–4

Revit Terms

When working in the Autodesk Revit software, it is important to know the typical terms used to describe items. Views and reports display information about the elements that make up a project. There are three types of elements: Model, Datum, and View-specific, (as shown in Figure 1–5) as described below.

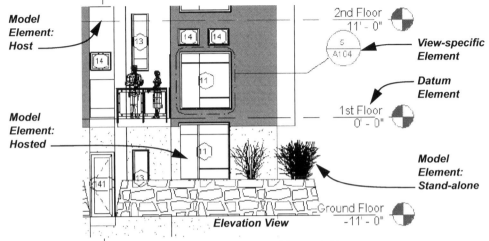

Model Element: Host

Model Element: Hosted

2nd Floor
11' - 0"

View-specific Element

Datum Element

1st Floor
0' - 0"

Model Element: Stand-alone

Ground Floor
-11' - 0"

Elevation View

Figure 1–5

Views	Enable you to display and manipulate the model. For example, you can view and work in floor plans, ceiling plans, elevations, sections, schedules, and 3D views. You can change a design from any view. All views are stored in the project.
Reports	Reports, including schedules, gather information from the building model element that can be presented in the construction documents or used for analysis.
Model Elements	Include all parts of a building such as walls, floors, roofs, ceilings, doors, windows, plumbing fixtures, lighting fixtures, mechanical equipment, columns, beams, furniture, plants and many more. • Host elements support other categories of elements. • Hosted elements must be attached to a host element. • Standalone elements do not require hosts.
Datum Elements	Define the project context such as the levels for the floors and other vertical distances, column grids, and reference planes.
View-specific Elements	Only display in the view in which they are placed. The view scale controls their size. These include annotation elements such as dimensions, text, tags, and symbols as well as detail elements such as detail lines, filled regions, and 2D detail components.

The software includes tools for architectural, mechanical, electrical, plumbing, and structural design.

Revit and Construction Documents

- Autodesk Revit elements are "smart": the software recognizes them as walls, columns, plants, ducts or lighting fixtures. This means that the information stored in their properties automatically updates in schedules, which ensures that views and reports are coordinated across an entire project, generated from a single model.

In the traditional workflow, the most time-consuming part of the project is the construction documents. With BIM, the base views of those documents (i.e., plans, elevations, sections, and schedules) are produced automatically and update as the model is updated, saving hours of work. The views are then placed on sheets that form the construction document set.

For example, a plan view of the model is duplicated to create a materials and layout plan. Then, all but the required categories of elements are hidden or set to halftone and dimensions are added. The plan is then placed on a sheet, as shown in Figure 1–6.

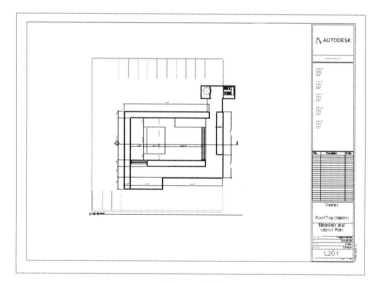

Figure 1–6

- Work can continue on a view and is automatically updated on the sheet.

- Annotating views in the preliminary design phase is often not required. You might be able to wait until you are further along in the project.

1.2 Overview of the Interface

The Autodesk Revit interface is designed for intuitive and efficient access to commands and views. It includes the Ribbon, Quick Access Toolbar, *File* tab, Navigation Bar, and Status Bar, which are common to most of the Autodesk® software. It also includes tools that are specific to the Autodesk Revit software, including the Properties Palette, Project Browser, and View Control Bar. The interface is shown in Figure 1–7.

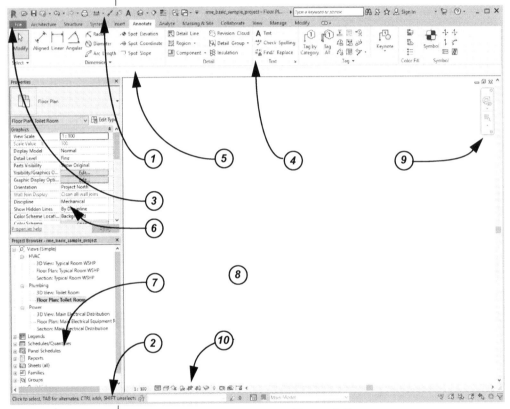

Figure 1–7

1. Quick Access Toolbar	6. Properties Palette
2. Status Bar	7. Project Browser
3. File Tab	8. View Window
4. Ribbon	9. Navigation Bar
5. Options Bar	10. View Control Bar

1. Quick Access Toolbar

Enhanced
in 2018

The Quick Access Toolbar (shown in Figure 1–8) includes commonly used commands, such as **Open**, **Save**, **Undo**, **Redo**, and **Print**. It also includes frequently used annotation tools, including measuring tools, **Aligned Dimension**, **Tag by Category**, and **Text**. Viewing tools, including several different 3D Views and **Sections**, are also easily accessed here.

Figure 1–8

Hint: Customizing the Quick Access Toolbar

Right-click on the Quick Access Toolbar to change the docked location of the toolbar to be above or below the ribbon, or to add, relocate, or remove tools on the toolbar. You can also right-click on a tool in the ribbon and select **Add to Quick Access Toolbar**, as shown in Figure 1–9.

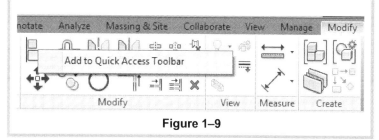

Figure 1–9

The top toolbar also hosts the InfoCenter (as shown in Figure 1–10) which includes a search field to find help on the web as well as access to the Communication Center, Autodesk A360 sign-in, the Autodesk App Store, and other help options.

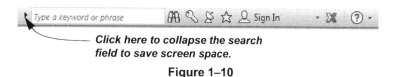

Click here to collapse the search field to save screen space.

Figure 1–10

2. Status Bar

The Status Bar provides information about the current process, such as the next step for a command, as shown in Figure 1–11.

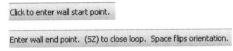

Click to enter wall start point.

Enter wall end point. (SZ) to close loop. Space flips orientation.

Figure 1–11

- Other options in the Status Bar are related to Worksets and Design Options (advanced tools), as well as selection methods and filters.

Hint: Shortcut Menus

Shortcut menus, accessed by right-clicking in the view window, enable you to smoothly and efficiently by quickly selecting commands. These menus include basic viewing commands, recently used commands, and the available Browsers, as shown in Figure 1–12. Additional options vary depending on the element or command that you are using.

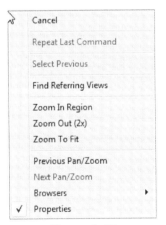

Figure 1–12

---

3. File Tab

The File Tab provides access to file commands, settings, and documents, as shown in Figure 1–13. Hover the cursor over a command to display a list of additional tools.

If you click the primary icon, rather than the arrow, it starts the default command.

Figure 1–13

- To display a list of recently used documents, click

  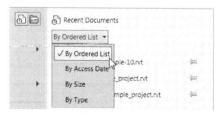 (Recent Documents). The documents can be reordered as shown in Figure 1–14.

Click ⚲ (Pin) next to a document name to keep it available.

Figure 1–14

- To display a list of open documents and views, click

  📁 (Open Documents). The list displays the open documents and each view that is open, as shown in Figure 1–15.

You can use the Open Documents list to change between views.

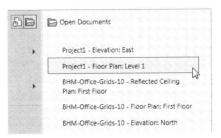

Figure 1–15

- Click 🗔 (Close) to close the current project.

- At the bottom of the menu, click **Options** to open the Options dialog box or click **Exit Revit** to exit the software.

4. Ribbon

The ribbon contains tools in a series of tabs and panels as shown in Figure 1–16. Selecting a tab displays a group of related panels. The panels contain a variety of tools, grouped by task.

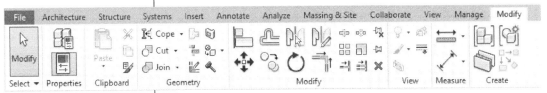

Figure 1–16

When you start a command that creates new elements or you select an element, the ribbon displays the *Modify | contextual* tab. This contains general editing commands and command specific tools, as shown in Figure 1–17.

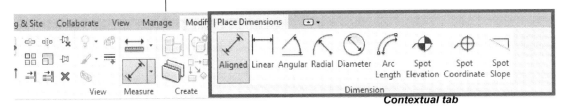

Contextual tab

Figure 1–17

- When you hover over a tool on the ribbon, tooltips display the tool's name and a short description. If you continue hovering over the tool, a graphic displays (and sometimes a video), as shown in Figure 1–18.

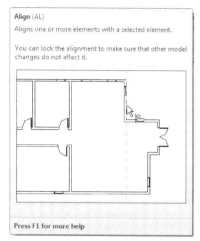

Figure 1–18

- Many commands have shortcut keys. For example, type **AL** for **Align** or **MV** for **Move**. They are listed next to the name of the command in the tooltips. Do not press <Enter> when typing shortcuts.

- To arrange the order in which the tabs on the ribbon display, select the tab, hold <Ctrl>, and drag it to a new location. The location is remembered when you restart the software.

- Any panel can be dragged by its title into the view window to become a floating panel. Click the **Return Panels to Ribbon** button (as shown in Figure 1–19) to reposition the panel in the ribbon.

Figure 1–19

Hint: You are always in a command when using the Autodesk Revit software.

When you are finished working with a tool, you typically default back to the **Modify** command. To end a command, use one of the following methods:

- In any tab on the ribbon, click ⌖ (Modify).
- Press <Esc> once or twice to revert to **Modify**.
- Right-click and select **Cancel...** once or twice.
- Start another command.

5. Options Bar

The Options Bar displays options that are related to the selected command or element. For example, when the **Rotate** command is active it displays options for rotating the selected elements, as shown at the top in Figure 1–20. When the **Place Dimensions** command is active it displays dimension related options, as shown at the bottom in Figure 1–20.

Options Bar for Rotate Command

Options Bar for Dimension Command

Figure 1–20

6. Properties Palette

The Properties palette includes the Type Selector, which enables you to choose the size or style of the element you are adding or modifying. This palette is also where you make changes to information (parameters) about elements or views, as shown in Figure 1–21. There are two types of properties:

- **Instance Properties** are set for the individual element(s) you are creating or modifying.

- **Type Properties** control options for all elements of the same type. If you modify these parameter values, all elements of the selected type change.

The Properties palette is usually kept open while working on a project to easily permit changes at any time. If it does not display, in the Modify tab>Properties panel

click 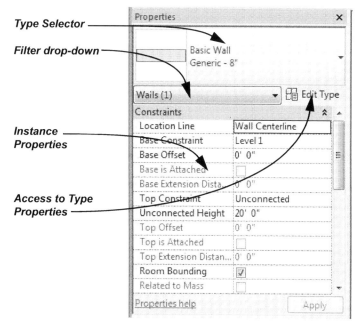 (Properties) or type **PP.**

Type Selector

Filter drop-down

Instance Properties

Access to Type Properties

Figure 1–21

Some parameters are only available when you are editing an element. They are grayed out when unavailable.

- Options for the current view display if the **Modify** command is active, but you have not selected an element.

- If a command or element is selected, the options for the associated element display.

- You can save the changes by either moving the cursor off of the palette, or by pressing <Enter>, or by clicking **Apply**.

- When you start a command or select an element, you can set the element type in the Type Selector, as shown in Figure 1–22.

You can limit what shows in the drop-down list by typing in the search box.

Search Box

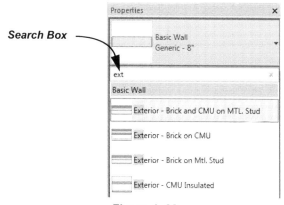

Figure 1–22

- When multiple elements are selected, you can filter the type of elements that display using the drop-down list, as shown in Figure 1–23.

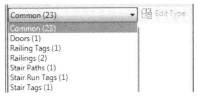

Figure 1–23

- The Properties palette can be placed on a second monitor, or floated, resized, and docked on top of the Project Browser or other dockable palettes, as shown in Figure 1–24. Click the tab to display its associated panel.

Figure 1–24

7. Project Browser

The Project Browser lists the views that can be opened in the project, as shown in Figure 1–25. This includes all views of the model in which you are working and any additional views that you create, such as floor plans, ceiling plans, 3D views, elevations, sections, etc. It also includes views of schedules, legends, sheets (for plotting), groups, and Autodesk Revit Links.

The Project Browser displays the name of the active project in the title bar.

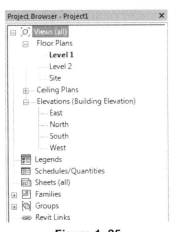

Figure 1–25

- Double-click on an item in the list to open the associated view.

- To display the views associated with a view type, click ⊞ (Expand) next to the section name. To hide the views in the section, click ⊟ (Contract).

- Right-click on a view and select **Rename** or press <F2> to rename a view in the Project Browser.

- If you no longer need a view, you can remove it. Right-click on its name in the Project Browser and select **Delete**.

- The Project Browser can be floated, resized, docked on top of the Properties palette, and customized. If the Properties palette and the Project Browser are docked on top of each other, use the appropriate tab to display the required panel.

How To: Search the Project Browser

1. In the Project Browser, right-click on the top level Views node as shown in Figure 1–26.

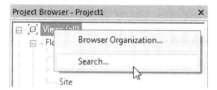

Figure 1–26

2. In the Search in Project Browser dialog box, type the words that you want to find (as shown in Figure 1–27), and click **Next**.
3. In the Project Browser, the first instance of that search displays as shown n Figure 1–28.

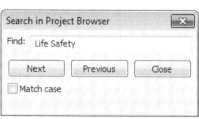

Figure 1–27

Figure 1–28

4. Continue using **Next** and **Previous** to move through the list.
5. Click **Close** when you are done.

8. View Window

Each view of a project opens in its own window. Each view displays a Navigation Bar (for quick access to viewing tools) and the View Control Bar, as shown in Figure 1–29.

In 3D views you can also use the ViewCube to rotate the view.

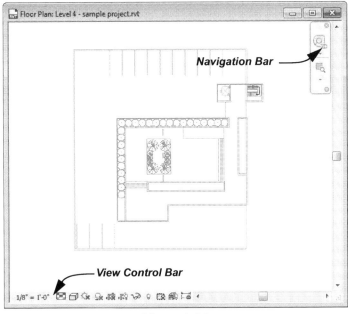

Figure 1–29

- To cycle through multiple views you can use several different methods:

    - Press <Ctrl>+<Tab>.
    - Select the view in the Project Browser.
    - In the Quick Access Toolbar or *View* tab>Windows panel, expand 🗗 (Switch Windows) and select the view from the list.

- You can Tile or Cascade views. In the *View* tab>Windows panel, click 🗗 (Cascade Windows) or 🗗 (Tile Windows). You can also type the shortcuts **WC** to cascade the windows or **WT** to tile the windows.

9. Navigation Bar

The Navigation Bar enables you to access various viewing commands, as shown in Figure 1–30.

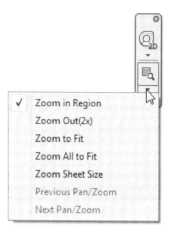

Figure 1–30

10. View Control Bar

The number of options in the View Control Bar change when you are in a 3D view.

The View Control Bar (shown in Figure 1–31), displays at the bottom of each view window. It controls aspects of that view, such as the scale and detail level. It also includes tools that display parts of the view and hide or isolate elements in the view.

Figure 1–31

1.3 Starting Projects

File operations to open existing files, create new files from a template, and save files in the Autodesk Revit software are found in the *File* tab, as shown in Figure 1–32.

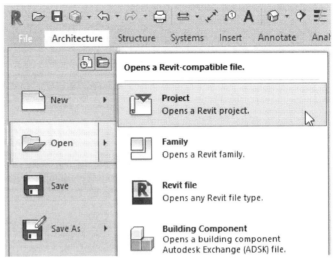

Figure 1–32

There are three main file formats:

*   **Project files (.RVT):** These are where you do the majority of your work in the building model by adding elements, creating views, annotating views, and setting up printable sheets. They are initially based on template files.

*   **Family files (.RFA):** These are separate components that can be inserted in a project. They include elements that can stand alone (e.g., a table or piece of mechanical equipment) or are items that are hosted in other elements (e.g., a door in a wall or a lighting fixture in a ceiling). Title block and Annotation Symbol files are special types of family files.

*   **Template files (.RTE):** These are the base files for any new project or family. They are designed to hold standard information and settings for creating new project files. The software includes several templates for various types of projects. You can also create custom templates.

Opening Projects

To open an existing project, in the Quick Access Toolbar or *File* tab click 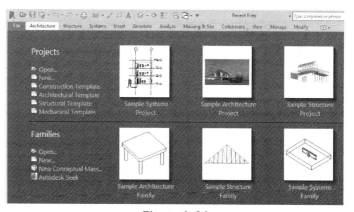 (Open), or press <Ctrl>+<O>. The Open dialog box opens (as shown in Figure 1–33), in which you can navigate to the required folder and select a project file.

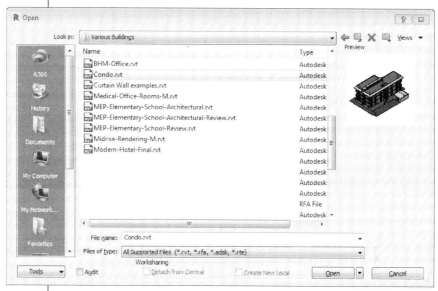

Figure 1–33

- When you first open the Autodesk Revit software, the Startup Screen displays, showing lists of recently used projects and family files as shown in Figure 1–34. This screen also displays if you close all projects.

Figure 1–34

- You can select the picture of a recently opened project or use one of the options on the left to open or start a new project using the default templates.

- It is very important that everyone working on a project uses the same software release. You can open files created in earlier versions of the software in comparison to your own, but you cannot open files created in newer versions of the software.

- When you open a file created in an earlier version, the Model Upgrade dialog box (shown in Figure 1–35) indicates the release of a file and the release to which it will be upgraded. If required, you can cancel the upgrade before it completes.

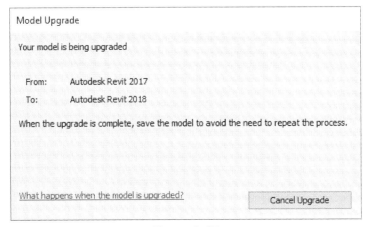

Figure 1–35

Starting New Projects

New projects are based on a template file. The template file includes preset levels, views, and some families, such as wall styles and text styles. Check with your BIM Manager about which template you need to use for your projects. Your company might have more than one based on the types of projects that you are designing.

How To: Start a New Project

1. In the *File* tab, expand (New) and click (Project) (as shown in Figure 1–36), or press <Ctrl>+<N>.

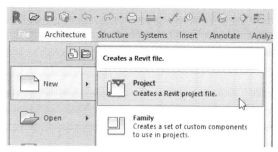

Figure 1–36

2. In the New Project dialog box (shown in Figure 1–37), select the template that you want to use and click **OK**.

The list of Template files is set in the Options dialog box in the File Locations pane. It might vary depending on the installed product and company standards.

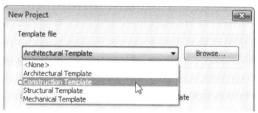

Figure 1–37

• You can select from a list of templates if they have been set up by your BIM Manager.

• You can add ⬜ (New) to the Quick Access Toolbar. At the end of the Quick Access Toolbar, click ▾ (Customize Quick Access Toolbar) and select **New**, as shown in Figure 1–38.

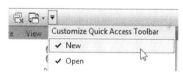

Figure 1–38

Saving Projects

Saving your project frequently is a good idea. In the Quick Access Toolbar or *File* tab click 💾 (Save), or press <Ctrl>+<S> to save your project. If the project has not yet been saved, the Save As dialog box opens, where you can specify a file location and name.

• To save an existing project with a new name, in the *File* tab, expand 💾 (Save As) and click 📄 (Project).

- If you have not saved in a set amount of time, the software opens the Project Not Saved Recently alert box, as shown in Figure 1–39. Select **Save the project**. If you want to set reminder intervals or not save at this time, select the other options.

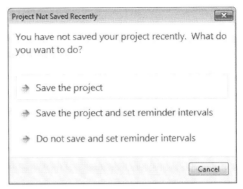

Figure 1–39

- You can set the *Save Reminder interval* to **15** or **30 minutes**, **1**, **2**, or **4 hours**, or to have **No reminders** display. In the *File* tab, click **Options** to open the Options dialog box. In the left pane, select **General** and set the interval as shown in Figure 1–40.

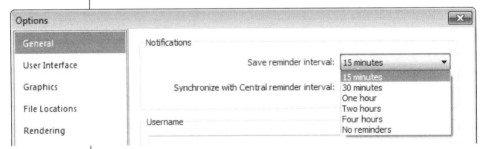

Figure 1–40

Saving Backup Copies

By default, the software saves a backup copy of a project file when you save the project. Backup copies are numbered incrementally (e.g., **My Project.0001.rvt**, **My Project.0002.rvt**, etc.) and are saved in the same folder as the original file. In the Save As dialog box, click **Options...** to control how many backup copies are saved. The default number is three backups. If you exceed this number, the software deletes the oldest backup file.

1.4 Viewing Commands

Viewing commands are crucial to working efficiently in most drawing and modeling programs and the Autodesk Revit software is no exception. Once in a view, you can use the Zoom controls to navigate in it. You can zoom in and out and pan in any view. There are also special tools for viewing in 3D.

Zooming and Panning

Using The Mouse to Zoom and Pan

Use the mouse wheel (shown in Figure 1–41) as the main method of moving around the models.

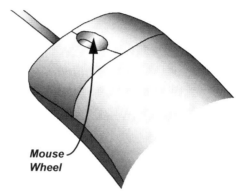

Mouse Wheel

Figure 1–41

- Scroll the wheel on the mouse up to zoom in and down to zoom out.
- Hold the wheel and move the mouse to pan.
- Double-click on the wheel to zoom to the extents of the view.
- In a 3D view, hold <Shift> and the mouse wheel and move the mouse to rotate around the model.
- When you save a model and exit the software, the pan and zoom location of each view is remembered. This is especially important for complex models.

Zoom Controls

A number of additional zoom methods enable you to control the screen display. **Zoom** and **Pan** can be performed at any time while using other commands.

- You can access the **Zoom** commands in the Navigation Bar in the upper right corner of the view (as shown in Figure 1–42). You can also access them from most shortcut menus and by typing the shortcut commands.

*(2D Wheel) provides cursor-specific access to **Zoom** and **Pan**.*

Figure 1–42

Zoom Commands

	Zoom In Region (ZR)	Zooms into a region that you define. Drag the cursor or select two points to define the rectangular area you want to zoom into. This is the default command.
	Zoom Out(2x) (ZO)	Zooms out to half the current magnification around the center of the elements.
	Zoom To Fit (ZF or ZE)	Zooms out so that the entire contents of the project only display on the screen in the current view.
	Zoom All To Fit (ZA)	Zooms out so that the entire contents of the project display on the screen in all open views.
	Zoom Sheet Size (ZS)	Zooms in or out in relation to the sheet size.
N/A	**Previous Pan/Zoom (ZP)**	Steps back one **Zoom** command.
N/A	**Next Pan/Zoom**	Steps forward one **Zoom** command if you have done a **Previous Pan/Zoom**.

Viewing in 3D

*There are two types of 3D views: isometric views created by the **3D View** command and perspective views created by the **Camera** command.*

Even if you started a project entirely in plan views, you can quickly create 3D views of the model, as shown in Figure 1–43.

Figure 1–43

Enhanced
in 2018

Working in 3D views can help you visualize the project and position some of the elements correctly. You can create and modify elements in both isometric and perspective 3D views, just as you can in plan views.

- Once you have created a 3D view, you can save it and easily return to it.

How To: Create and Save a 3D Isometric View

1. In the Quick Access Toolbar or *View* tab>Create panel, click
   (Default 3D View). The default 3D Southeast isometric view opens, as shown in Figure 1–44.

You can spin the view to a different angle using the mouse wheel or the middle button of a three-button mouse. Hold <Shift> as you press the wheel or middle button and drag the cursor.

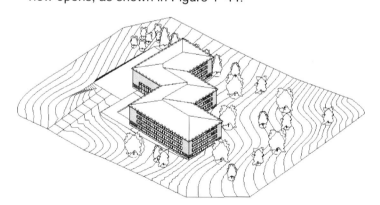

Figure 1–44

2. Modify the view to display the building from other directions.
3. In the Project Browser, right-click on the {3D} view and select **Rename...**

4. Type a new name in the Rename View dialog box, as shown in Figure 1–45, and click **OK**.

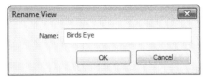

Figure 1–45

• When changes to the default 3D view are saved and you start another default 3D view, it displays the Southeast isometric view once again. If you modified the default 3D view but did not save it to a new name, the **Default 3D View** command opens the view in the last orientation you specified.

How To: Create a Perspective View

1. Switch to a Floor Plan view.
2. In the Quick Access Toolbar or *View* tab>Create panel, expand 🏠 (Default 3D View) and click 📷 (Camera).
3. Place the camera on the view.
4. Point the camera in the direction in which you want it to shoot by placing the target on the view, as shown in Figure 1–46.

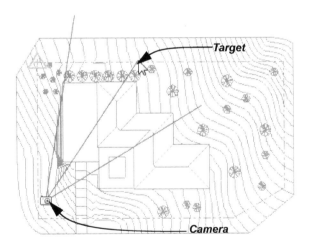

Figure 1–46

Use the round controls to modify the display size of the view and press <Shift> + the mouse wheel to change the view.

A new view displays, as shown in Figure 1–47.

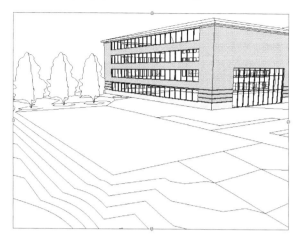

Figure 1–47

5. In the Properties palette, scroll down and adjust the *Eye Elevation* and *Target Elevation*, as required.

• You can rename perspective views.

• If the view becomes distorted, reset the target so that it is centered in the boundary of the view (called the crop region).

   In the *Modify | Cameras* tab>Camera panel, click (Reset Target).

• You can further modify a view by adding shadows, as shown in Figure 1–48. In the View Control Bar, toggle (Shadows Off) and (Shadows On). Shadows display in any model view, not just in the 3D views.

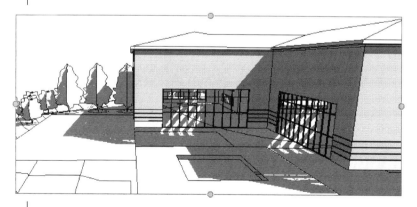

Figure 1–48

Hint: Using the ViewCube

The ViewCube provides visual clues as to where you are in a 3D view. It helps you move around the model with quick access to specific views (such as top, front, and right), as well as corner and directional views, as shown in Figure 1–49.

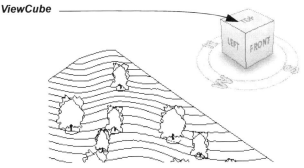

Figure 1–49

Move the cursor over any face of the ViewCube to highlight it. Once a face is highlighted, you can select it to reorient the model. You can also click and drag on the ViewCube to rotate the box, which rotates the model.

- ⌂ (Home) displays when you hover the cursor over the ViewCube. Click it to return to the view defined as **Home**. To change the Home view, set the view as you want it, right-click on the ViewCube, and select **Set Current View as Home**.

- The ViewCube is available in isometric and perspective views.

- If you are in a camera view, you can switch between Perspective and Isometric mode. Right-click on the ViewCube and click **Toggle to Parallel-3D View** or **Toggle to Perspective-3D View**. You can make more changes to the model in a parallel view.

Visual Styles

Any view can have a visual style applied. The **Visual Style** options found in the View Control Bar (as shown in Figure 1–50), specify the shading of the building model. These options apply to plan, elevation, section, and 3D views.

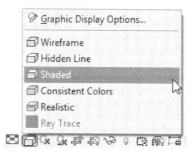

Figure 1–50

- (Wireframe) displays the lines and edges that make up elements, but hides the surfaces. This can be useful when you are dealing with complex intersections.

- (Hidden Line) displays the lines, edges, and surfaces of the elements, but it does not display any colors. This is the most common visual style to use while working on a design.

- (Shaded) and (Consistent Colors) give you a sense of the materials, including transparent glass. An example that uses Consistent Colors is shown in Figure 1–51.

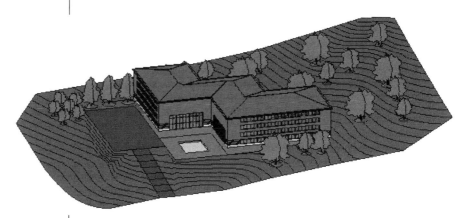

Figure 1–51

- (Realistic) displays what is shown when you render the view, including RPC (Rich Photorealistic Content) components and artificial lights. It takes a lot of computer power to execute this visual style. Therefore, it is better to use the other visual styles most of the time as you are working.

- (Ray Trace) is useful if you have created a 3D view that you want to render. It gradually moves from draft resolution to photorealistic. You can stop the process at any time.

Hint: Rendering

Rendering is a powerful tool which enables you to display a photorealistic view of the model you are working on, such as the example shown in Figure 1–52. This can be used to help clients and designers to understand a building's design in better detail.

Figure 1–52

- In the View Control Bar, click (Show Rendering Dialog) to set up the options. **Show Rendering Dialog** is only available in 3D views.

Practice 1a

Open and Review a Project

Practice Objectives

- Navigate the graphic user interface.
- Manipulate 2D and 3D views by zooming and panning.
- Create 3D Isometric and Perspective views.
- Set the Visual Style of a view.

Estimated time for completion: 15 minutes

In this practice you will open a project file and view each of the various areas in the interface. You will investigate elements, commands, and their options. You will also open views through the Project Browser and view the model in 3D, as shown in Figure 1–53.

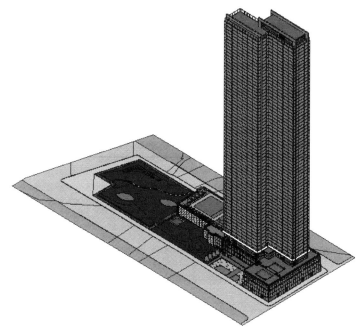

Figure 1–53

- This is a version of the main project you will work on throughout the learning guide.

Task 1 - Explore the interface.

1. In the *File* tab, expand ![Open icon] (Open) and click ![Project icon] (Project).

2. In the Open dialog box, navigate to the practice files folder and select **Urban-Garden-Intro.rvt**.

If the Project Browser and Properties palette are docked over each other, use the Project Browser tab at the bottom to display it.

3. Click **Open**. The 3D view of the building and site opens in the view window.

4. Take time to review the project to get acquainted with it. Review the various parts of the screen.

5. In the Project Browser, expand the *Floor Plans* node. Double-click on **-01 Motor Court** to open it. This view is referred to as **Floor Plans: -01 Motor Court**.

    *   The hyphen in front of the view name means that this is a working view. The other view names are designed to be placed on sheets for construction documents.

6. In the view window, hover the cursor over one of the trees. A tooltip displays describing the element, as shown in Figure 1–54.

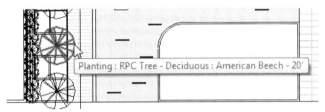

Planting : RPC Tree - Deciduous : American Beech - 20'

Figure 1–54

7. Hover the cursor over another element to display its description.

8. Select a wall. The ribbon changes to the *Modify | Walls* tab.

9. Click in an empty space to release the selection.

10. Hold <Ctrl> and select several elements of different types. The ribbon changes to the *Modify | Multi-Select* tab.

11. Click in an empty space to release the selection set.

12. In the *Architecture* tab>Build panel, click 📄 (Wall). The ribbon changes to the *Modify | Place Wall* tab and at the end of the ribbon, the Draw panel displays. It contains tools that enable you to create walls. The rest of the ribbon displays the same tools found on the *Modify* tab.

13. In the Select panel, click ⌖ (Modify) to return to the main ribbon.

14. In the *Architecture* tab>Build panel, click ▱ (Component). The ribbon changes to the *Modify | Place Component* tab and displays the options and tools that you can use to add components such as trees.

15. In the Select panel, click ⌖ (Modify) to return to the main ribbon.

Task 2 - Look at views.

1. In the Project Browser, verify that the *Floor Plans* node is open. Double-click on the **01 Motor Court - Materials and Layout Plan** view.

2. The basic floor plan displays with the walls, but without the trees and shrubs that were displayed in the working view.

3. Double-click on the **01 Motor Court - Paving and Grading Plan** view to open it.

4. The walls, the floors, and the patterns on the floors display.

5. Double-click on the **01 Motor Court - Planting Plan** view to open it. The planting displays again but the floor patterns are toggled off.

6. In the Project Browser, scroll down and expand *Sections (Building Section)*. Double-click on **Section 1** to open the view.

7. At the bottom of the view window, in the View Control Bar, click ▱ (Visual Style) and select **Shaded**. The elements in the section are now easier to read.

8. In the Project Browser, scroll down and expand the *Sheets (all)* node.

You might need to widen the Project Browser to display the full names of the views.

*This view is referred to as **Sections (Building Section): Section1** view.*

9. View several of the sheets. Some have views already applied, (e.g., **L101 Motor Court Materials & Layout Plan** as shown in Figure 1–55).

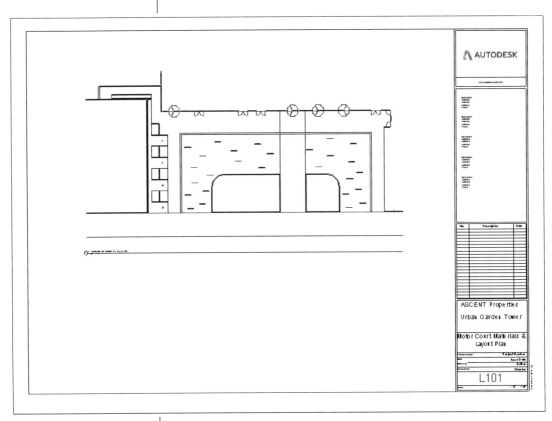

Figure 1–55

10. Which sheet displays the view that you just set to **Shaded**?

Task 3 - Practice viewing tools.

1. Open the **Floor Plans: - 02 Roof Garden** view.

2. In the Navigation Bar, click and select **Zoom to Fit** or type **ZF**. Zoom in on one of the planting beds.

3. Pan to another part of the building by holding and dragging the middle mouse button or wheel. Alternatively, you can use the 2D Wheel in the Navigation Bar.

4. Double-click on the mouse wheel to zoom out to fit the extents of the view.

5. In the Quick Access Toolbar, click 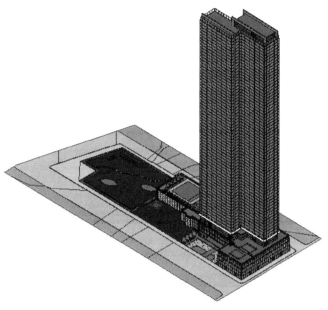 (Default 3D View) to open the default 3D view, as shown in Figure 1–56.

Figure 1–56

6. Hold <Shift> and use the middle mouse button or wheel to rotate the model in the 3D view.

7. Drag the ViewCube to find a view that shows the three landscaped areas in a birds-eye-like view.

8. In the View Control Bar, change the *Visual Style* to ◻ (Realistic).

9. In the Project Browser, expand *3D Views* and right-click on the **{3D}** view and select **Rename....** In the Rename View dialog box, type the required name.

10. Review the other 3D views that have already been created.

11. Press <Ctrl>+<Tab> to cycle through the open views.

12. In the Quick Access Toolbar, expand ⬚ (Switch Windows) and select the **Urban Garden-Intro.rvt - Floor Plan: 02 Roof Garden** view.

13. In the Quick Access Toolbar, click 🖳 (Close Hidden Windows). This closes all of the other windows except the one in which you are working.

14. Open the **Floor Plans: 02 Roof Garden-Paving and Grading Plan** view.

15. In the Quick Access Toolbar, expand 🏠 (Default 3D View) and click 📷 (Camera).

16. Click the first point in the open area and click the second point (target) outside the building, as shown in Figure 1–57.

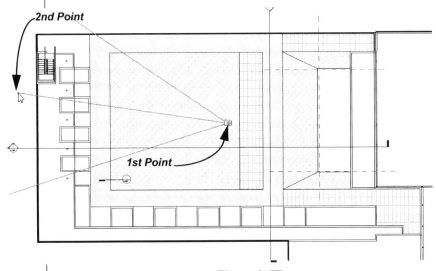

Figure 1–57

17. The plants display although they did not display in the floor plan view.

18. In the View Control Bar, set the *Visual Style* to 🗔 (Realistic).

19. In the Project Browser, right-click on the new camera view and select **Rename...** In the Rename View dialog box, type **Roof Garden Seating Area** and click **OK**.

20. In the Quick Access Toolbar, click 💾 (Save) to save the project.

21. In the *File* tab, click 🗔 (Close). This closes the entire project.

Chapter Review Questions

1. When you create a project in the Autodesk Revit software, do you work in 3D (as shown on the left in Figure 1–58) or 2D (as shown on the right in Figure 1–59)?

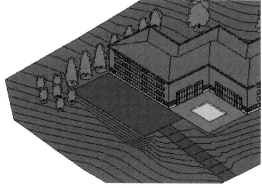

Figure 1–58

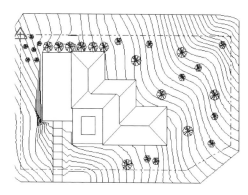

Figure 1–59

   a. You work in 2D in plan views and in 3D in non-plan views.

   b. You work in 3D almost all of the time, even when you are using what looks like a flat view.

   c. You work in 2D or 3D depending on how you toggle the 2D/3D control.

   d. You work in 2D in plan and section views and in 3D in isometric views.

2. What is the purpose of the Project Browser?

   a. It enables you to browse through the building project, similar to a walk through.

   b. It is the interface for managing all of the files that are required to create the complete architectural model of the building.

   c. It manages multiple Autodesk Revit projects as an alternative to using Windows Explorer.

   d. It is used to access and manage the views of the project.

3. Which part(s) of the interface changes according to the command you are using? (Select all that apply.)

   a. Ribbon

   b. View Control Bar

   c. Options Bar

   d. Properties Palette

4. The difference between Type Properties and Properties (the ribbon location is shown in Figure 1–60) is...

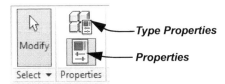

Figure 1–60

   a. Properties stores parameters that apply to the selected individual element(s). Type Properties stores parameters that impact every element of the same type in the project.

   b. Properties stores the location parameters of an element. Type Properties stores the size and identity parameters of an element.

   c. Properties only stores parameters of the view. Type Properties stores parameters of model components.

5. When you start a new project, how do you specify the base information in the new file?

   a. Transfer the base information from an existing project.

   b. Select the right template for the task.

   c. The Autodesk Revit software automatically extracts the base information from imported or linked file(s).

6. What is the main difference between a view made using (Default 3D View) and a view made using (Camera)?

   a. Use **Default 3D View** for exterior views and **Camera** for interiors.

   b. **Default 3D View** creates a static image and a **Camera** view is live and always updated.

   c. **Default 3D View** is isometric and a **Camera** view is perspective.

   d. **Default 3D View** is used for the overall building and a **Camera** view is used for looking in tight spaces.

Command Summary

Button	Command	Location
General Tools		
	Modify	• **Ribbon:** All tabs>Select panel • **Shortcut:** MD
	New	• **Quick Access Toolbar** (Optional) • *File* tab • **Shortcut:** <Ctrl>+<N>
	Open	• **Quick Access Toolbar** • *File* tab • **Shortcut:** <Ctrl>+<O>
	Open Documents	• *File* tab
	Properties	• **Ribbon:** *Modify* tab>Properties panel • **Shortcut:** PP
	Recent Documents	• *File* tab
	Save	• **Quick Access Toolbar** • *File* tab • **Shortcut:** <Ctrl>+<S>
	Synchronize and Modify Settings	• **Quick Access Toolbar**
	Synchronize Now/	• **Quick Access Toolbar**>expand Synchronize and Modify Settings
	Type Properties	• **Ribbon:** *Modify* tab>Properties panel • **Properties palette**
Viewing Tools		
	Camera	• **Quick Access Toolbar**> Expand Default 3D View • **Ribbon:** *View* tab>Create panel> expand Default 3D View
	Default 3D View	• **Quick Access Toolbar** • **Ribbon:** *View* tab>Create panel
	Home	• **ViewCube**
N/A	Next Pan/Zoom	• **Navigation Bar** • **Shortcut Menu**
N/A	Previous Pan/Zoom	• **Navigation Bar** • **Shortcut Menu** • **Shortcut:** ZP
	Shadows On/Off	• **View Control Bar**

	Show Rendering Dialog/ Render	• **View Control Bar** • **Ribbon:** *View* tab>Graphics panel • **Shortcut:** RR
	Zoom All to Fit	• **Navigation Bar** • **Shortcut:** ZA
	Zoom in Region	• **Navigation Bar** • **Shortcut Menu** • **Shortcut:** ZR
	Zoom Out (2x)	• **Navigation Bar** • **Shortcut Menu** • **Shortcut:** ZO
	Zoom Sheet Size	• **Navigation Bar** • **Shortcut:** ZS
	Zoom to Fit	• **Navigation Bar** • **Shortcut Menu** • **Shortcut:** ZF, ZE

Visual Styles

	Consistent Colors	• **View Control Bar**
	Hidden Line	• **View Control Bar** • **Shortcut:** HL
	Ray Trace	• **View Control Bar**
	Realistic	• **View Control Bar**
	Shaded	• **View Control Bar** • **Shortcut:** SD
	Wireframe	• **View Control Bar** • **Shortcut:** WF

Chapter
2

Basic Sketching and Modify Tools

Basic sketching, selecting, and modifying tools are the foundation of working with all types of elements in the Autodesk® Revit® software. Using these tools with drawing aids helps you to place and modify elements to create accurate building models.

Learning Objectives in this Chapter

- Sketch linear elements such as walls, beams, and pipes.
- Ease the placement of elements by incorporating drawing aids, such as alignment lines, temporary dimensions, and snaps.
- Place Reference Planes as temporary guide lines.
- Use techniques to select and filter groups of elements.
- Modify elements using a contextual tab, Properties, temporary dimensions, and controls.
- Move, copy, rotate, and mirror elements and create array copies in linear and radial patterns.
- Align, trim, and extend elements with the edges of other elements.
- Split linear elements anywhere along their length.
- Offset elements to create duplicates a specific distance away from the original.

2.1 Using General Sketching Tools

When you start a command, the contextual tab on the ribbon, the Options Bar, and the Properties palette enable you to set up features for each new element you are placing in the project. As you are working, several features called *drawing aids* display, as shown in Figure 2–1. They help you create designs quickly and accurately.

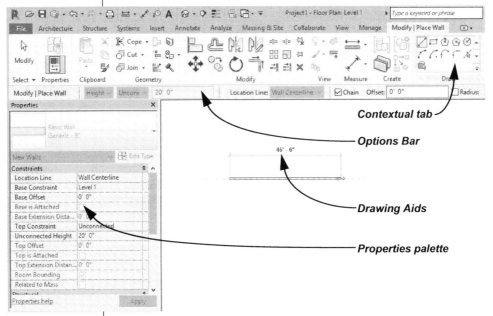

Figure 2–1

- In the Autodesk Revit software, you are most frequently creating 3D model elements rather than 2D sketches. These tools work with both 3D and 2D elements in the software.

Draw Tools

Many linear elements (such as walls, beams, ducts, pipes, and conduits) are modeled using the tools on the contextual tab on the *Draw* panel, as shown for walls in Figure 2–1. Other elements (such as floors, ceilings, roofs, and slabs) have boundaries that are sketched using many of the same tools. Draw tools are also used when you create details or schematic drawings.

Two methods are available:

- *Draw* the element using a geometric form.
- *Pick* an existing element (such as a line, face, or wall) as the basis for the new element's geometry and position.

The exact tools vary according to the element being modeled.

How To: Create Linear Elements

1. Start the command you want to use.
2. In the contextual tab>Draw panel, as shown in Figure 2–2, select a drawing tool.
3. Select points to define the elements.

You can change from one Draw tool shape to another in the middle of a command.

Figure 2–2

4. Finish the command using one of the standard methods:

- Click ⌖ (Modify).
- Press <Esc> twice.
- Right-click and select **Cancel** twice.
- Start another command.

Draw Options

When you are in Drawing mode, several options display in the Options Bar, as shown in Figure 2–3.

Figure 2–3

Different options display according to the type of element that is selected or the command that is active.

- **Chain**: Controls how many segments are created in one process. If this option is not selected, the **Line** and **Arc** tools only create one segment at a time. If it is selected, you can continue adding segments until you select the command again.

- **Offset**: Enables you to enter values so you can create linear elements at a specified distance from the selected points or element.

- **Radius**: Enables you to enter values when using a radial tool.

Draw Tools

/	**Line**	Draws a straight line defined by the first and last points. If Chain is enabled, you can continue selecting end points for multiple segments.
▱	**Rectangle**	Draws a rectangle defined by two opposing corner points. You can adjust the dimensions after selecting both points.
⬠	**Inscribed Polygon**	Draws a polygon inscribed in a hypothetical circle with the number of sides specified in the Options Bar.
⬠	**Circumscribed Polygon**	Draws a polygon circumscribed around a hypothetical circle with the number of sides specified in the Options Bar.
◉	**Circle**	Draws a circle defined by a center point and radius.
⌒	**Start-End-Radius Arc**	Draws a curve defined by a start, end, and radius of the arc. The outside dimension shown is the included angle of the arc. The inside dimension is the radius.
⌒	**Center-ends Arc**	Draws a curve defined by a center, radius, and included angle. The selected point of the radius also defines the start point of the arc.
⌒	**Tangent End Arc**	Draws a curve tangent to another element. Select an end point for the first point, but do not select the intersection of two or more elements. Then select a second point based on the included angle of the arc.
⌒	**Fillet Arc**	Draws a curve defined by two other elements and a radius. Because it is difficult to select the correct radius by clicking, this command automatically moves to edit mode. Select the dimension and then modify the radius of the fillet.
⋏	**Spline**	Draws a spline curve based on selected points. The curve does not actually touch the points (Model and Detail Lines only).
⬯	**Ellipse**	Draws an ellipse from a primary and secondary axis (Model and Detail Lines only).
⊃	**Partial Ellipse**	Draws only one side of the ellipse, like an arc. A partial ellipse also has a primary and secondary axis (Model and Detail Lines only).

Pick Tools

![]	**Pick Lines**	Use this option to select existing linear elements in the project. This is useful when you start the project from an imported 2D drawing.
![]	**Pick Face**	Use this option to select the face of a 3D massing element (walls and 3D views only).
![]	**Pick Walls**	Use this option to select an existing wall in the project to be the basis for a new sketch line (floors, ceilings, etc.).

Hint: Model Lines and Detail Lines

While most of the elements that you create are representations of actual building elements, there are times you may need to add lines to clarify the design intent or to actually build a structure based on lines. For example, when you are working with Site Designer you can build a swale based on a model (or detail) line as shown in Figure 2–4.

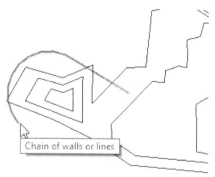

Figure 2–4

- Model Lines (*Architecture* or *Structure* tab>Model panel

  ![] (Model Line)) function as 3D elements and display in all views.

- Detail Lines (*Annotate* tab>Detail panel>![] (Detail Lines) are strictly 2D elements that only display in the view in which they are drawn.

- In the *Modify* contextual tab, select a Line Style and then the Draw tool that you want to use to draw the model or detail line.

Drawing Aids

As soon as you start sketching or placing elements, three drawing aids display, as shown in Figure 2–5:

- Alignment lines
- Snaps
- Temporary dimensions

These aids are available with most modeling and many modification commands.

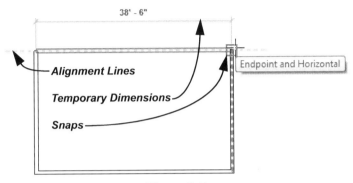

Figure 2–5

Alignment lines display as soon as you select your first point. They help keep lines horizontal, vertical, or at a specified angle. They also line up with the implied intersections of walls and other elements.

- Hold <Shift> to force the alignments to be orthogonal (90 degree angles only).

Snaps are key points that help you reference existing elements to exact points when modeling, as shown in Figure 2–6.

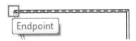

Figure 2–6

- When you move the cursor over an element, the snap symbol displays. Each snap location type displays with a different symbol.

Hint: Snap Settings and Overrides

In the *Manage* tab>Settings panel, click 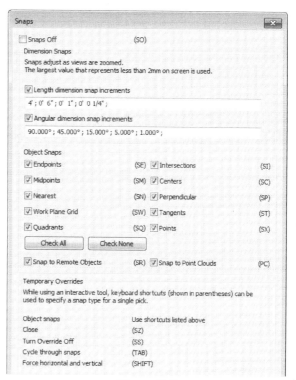 (Snaps) to open the Snaps dialog box, which is shown in Figure 2–7. The Snaps dialog box enables you to set which snap points are active, and set the dimension increments displayed for temporary dimensions (both linear and angular).

Figure 2–7

*   Keyboard shortcuts for each snap can be used to override the automatic snapping. Temporary overrides only affect a single pick, but can be very helpful when there are snaps nearby other than the one you want to use.

Temporary dimensions display to help place elements at the correct length, angle and location.

- You can type in the dimension and then move the cursor until you see the dimension you want, or you can place the element and then modify the dimension as required.
- The length and angle increments shown vary depending on how far in or out the view is zoomed.
- For Imperial measurements (feet and inches), the software uses a default of feet. For example, when you type **4** and press <Enter>, it assumes 4'-0". For a distance such as 4'-6", you can type any of the following: **4'-6"**, **4'6**, **4-6**, or **4 6** (the numbers separated by a space). To indicate distances less than one foot, type the inch mark (") after the distance, or enter **0**, a space, and then the distance.

Hint: Temporary Dimensions and Permanent Dimensions

Temporary dimensions disappear as soon as you finish adding elements. If you want to make them permanent, select the control shown in Figure 2–8.

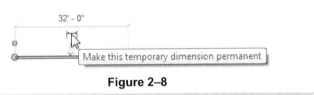

Figure 2–8

Using Dimensions as Drawing Aids

Dimensions are a critical part of construction documents that can also help you create the elements in your model. There are a variety of dimension types, but the most useful is the **Aligned Dimension** with the *Individual References* option.

How To: Add Aligned Dimensions to Individual References

1. In the Quick Access Toolbar or in the *Modify* tab>Measure panel, click 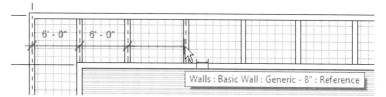 (Aligned Dimension), or type **DI**.
2. Select the elements in order.
3. To position the dimension string, click a point at the location where you want it to display, ensuring that the string is not overlapping anything else, as shown in Figure 2–9.

Figure 2–9

Hint: Setting Dimensions Equal

Using dimensions while you are modeling enables you to set a string of dimensions so that they are equal. Doing this updates the model elements, such as the location of windows in a wall, as shown in Figure 2–10.

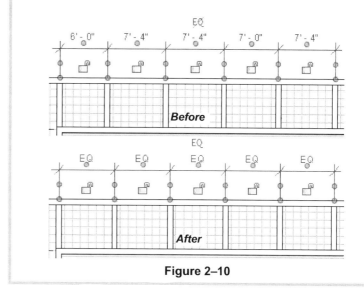

Figure 2–10

Reference Planes

As you develop designs in the Autodesk Revit software, there are times when you need lines to help you define certain locations. You can sketch reference planes (displayed as dashed green lines) and snap to them whenever you need to line up elements. For the example shown in Figure 2–11, the trees are placed using reference planes.

- To insert a reference plane, in the *Architecture, Structure*, or

  Systems tab>Work Plane panel, click 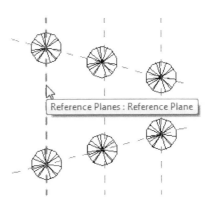 (Ref Plane) or type **RP**.

Reference planes do not display in 3D views.

Reference Planes : Reference Plane

Figure 2–11

- Reference planes display in associated views because they are infinite planes, and not just lines.

- You can name Reference planes by clicking on **<Click to name>** and typing in the text box, as shown in Figure 2–12.

Center Line

<Click to name>
3D
<Click to name>

Figure 2–12

- If you sketch a reference pane in Sketch Mode (used with floors and similar elements), it does not display once the sketch is finished.

- Reference planes can have different line styles if they have been defined in the project. In Properties, select a style from the Subcategory list.

Hint: Creating Tree Lines

Tree lines are easily created using an open revision cloud, as shown in Figure 2–13. In the *Annotate* tab>Detail panel, click

 (Revision Cloud). Use any of the Draw tools to sketch the

line. Then, in the Mode panel, click (Finish Edit Mode). The Spline tool makes the smoothest curves.

Figure 2–13

• Revision clouds are annotation tools and only display in the view in which they are created.

2.2 Editing Elements

Building design projects typically involve extensive changes to the model. The Autodesk Revit software was designed to make such changes quickly and efficiently. You can change an element using the following methods, as shown in Figure 2–14:

- Type Selector enables you to specify a different type. This is frequently used to change the size and/or style of the elements.

- Properties enables you to modify the information (parameters) associated with the selected elements.

- The contextual tab in the ribbon contains the Modify commands and element-specific tools.

- Temporary dimensions enable you to change the element's dimensions or position in relation to walls.

- Controls enable you to drag, flip, lock, and rotate the element.

- Shape handles (not shown) enable you to drag elements to modify their height or length.

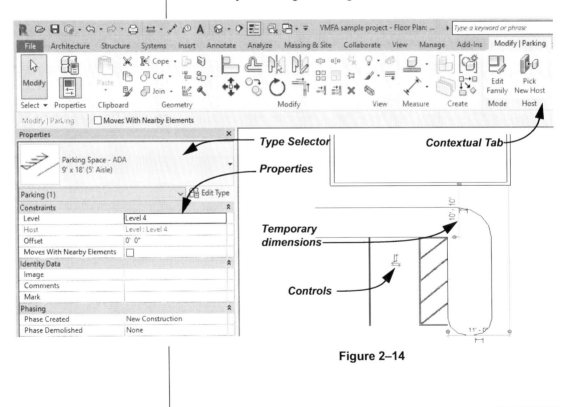

Figure 2–14

- To delete an element, select it and press <Delete>, right-click
  and select **Delete**, or in the Modify panel, click ✖ (Delete).

Working with Controls and Shape Handles

When you select an element, various controls and shape
handles display depending on the element and view. For
example, in plan view you can use controls to drag the ends of a
wall and change its orientation. You can also drag the wall ends
in a 3D view, and you can also use the arrow shape handles to
change the height of the wall, as shown in Figure 2–15

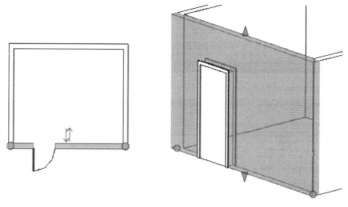

Figure 2–15

- If you hover the cursor over the control or shape handle, a
  tool tip displays showing its function.

Hint: Editing Temporary Dimensions

Temporary dimensions automatically link to the closest wall. To change this, drag the *Witness Line* control (as shown in Figure 2–16) to connect to a new reference. You can also click on the control to toggle between justifications in the wall.

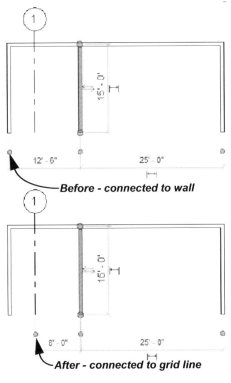

Figure 2–16

- The new location of a temporary dimension for an element is remembered as long as you are in the same session of the software.

Selecting Multiple Elements

- Once you have selected at least one element, hold <Ctrl> and select another item to add it to a selection set.

- To remove an element from a selection set, hold <Shift> and select the element.

- If you click and drag the cursor to *window* around elements, you have two selection options, as shown in Figure 2–17. If you drag from left to right, you only select the elements completely inside the window. If you drag from right to left, you select elements both inside and crossing the window.

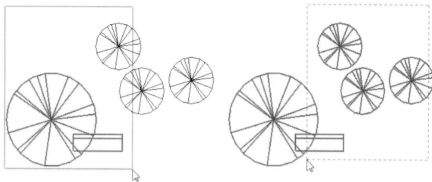

Window: Left to Right   *Crossing: Right to Left*

Figure 2–17

- If several elements are on or near each other, press <Tab> to cycle through them before you click. If there are elements that might be linked to each other, such as walls that are connected, pressing <Tab> selects the chain of elements.

- Press <Ctrl>+<Left Arrow> to reselect the previous selection set. You can also right-click in the view window with nothing selected and select **Select Previous**.

- To select all elements of a specific type, right-click on an element and select **Select All Instances>Visible in View** or **In Entire Project**, as shown in Figure 2–18.

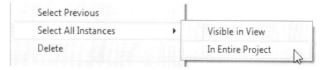

Figure 2–18

Hint: Measuring Tools

When modifying a model, it is useful to know the distance between elements. This can be done with temporary dimensions, or more frequently, by using the measuring tools found in the Quick Access Toolbar or on the *Modify* tab> Measure panel, as shown in Figure 2–19.

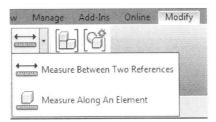

Figure 2–19

- (Measure Between Two References): Select two elements and the measurement displays.

- (Measure Along An Element): Select the edge of a linear element and the total length displays.

Filtering Selection Sets

When multiple element categories are selected, the *Multi-Select* contextual tab opens in the ribbon. This gives you access to all of the Modify tools and the **Filter** command. The **Filter** command enables you to specify the types of elements to select. For example, you might only want to select planting, as shown in Figure 2–20.

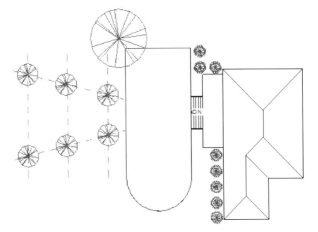

Figure 2–20

How To: Filter a Selection Set

1. Select everything in the required area.
2. in the *Modify | Multi-Select* tab>Selection panel, or in the Status Bar, click 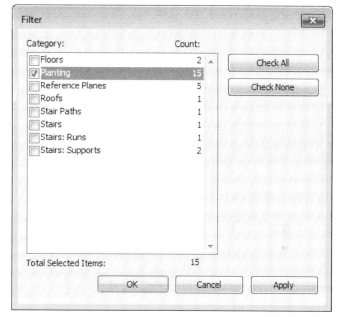 (Filter). The Filter dialog box opens, as shown in Figure 2–21.

The Filter dialog box displays all types of elements in the original selection.

Category:	Count:	
☐ Floors	2	Check All
☑ Planting	15	Check None
☐ Reference Planes	5	
☐ Roofs	1	
☐ Stair Paths	1	
☐ Stairs	1	
☐ Stairs: Runs	1	
☐ Stairs: Supports	2	

Total Selected Items: 15

OK   Cancel   Apply

Figure 2–21

3. Click **Check None** to clear all of the options or **Check All** to select all of the options. You can also select or clear individual categories as required.
4. Click **OK**. The selection set is now limited to the elements you specified.

- The number of elements selected displays on the right end of the status bar and in the Properties palette.

- Clicking **Filter** in the Status Bar also opens the Filter dialog box.

Hint: Selection Options

You can control how the software selects specific elements in a project by toggling Selection options on and off on the Status Bar, as shown in Figure 2–22. Alternatively, in any tab on the ribbon, expand the Select panel's title and select the option.

Figure 2–22

- **Select links:** When toggled on, you can selected linked CAD drawings or Autodesk Revit models. When it is toggled off you cannot select them when using **Modify** or **Move**.

- **Select underlay elements:** When toggled on, you can select underlay elements. When toggled off, you cannot select them when using **Modify** or **Move**.

- **Select pinned elements:** When toggled on, you can selected pinned elements. When toggled off, you cannot select them when using **Modify** or **Move**.

- **Select elements by face:** When toggled on you can select elements (such as the floors or walls in an elevation) by selecting the interior face or selecting an edge. When toggled off, you can only select elements by selecting an edge.

- **Drag elements on selection:** When toggled on, you can hover over an element, select it, and drag it to a new location. When toggled off, the Crossing or Box select mode starts when you press and drag, even if you are on top of an element. Once elements have been selected, they can still be dragged to a new location.

Practice 2a

Sketch and Edit Elements

Practice Objective

*   Use sketch tools and drawing aids.

Estimated time for completion: 10 minutes

In this practice, you will use the **Wall** command along with sketching tools and drawing aids, such as temporary dimensions and snaps. You will use the **Modify** command and modify the walls using grips, temporary dimensions, the Type Selector, and Properties. You will also add reference planes and a tree line, as shown in Figure 2–23.

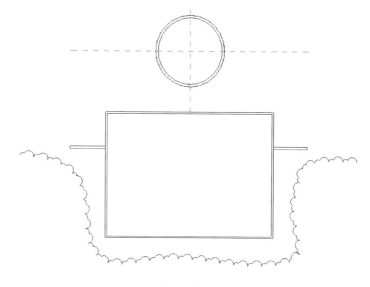

Figure 2–23

Task 1 - Draw and modify walls.

1. In the *File Tab*, click 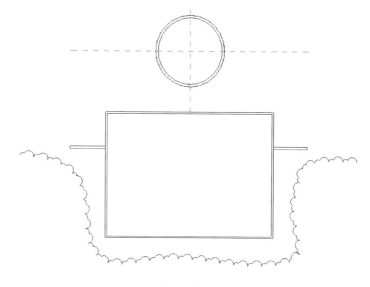 (New)> (Project).

2. In the New Project dialog box, select **Architectural Template** from the Template file drop-down list and click **OK**.

3. In the Quick Access Toolbar, click (Save). When prompted, name the project **Simple Landscape.rvt**.

4. In the *Architecture* tab>Build panel, click (Wall).

*By default, you are working in the **Floor Plans: Level 1** view.*

5. In the *Modify | Place Wall* tab>Draw panel, click

   (Rectangle) and sketch a rectangle approximately **70'-0" x 50'-0"**. You do not have to be precise because you can change the dimensions later.

6. Note that the dimensions are temporary. Select the vertical dimension text and type **50**, as shown in Figure 2–24. Press <Enter>.

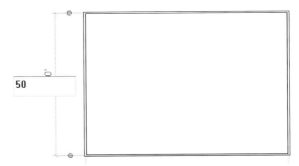

Figure 2–24

7. In the Select panel, click (Modify). You can also use one of the other methods to switch to **Modify:**

   - Type the shortcut **MD**.
   - Press <Esc> once or twice.
   - Right-click and select **Cancel**.

8. Select either vertical wall. The temporary dimension displays. Click the text and type **70**, as shown in Figure 2–25. Press <Enter>.

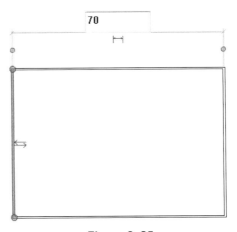

Figure 2–25

9. Click in an empty space to end the selection.

10. In the *Architecture* tab>Build panel, click 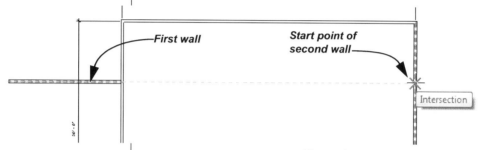 (Wall). In the Draw panel, verify that (Line) is selected.

11. In the Options Bar, set the *Height* to **Unconnected 4'-0"**.

12. Draw a wall out from the left of the building, similar to the one shown in Figure 2–26 (the exact location and length does not matter.)

13. Draw a wall out from the right of the building using alignment lines and snaps to specify the start point of the wall as shown in Figure 2–26.

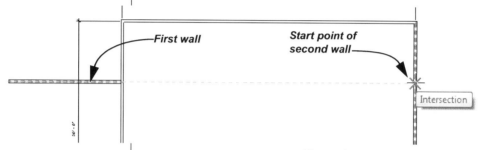

Figure 2–26

14. Click **Modify**.

15. Select the wall and use the **Drag Wall End** control to set the length of the retaining wall, as shown in Figure 2–27.

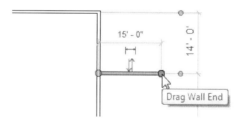

Figure 2–27

16. Select both of the retaining walls and in the Type Selector, change the type to **Basic Wall: Retaining - 12" Concrete**, as shown in Figure 2–28. The thickness of the walls change.

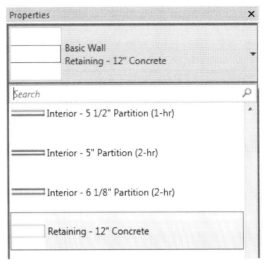

Figure 2–28

17. In the Quick Access Toolbar, click 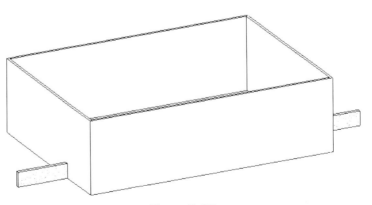 (Default 3D View).

18. Rotate the view so you can see the building walls and both retaining walls, as shown in Figure 2–29.

Figure 2–29

19. Save the project.

Task 2 - Add Reference Planes, Additional Walls, and a Tree Line.

1. Return to the **Floor Plans: Level 1** view using one of the following methods:

    *   Press <Ctrl>+<Tab> to cycle through the open views
    *   In the Project Browser, double-click on **Floor Plans: Level 1**.

    *   In the Quick Access Toolbar, expand ⬛ (Switch Windows) and select **Simple Landscape.rvt - Floor Plan: Level 1** from the drop-down list.

2. In the *Architecture* tab>Work Plane panel, click ⬛ (Ref Plane).

3. Draw a vertical reference plane from the midpoint of the north wall and a horizontal reference plane about 25'-0" above the north wall, as shown in Figure 2–30.

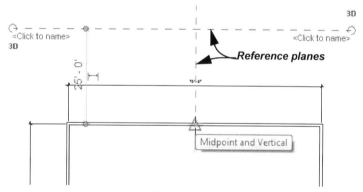

Figure 2–30

4. Start the **Wall** command.

5. In the Type Selector, select **Basic Wall: Retaining - 12" Concrete**.

6. In Properties, set the *Unconnected Height* to **3'-0"**.

7. In the Draw panel, click 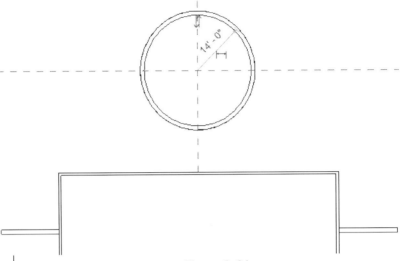 (Circle) and sketch a **14'-0"** radius circular wall at the intersection of the two reference planes, as shown in Figure 2–31.

Figure 2–31

8. In the *Annotate* tab>Detail panel, click (Revision Cloud).

9. In the Draw panel, select one of the linear options and draw a tree line, as shown in Figure 2–32.

10. In the *Modify | Create Revision Cloud Sketch* tab>Mode panel, click (Finish Edit Mode)

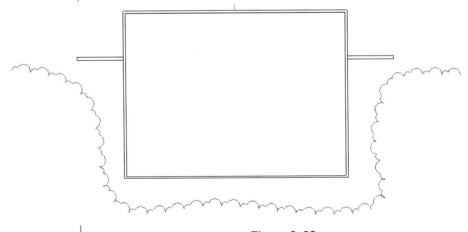

Figure 2–32

11. Open the default 3D view. Note that only the wall elements display (as shown in Figure 2–33), not the reference planes or revision cloud elements.

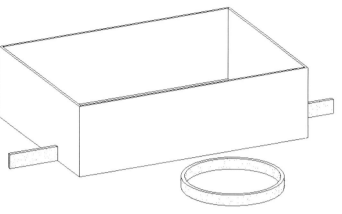

Figure 2–33

12. Save the project.

2.3 Working with Basic Modify Tools

The Autodesk Revit software contains controls and temporary dimensions that enable you to edit elements. Additional modifying tools can be used with individual elements or any selection of elements. They are found in the *Modify* tab>Modify panel, as shown in Figure 2–34, and in contextual tabs.

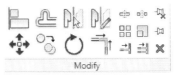

Figure 2–34

- The **Move**, **Copy**, **Rotate**, **Mirror**, and **Array** commands are covered in this topic. Other tools are covered later.

- For most modify commands, you can either select the elements and start the command, or start the command, select the elements, and press <Enter> to finish the selection and move to the next step in the command.

Hint: Adding Components

Stand-alone elements such as plants (as shown in Figure 2–35), benches, and parking spaces are added to a project using the **Component** command. Their location can then be modified using commands such as **Move** and **Copy**.

Figure 2–35

1. In the *Architecture* tab>Build panel, click  (Component).
2. In the Type Selector, select the required type and size from the drop-down list.
3. Click in the view to place the component.

Moving and Copying Elements

The **Move** and **Copy** commands enable you to select the element(s) and move or copy them from one place to another. You can use alignment lines, temporary dimensions, and snaps to help place the elements, as shown in Figure 2–36.

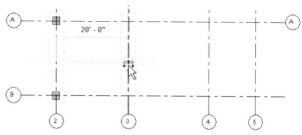

Figure 2–36

Hint: Nudge

Nudge enables you to move an element in short increments. When an element is selected, you can press one of the four arrow keys to move the element in that direction. The distance the element moves depends on how far in or out you are zoomed.

How To: Move or Copy Elements

1. Select the elements you want to move or copy.
2. In the Modify panel, click (Move) or (Copy). A boundary box displays around the selected elements.
3. Select a move start point on or near the element.
4. Select a second point. Use alignment lines and temporary dimensions to help place the elements.
5. When you are finished, you can start another modify command using the elements that remain selected, or switch back to **Modify** to end the command.

-   If you start the **Move** command and hold <Ctrl>, the elements are copied.

Move/Copy Elements Options

The **Move** and **Copy** commands have several options that display in the Options Bar, as shown in Figure 2–37.

Figure 2–37

*You can also use the shortcut for **Move, MV** or for **Copy, CO**.*

Constrain	Restricts the movement of the cursor to horizontal or vertical, or along the axis of an item that is at an angle. This keeps you from selecting a point at an angle by mistake. **Constrain** is off by default.
Disjoin (Move only)	Breaks any connections between the elements being moved and other elements. If **Disjoin** is on, the elements move separately. If it is off, the connected elements also move or stretch. **Disjoin** is off by default.
Multiple (Copy only)	Enables you to make multiple copies of one selection. **Multiple** is off by default.

- These commands only work in the current view, not between views or projects. To copy between views or projects, in the *Modify* tab>Clipboard panel, use ▯ (Copy to Clipboard), ✂ (Cut to the Clipboard), and ▯ (Paste from Clipboard).

- Many tools such as **Move**, **Copy**, and the clipboard commands can be used in perspective views.

Hint: Pinning Elements

If you do not want elements to be moved, you can pin them in place, as shown in Figure 2–38. Select the elements and in the *Modify* tab, in the Modify panel, click ▯ (Pin). Pinned elements can be copied, but not moved. If you try to delete a pinned element, a warning dialog displays reminding you that you must unpin the element before starting the command.

Figure 2–38

Select the element and click ▯ (Unpin) or type the shortcut **UP** to free it.

Rotating Elements

The **Rotate** command enables you to rotate selected elements around a center point or origin, as shown in Figure 2–39. You can use alignment lines, temporary dimensions, and snaps to help specify the center of rotation and the angle. You can also create copies of the element as it is being rotated.

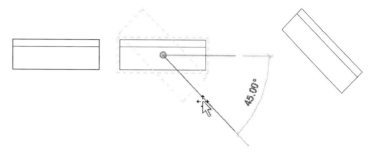

Figure 2–39

How To: Rotate Elements

1. Select the element(s) you want to rotate.

2. In the Modify panel, click ⟳ (Rotate) or type the shortcut **RO**.

3. The center of rotation is automatically set to the center of the element or group of elements, as shown on the left in Figure 2–40. To change the center of rotation, as shown on the right in Figure 2–40, use the following:

   - Drag the ⟳ (Center of Rotation) control to a new point.
   - In the Options Bar, next to **Center of rotation**, click **Place** and use snaps to move it to a new location.
   - Press <Spacebar> to select the center of rotation and click to move it to a new location.

*To start the **Rotate** command with a prompt to select the center of rotation, select the elements first and type **R3**.*

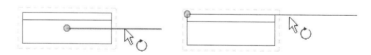

Figure 2–40

4. In the Options Bar, specify if you want to make a Copy (select **Copy**), type an angle in the *Angle* field (as shown in Figure 2–41), and press <Enter>. You can also specify the angle on screen using temporary dimensions.

Figure 2–41

5. The rotated element(s) remain highlighted, enabling you to start another command using the same selection, or click

    (Modify) to finish.

*   The **Disjoin** option breaks any connections between the elements being rotated and other elements. If **Disjoin** is on (selected), the elements rotate separately. If it is off (cleared), the connected elements also move or stretch, as shown in Figure 2–42. By default, **Disjoin** is toggled off.

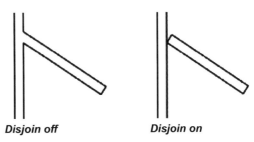

Disjoin off   *Disjoin on*

Figure 2–42

Mirroring Elements

The **Mirror** command enables you to mirror elements about an axis defined by a selected element, as shown in Figure 2–43, or by selected points.

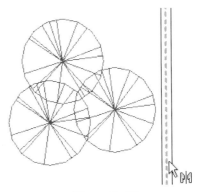

Figure 2–43

How To: Mirror Elements

1. Select the element(s) to mirror.
2. In the Modify panel, select the method you want to use:

   - Click 🪞 (Mirror - Pick Axis) or type the shortcut **MM**. This prompts you to select an element as the **Axis of Reflection** (mirror line).

   - Click 🪞 (Mirror - Draw Axis) or type the shortcut **DM**. This prompts you to select two points to define the axis about which the elements mirror.

3. The new mirrored element(s) remain highlighted, enabling you to start another command, or return to **Modify** to finish.

   - By default, the original elements that were mirrored remain. To delete the original elements, clear the **Copy** option in the Options Bar.

Hint: Scale

The Autodesk Revit software is designed with full-size elements. Therefore, not much should be scaled. For example, scaling a wall increases its length but does not impact the width, which is set by the wall type. However, you can use

📐 (Scale) in reference planes, images, and imported files from other programs.

Creating Linear and Radial Arrays

A linear array creates a straight line pattern of elements, while a radial array creates a circular pattern around a center point.

The **Array** command creates multiple copies of selected elements in a linear or radial pattern, as shown in Figure 2–44. For example, you can array a row of columns to create a row of evenly spaced columns on a grid, or array a row of parking spaces. The arrayed elements can be grouped or placed as separate elements.

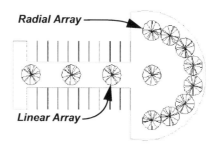

Figure 2–44

How To: Create a Linear Array

1. Select the element(s) to array.
2. In the Modify panel, click ⬜⬜ (Array) or type the shortcut **AR**.
3. In the Options Bar, click 🎚 (Linear).
4. Specify the other options, as required.
5. Select a start point and an end point to set the spacing and direction of the array. The array displays.
6. If **Group and Associate** is selected, you are prompted again for the number of items, as shown in Figure 2–45. Type a new number or click on the screen to finish the command.

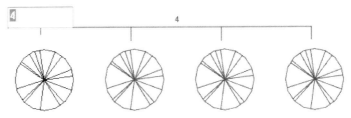

Figure 2–45

- To make a linear array in two directions, you need to array one direction first, select the arrayed elements, and then array them again in the other direction.

Array Options

In the Options Bar, set up the **Array** options for **Linear Array** (top of Figure 2–46) or **Radial Array** (bottom of Figure 2–46).

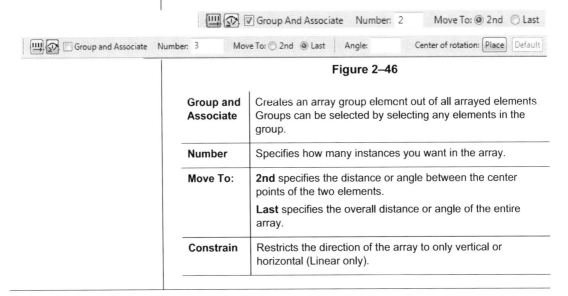

Figure 2–46

Group and Associate	Creates an array group element out of all arrayed elements. Groups can be selected by selecting any elements in the group.
Number	Specifies how many instances you want in the array.
Move To:	**2nd** specifies the distance or angle between the center points of the two elements. **Last** specifies the overall distance or angle of the entire array.
Constrain	Restricts the direction of the array to only vertical or horizontal (Linear only).

Angle	Specifies the angle (Radial only).
Center of rotation	Specifies a location for the origin about which the elements rotate (Radial only).

How To: Create a Radial Array

1. Select the element(s) to array.

2. In the Modify panel, click □□ (Array).

3. In the Options Bar, click ☜ (Radial).

4. Drag ○ (Center of Rotation) or use **Place** to the move the center of rotation to the appropriate location, as shown in Figure 2–47.

Remember to set the ***Center of Rotation*** *control first, because it is easy to forget to move it before specifying the angle.*

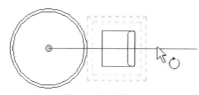

Figure 2–47

5. Specify the other options as required.
6. In the Options Bar, type an angle and press <Enter>, or specify the rotation angle by selecting points on the screen.

Modifying Array Groups

When you select an element in an array that has been grouped, you can change the number of instances in the array, as shown in Figure 2–48. For radial arrays you can also modify the distance to the center.

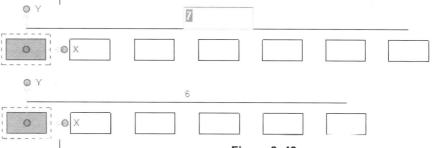

Figure 2–48

•   Dashed lines surround the element(s) in a group, and the XY control lets you move the origin point of the group

If you move one of the elements in the array group, the other elements move in response based on the distance and/or angle, as shown in Figure 2–49.

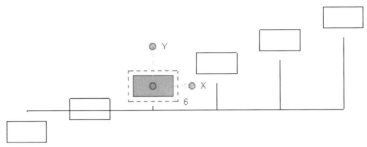

Figure 2–49

- To remove the array constraint on the group, select all of the elements in the array group and, in the *Modify* contextual tab>Group panel, click (Ungroup).

- If you select an individual element in an array and click (Ungroup), the element you selected is removed from the array, while the rest of the elements remain in the array group.

- You can use (Filter) to ensure that you are selecting only **Model Groups**.

Practice 2b

Work with Basic Modify Tools

Practice Objective

- Use basic modify tools such as Move, Copy, Rotate, and Array Elements.

Estimated time for completion: 15 minutes

In this practice, you will add tree components of different types and sizes using **Move** and **Copy** to place them around the site. You will also array a tree component around a sunken garden area. Finally, you will place a parking space component and then array and rotate it to create a parking area, as shown in Figure 2–50.

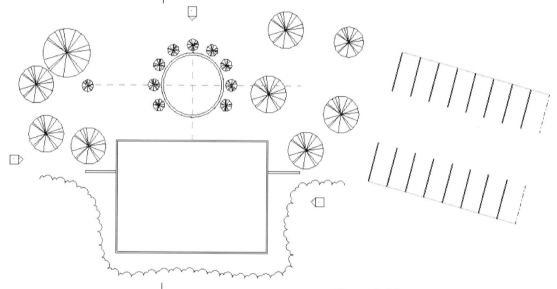

Figure 2–50

Task 1 - Add and modify tree components.

1. Open the project **Simple-Landscape-1.rvt** from your practice files folder.

2. Open the **Floor Plans: Level 1** view.

3. In the *Architecture* tab>Build panel, click (Component).

4. In the Type Selector, select one of the smaller versions of the **RPC Tree - Deciduous** type and place it close to the building, as shown in Figure 2–51.

5. Click **Modify** and select the tree. Change the type to one of the larger trees, as shown in Figure 2–52.

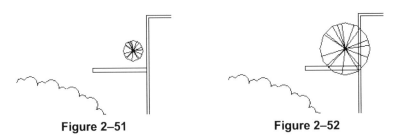

Figure 2–51   Figure 2–52

6. Drag the tree away from the building.

7. With the tree still selected, in the *Modify | Planting* tab> Modify panel, click ⊙ (Copy).

8. Select the center of the tree as the move start point.

9. In the Options Bar, select **Multiple**.

10. Place several trees around the area, as shown in Figure 2–53 and click **Modify** to finish.

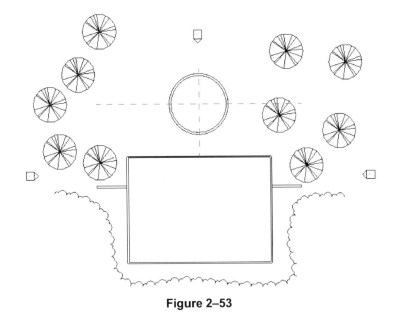

Figure 2–53

11. Select individual trees and change the type so that you have a variety of species.

12. Save the project.

Task 2 - Create a Radial Array of plants.

1. Start the **Component** command again and place a small tree near the circular wall on the horizontal reference plane, as shown in Figure 2–54.

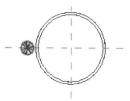

Figure 2–54

2. Click **Modify** and select the new tree.

3. In the Modify panel, click ⠿ (Array).

4. In the Options Bar, click 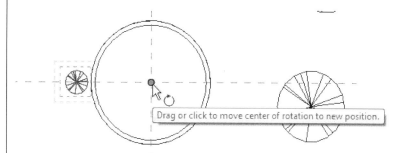 (Radial). Clear the **Group and Associate** option, set the *Number* field to 12, and set the *Move To:* field to **2nd.**

5. Drag the center of rotation from the center of the tree to the intersection of the reference planes, as shown in Figure 2–55.

Drag or click to move center of rotation to new position.

Figure 2–55

*Sometimes it is easier to
create more elements
then you need and then
delete the ones that are
not required, as it is
done in this example.*

6. Return to the Options Bar and set the *Angle* to **360**. Press
   <Enter>. The array displays as shown in Figure 2–56.

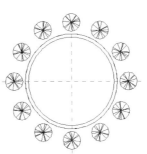

Figure 2–56

7. Delete the three trees closest to the building.

8. Zoom out to display the entire view.

Task 3 - Array, Mirror, and Rotate parking spaces.

1. With the **Modify** command active, select the elevation marker
   on the right of the building and drag it down and over below
   the tree line, as shown in Figure 2–57. Use the window
   selection method or hold <Ctrl> to select both parts.

2. Start the **Component** command and in the Type Selector,
   select **Parking Space: 9' x 18' - 90 deg**.

3. Place the component as shown in Figure 2–57 and click the
   vertical **Flip the instance facing** control.

*These steps show you
the power of controls
and temporary
dimensions. You could
also move the parking
space to the correct
location.*

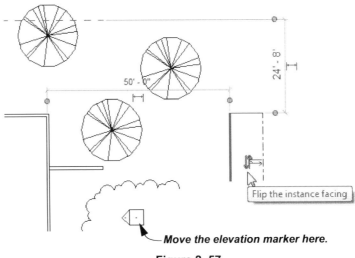

Move the elevation marker here.

Figure 2–57

4. Click **Modify** and select the parking space.

5. Drag the temporary dimension **Move Witness Line** control to the end of the parking space closest to the reference plane, as shown in Figure 2–58.

6. Change the temporary dimension to **12'-0"**, as shown in Figure 2–59.

Figure 2–58   Figure 2–59

7. With the parking space still selected, type **AR** to start the **Array** command.

8. In the Options Bar, verify that ▥ (Linear) is selected. Clear the **Group and Associate** option and set the *Number* to **8** and *Move To:* to **2nd.**

9. Select the points shown in Figure 2–60 and the array is created.

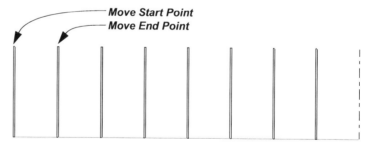

Figure 2–60

10. Select all of the new parking spaces.

11. In the *Modify | Parking* tab>Modify panel, click ▯ (Mirror - Pick Access).

12. Click the horizontal reference plane and the additional parking spaces are placed.

13. Select both groups of parking spaces and type **RO** to start the **Rotate** command.

14. Drag the center of rotation to the corner of the building, as shown in Figure 2–61.

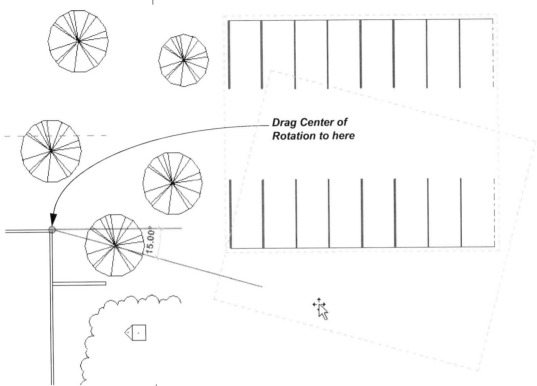

Drag Center of Rotation to here

Figure 2–61

15. Click horizontally to the right of the center point and then 15 degrees down, as shown in Figure 2–61.

16. Type **ZF** zoom out to see the full site.

17. Save the project.

2.4 Working with Additional Modify Tools

As you work on a project, some additional tools on the *Modify* tab>Modify panel, as shown in Figure 2–62, can help you with placing, modifying, and constraining elements. **Align** can be used with a variety of elements, while **Split Element**, **Trim/Extend**, and **Offset** can only be used with linear elements.

Figure 2–62

Aligning Elements

The **Align** command enables you to line up one element with another, as shown in Figure 2–63. Most Autodesk Revit elements can be aligned. For example, you can line up the tops of windows with the top of a door, or line up furniture with a wall.

First Pick   *Second Pick*

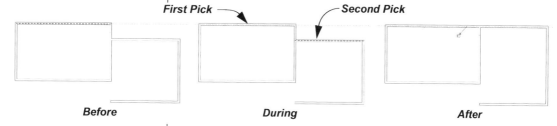

Before   *During*   *After*

Figure 2–63

How To: Align Elements

1. In the *Modify* tab>Modify panel, click ⬚ (Align).
2. Select a line or point on the element that is going to remain stationary. For walls, press <Tab> to select the correct wall face.
3. Select a line or point on the element to be aligned. The second element moves into alignment with the first one.

• The **Align** command works in all model views, including parallel and perspective 3D views.

Locking elements enlarges the size of the project file, so use this option carefully.

- You can lock alignments so that the elements move together if either one is moved. Once you have created the alignment, a padlock displays. Click on the padlock to lock it, as shown in Figure 2–64.

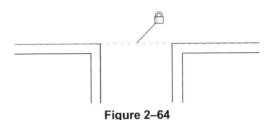

Figure 2–64

- Select **Multiple Alignment** to select multiple elements to align with the first element. You can also hold <Ctrl> to make multiple alignments.

- For walls, you can specify if you want the command to prefer **Wall centerlines**, **Wall faces**, **Center of core**, or **Faces of core**, as shown in Figure 2–65. The core refers to the structural members of a wall as opposed to facing materials, such as sheet rock.

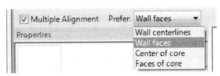

Figure 2–65

Splitting Linear Elements

The **Split** Element command enables you to break a linear element at a specific point. You can use alignment lines, snaps, and temporary dimensions to help place the split point. After you have split the linear element, you can use other editing commands to modify the two parts, or change the type of one part, as shown with walls in Figure 2–66.

You can split walls in plan, elevation or 3D views.

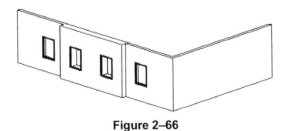

Figure 2–66

How To: Split Linear Elements

1. In the *Modify* tab>Modify panel, click ⊕ (Split Element) or type the shortcut **SL**.
2. In the Options Bar, select or clear the **Delete Inner Segment** option.
3. Move the cursor to the point you want to split and select the point.
4. Repeat for any additional split locations.
5. Modify the elements that were split, as required.

- The **Delete Inner Segment** option is used when you select two split points along a linear element. When the option is selected, the segment between the two split points is automatically removed.

- An additional option, ⁰⁞ᵒ (Split with Gap), splits the linear element at the point you select (as shown in Figure 2–67), but also creates a *Joint Gap* specified in the Options Bar.

This command is typically used with structural precast slabs.

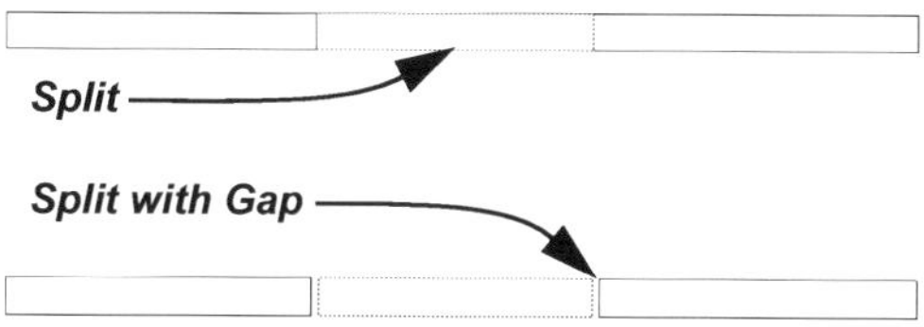

Figure 2–67

Trimming and Extending

There are three trim/extend methods that you can use with linear elements: **Trim/Extend to Corner**, **Trim/Extend Single Element**, and **Trim/Extend Multiple Elements**.

- When selecting elements to trim, click the part of the element that you want to keep. The opposite part of the line is then trimmed.

How To: Trim/Extend to Corner

1. In the *Modify* tab>Modify panel, click ⌐ (Trim/Extend to Corner) or type the shortcut **TR**.
2. Select the first linear element on the side you want to keep.

3. Select the second linear element on the side you want to keep, as shown in Figure 2–68.

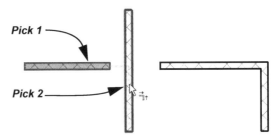

Figure 2–68

How To: Trim/Extend a Single Element

1. In the *Modify* tab>Modify panel, click ⇥ǁ (Trim/Extend Single Element).
2. Select the cutting or boundary edge.
3. Select the linear element to be trimmed or extended, as shown in Figure 2–69.

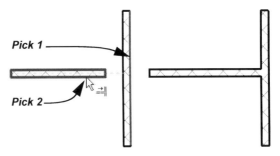

Figure 2–69

How To: Trim/Extend Multiple Elements

1. In the *Modify* tab>Modify panel, click ⇥ǁ (Trim/Extend Multiple Elements).
2. Select the cutting or boundary edge.
3. Select the linear elements that you want to trim or extend by selecting one at a time, or by using a crossing window, as shown in Figure 2–70. For trimming, select the side you want to keep.

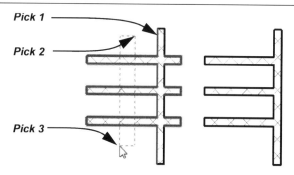

Figure 2–70

- You can click in an empty space to clear the selection and select another cutting edge or boundary.

Offsetting Elements

The **Offset** command is an easy way of creating parallel copies of linear elements at a specified distance, as shown in Figure 2–71. Walls, beams, braces, and lines are among the elements that can be offset.

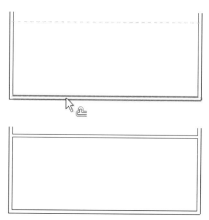

Figure 2–71

- If you offset a wall that has a door or window embedded in it, the elements are copied with the offset wall.

The offset distance can be set by typing the distance (**Numerical** method shown in Figure 2–72) or by selecting points on the screen (**Graphical** method).

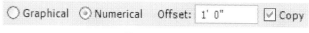

Figure 2–72

How To: Offset using the Numerical Method

*The **Copy** option (which is on by default) makes a copy of the element being offset. If this option is not selected, the **Offset** command moves the element the set offset distance.*

1. In the *Modify* tab>Modify panel, click  (Offset) or type the shortcut **OF**.
2. In the Options Bar, select **Numerical**.
3. In the Options Bar, type the required distance in the *Offset* field.
4. Move the cursor over the element you want to offset. A dashed line previews the offset location. Move the cursor to flip the sides, as required.
5. Click to create the offset.
6. Repeat Steps 4 and 5 to offset other elements by the same distance, or to change the distance for another offset.

- With the **Numerical** option, you can select multiple connected linear elements for offsetting. Hover the cursor over an element and press <Tab> until the other related elements are highlighted. Select the element to offset all of the elements at the same time.

How To: Offset using the Graphical Method

1. Start the **Offset** command.
2. In the Options Bar, select **Graphical**.
3. Select the linear element to offset.
4. Select two points that define the distance of the offset and which side to apply it. You can type an override in the temporary dimension for the second point.

- Most linear elements connected at a corner automatically trim or extend to meet at the offset distance, as shown in Figure 2–73.

Figure 2–73

Hint: Create Similar

To place elements exactly like those in your current project, right-click on an existing element and select **Create Similar**, as shown in Figure 2–74. The related command starts with the type and properties set to match the selected element. This works with all types of elements such as walls and components.

Figure 2–74

Practice 2c

Work with Additional Modify Tools

Practice Objective

- Split, Trim/Extend, and Offset elements.

Estimated time for completion: 15 minutes

In this practice, you will add walls around the parking area and create walls that function as curbs for walkways. You will then use Offset, Trim/Extend, and Split to clean up the walls, as shown in Figure 2–75.

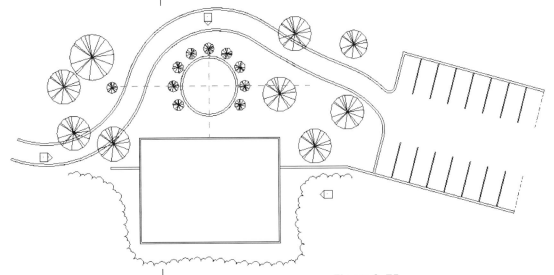

Figure 2–75

Task 1 - Add walls around the parking area.

1. Open the project **Simple-Landscape-2.rvt** from the practice files folder.

2. Zoom in on the parking lot and the side of the building.

3. Right-click on the retaining wall that is coming off the side of the building and select **Create Similar**.

4. Note that the **Wall** command starts with the same type and properties as the selected wall.

5. Sketch a wall along three sides of the parking area, as shown in Figure 2–76.

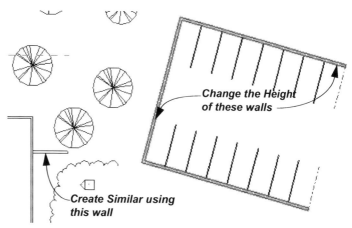

Figure 2–76

6. Select the two walls shown in Figure 2–76. In Properties, change the *Unconnected Height* to **6"**. (These are now curb height while the other wall remains at retaining wall height.)

7. In the *Modify* tab>Modify panel, click ↱ (Trim/Extend to corner) and select the two walls to extend as shown in Figure 2–77.

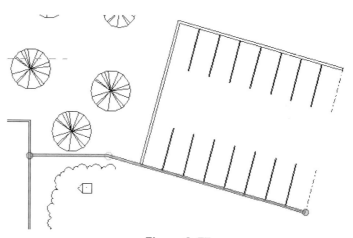

Figure 2–77

8. Switch to a 3D view to see the new walls.

9. Save the project.

Task 2 - Create a curved path using low walls as a curb.

1. Return to the **Floor Plans: Level 1** view.

2. Right-click on the low curb wall around the parking lot and select **Create Similar.**

3. Note that the **Wall** command starts with the same type and properties as the selected wall.

4. In the *Modify | Place Wall* tab>Draw panel, click

   ⌐ (Start-End-Radius Arc).

5. In the Options Bar, select **Chain**.

6. Sketch a curved wall similar to that shown in Figure 2–78. As you are sketching, ensure that you use the Tangent snap so that the walls curve smoothly.

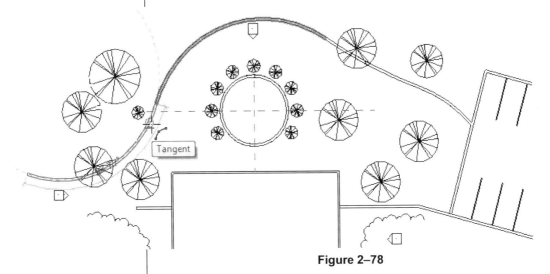

Figure 2–78

7. Click **Modify**.

8. In the *Modify* tab>Modify panel, click ⌐ (Offset).

9. In the Options Bar, set the *Offset* to **10'-0"** and verify that **Copy** is selected.

10. Hover over the first wall and then press <Tab> so the rest are highlighted, as shown in Figure 2–79. Ensure that the dashed lines are on the lower side of the wall and then click to place the offset walls.

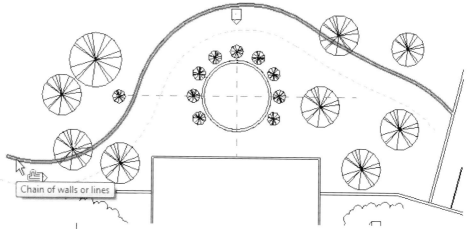

Figure 2–79

11. Save the project.

Task 3 - Clean up the curb intersections.

1. In the *Modify* tab>Modify panel, click ⌐╢ (Trim/Extend Single Element).

2. Select the angled parking lot curb wall and then the curved wall as shown in Figure 2–80.

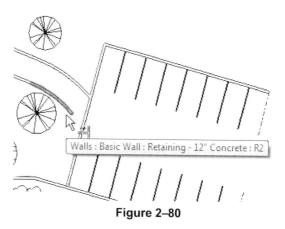

Figure 2–80

3. In the *Modify* tab>Modify panel, click ⊕ (Split Element).

4. In the Options Bar, select **Delete Inner Segment**.

5. Click on the angled wall where it intersects with the curved wall at both ends. The wall segment between these points is removed, as shown in Figure 2–81.

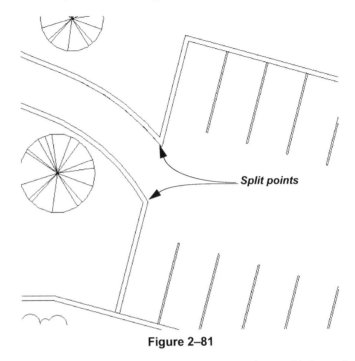

Split points

Figure 2–81

6. Start the **Wall** command. (The most recently used information is set by default.)

7. In the *Modify | Place Wall* tab>Draw panel, click (Fillet Arc).

8. In the Options Bar, select **Radius** and type **12'-0"**.

9. Select the two intersecting curbs at the lower end of the opening.

10. Change the *Radius* to **3'-0"** and select the two intersecting curbs at the upper end of the opening, as shown in Figure 2–82.

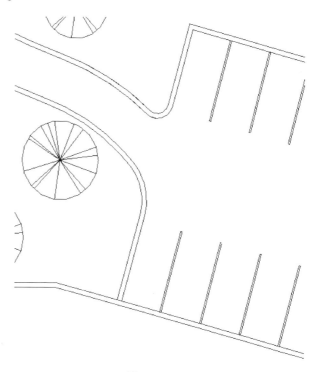

Figure 2–82

11. Select and adjust the radiuses of the arcs as required, using temporary dimensions.

12. Zoom out to see the entire site.

13. View the site in 3D.

14. Save the project.

Chapter Review Questions

1. What is the purpose of an alignment line?

   a. Displays when the new element you are placing or modeling is aligned with the grid system.

   b. Indicates that the new element you are placing or modeling is aligned with an existing object.

   c. Displays when the new element you are placing or modeling is aligned with a selected tracking point.

   d. Indicates that the new element is aligned with true north rather than project north.

2. When you are modeling (not editing) a linear element, how do you edit the temporary dimension, as that shown in Figure 2–83?

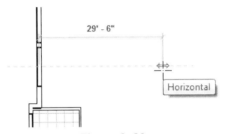

Figure 2–83

   a. Select the temporary dimension and enter a new value.

   b. Type a new value and press <Enter>.

   c. Type a new value in the Distance/Length box in the Options Bar and press <Enter>.

3. How do you select all door types, but no other elements in a view?

   a. In the Project Browser, select the *Door* category.

   b. Select one door, right-click and select **Select All Instances>Visible in View**.

   c. Select all of the objects in the view and use ▽ (Filter) to clear the other categories.

   d. Select one door, and click ⬛ (Select Multiple) in the ribbon.

4. What are the two methods for starting 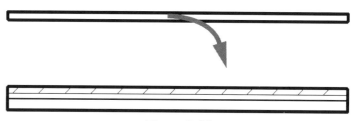 (Move) or

   (Copy)?

   a. Start the command first and then select the objects, or select the objects and then start the command.

   b. Start the command from the *Modify* tab, or select the object and then select **Move** or **Copy** from the shortcut menu.

   c. Start the command from the *Modify* tab, or select the objects and select **Auto-Move**.

   d. Use the **Move/Copy** command or **Cut/Copy** and **Paste** using the Clipboard.

5. Where do you change the wall type for a selected wall, as shown in Figure 2–84?

Figure 2–84

   a. In the *Modify | Walls* tab>Properties panel, click (Type Properties) and select a new wall type in the dialog box.

   b. In the Options Bar, click **Change Element Type**.

   c. Select the dynamic control next to the selected wall and select a new type in the drop-down list.

   d. In Properties, select a new type in the Type Selector drop-down list.

6. Both ⟳ (Rotate) and ⊞ (Array) with ⧉ (Radial) have a center of rotation that defaults to the center of the element or group of elements you have selected. How do you move the center of rotation to another point as shown in Figure 2–85? (Select all that apply.)

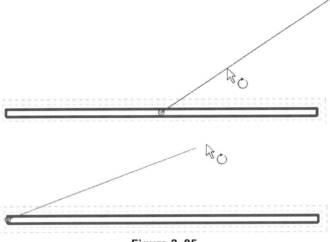

Figure 2–85

a. Select the center of rotation and drag it to a new location.

b. In the Options Bar, click **Place** and select the new point.

c. In the *Modify* tab>Placement panel, click ⊙ (Center) and select the new point.

d. Right-click and select **Snap Overrides>Centers** and select the new point.

7. Which command would you use to remove part of a wall?

a. ⊏⊐ (Split Element)

b. ⟋ (Wall Joins)

c. ⬡ (Cut Geometry)

d. ⬟ (Demolish)

8. Which of the following are ways in which you can create additional parallel walls, as shown in Figure 2–86? (Select all that apply.)

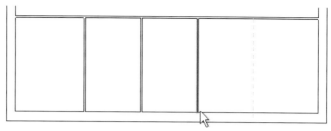

Figure 2–86

a. Select an existing wall, right-click and select **Create Offset**.

b. Use the **Offset** tool in the *Modify* tab.

c. Select an existing wall, hold <Ctrl>, and drag the wall to a new location.

d. Use the **Wall** tool and set an offset in the Options Bar.

9. Which command do you use if you want two walls that are not touching to come together, as shown in Figure 2–87?

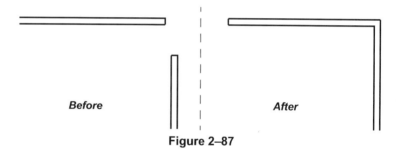

Before　　　　　　　　*After*

Figure 2–87

a. 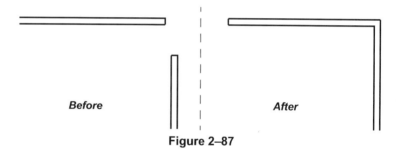 (Edit Wall Joins)

b. (Trim/Extend to Corner)

c. (Join Geometry)

d. (Edit Profile)

Command Summary

Button	Command	Location
Draw Commands and Tools		
	Detail Lines	• **Ribbon**: *Annotate* tab>Detail panel • **Shortcut**: DL
	Model Line	• **Ribbon**: *Architecture* or *Structure* tab> Model panel • **Shortcut**: LI
	Revision Cloud	• **Ribbon**: *Annotate* tab>Detail panel
	Center-ends Arc	• **Ribbon**: *Modify*	*(various linear elements)* tab>Draw panel
	Circle	• **Ribbon**: *Modify*	*(various linear elements)* tab>Draw panel
	Circumscribed Polygon	• **Ribbon**: *Modify*	*(various linear elements)* tab>Draw panel
	Ellipse	• **Ribbon**: *Modify*	*Place Lines, Place Detail Lines, and various boundary sketches*>Draw panel
	Ellipse Arc	• **Ribbon**: *Modify*	*Place Lines, Place Detail Lines, and various boundary sketches*>Draw panel
	Fillet Arc	• **Ribbon**: *Modify*	*(various linear elements)* tab>Draw panel
	Inscribed Polygon	• **Ribbon**: *Modify*	*(various linear elements)* tab>Draw panel
	Line	• **Ribbon**: *Modify*	*(various linear elements)* tab>Draw panel
	Pick Faces	• **Ribbon**: *Modify*	*Place Wall*> Draw panel
	Pick Lines	• **Ribbon**: *Modify*	*(various linear elements)* tab>Draw panel
	Pick Walls	• **Ribbon**: *Modify*	*(various boundary sketches)*>Draw panel
	Rectangle	• **Ribbon**: *Modify*	*(various linear elements)* tab>Draw panel
	Spline	• **Ribbon**: *Modify*	*Place Lines, Place Detail Lines, and various boundary sketches*>Draw panel
	Start-End-Radius Arc	• **Ribbon**: *Modify*	*(various linear elements)* tab>Draw panel
	Tangent End Arc	• **Ribbon**: *Modify*	*(various linear elements)* tab>Draw panel

Modify Tools

	Align	• **Ribbon:** *Modify* tab>Modify panel • **Shortcut:** AL
	Array	• **Ribbon:** *Modify* tab>Modify panel • **Shortcut:** AR
	Copy	• **Ribbon:** *Modify* tab>Modify panel • **Shortcut:** CO
	Copy to Clipboard	• **Ribbon:** *Modify* tab>Clipboard panel • **Shortcut:** <Ctrl>+<C>
	Delete	• **Ribbon:** *Modify* tab>Modify panel • **Shortcut:** DE
	Mirror - Draw Axis	• **Ribbon:** *Modify* tab>Modify panel • **Shortcut:** DM
	Mirror - Pick Axis	• **Ribbon:** *Modify* tab>Modify panel • **Shortcut:** MM
	Move	• **Ribbon:** *Modify* tab>Modify panel • **Shortcut:** MV
	Offset	• **Ribbon:** *Modify* tab>Modify panel • **Shortcut:** OF
	Paste	• **Ribbon:** *Modify* tab>Clipboard panel • **Shortcut:** <Ctrl>+<V>
	Pin	• **Ribbon:** *Modify* tab>Modify panel • **Shortcut:** PN
	Rotate	• **Ribbon:** *Modify* tab>Modify panel • **Shortcut:** RO
	Scale	• **Ribbon:** *Modify* tab>Modify panel • **Shortcut:** RE
	Split Element	• **Ribbon:** *Modify* tab>Modify panel • **Shortcut:** SL
	Split with Gap	• **Ribbon:** *Modify* tab>Modify panel
	Trim/Extend Multiple Elements	• **Ribbon:** *Modify* tab>Modify panel
	Trim/Extend Single Element	• **Ribbon:** *Modify* tab>Modify panel
	Trim/Extend to Corner	• **Ribbon:** *Modify* tab>Modify panel • **Shortcut:** TR
	Unpin	• **Ribbon:** *Modify* tab>Modify panel • **Shortcut:** UP

Select Tools

	Drag elements on selection	• **Ribbon:** All tabs>Expanded Select panel • **Status Bar**
	Filter	• **Ribbon:** *Modify | Multi-Select* tab> Filter panel • **Status Bar**
	Select Elements By Face	• **Ribbon:** All tabs>Expanded Select panel • **Status Bar**
	Select Links	• **Ribbon:** All tabs>Expanded Select panel • **Status Bar**
	Select Pinned Elements	• **Ribbon:** All tabs>Expanded Select panel • **Status Bar**
	Select Underlay Elements	• **Ribbon:** All tabs>Expanded Select panel • **Status Bar**

Additional Tools

	Measure Between Two References	• **Ribbon:** *Modify* tab>Measure panel • **Quick Access Toolbar**
	Measure Along An Element	• **Ribbon:** *Modify* tab>Measure panel> Expand Measure • **Quick Access Toolbar**>Expand Measure
	Reference Plane	• **Ribbon:** *Architecture/Structure/ Systems* tab> Work Plane panel

Chapter

3

Starting Model-Based Projects

Landscape projects typically use information provided by the architect as the base for the project and are therefore only started after an architectural project is well underway. You can link Autodesk® Revit® models and then build the landscape model around them, copying and monitoring the required information from the architectural model into the landscape project.

Learning Objectives in this Chapter

- Link Revit models into the project so that you can design the landscape project.
- Add levels to define floor to floor heights and other vertical references.
- Copy and monitor elements from linked Revit models so that you know when changes have been made.
- Run Coordination Reviews to identify changes between the current project and any linked models.

3.1 Linking Revit Models

You can link an Autodesk Revit project into any other project. A linked model automatically updates if the original file is changed. This method can be used in many ways. For example, you can use it when you have a number of identical buildings on one site plan, as shown in Figure 3–1.

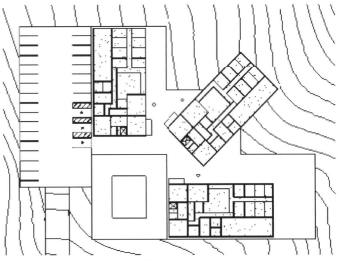

Figure 3–1

- Landscape projects typically use the architectural model as the base for their projects.

- Architectural, structural, and MEP models created in the Autodesk Revit software can be linked to each other as long as they are from the same release cycle.

- When you use linked models, clashes between disciplines can be detected and information can be passed between disciplines.

- Elements can be copied and monitored for even better coordination.

Hint: Project Base Point

The origin of a project coordinate system is specified by the project base point, as shown in Figure 3–2. This should be set early in the project and before you start linking files together. It can be (but is not always) connected with the Survey Point, which is set to exact survey information.

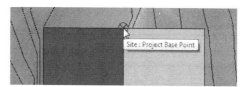

Figure 3–2

- Project base points and survey points are visible in the Site view of the default architectural template. You can toggle them on in any view. In the Visibility/Graphic Overrides dialog box, in the *Model* Category tab, expand the **Site** category.

- Spot Coordinates and Spot Elevations are relative to the project base point, survey base point, or relative to the level depending on the type of tag you use and its settings.

How To: Add a Linked Model to a Host Project

1. In the *Insert* tab>Link panel, click [icon] (Link Revit).
2. In the Import/Link RVT dialog box, select the file that you want to link. Before opening the file, set the *Positioning*, as shown in Figure 3–3.

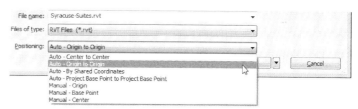

Figure 3–3

3. Click **Open**.
4. Depending on how you decide to position the file, it is automatically placed in the project or you can manually place it with the cursor.

- As the links are loading, do not click on the screen or click any buttons. The more links are present in a project, the longer it takes to load.

Hint: Preventing Linked Model from being moved

Once a linked model is in the correct location, you can lock it in place to ensure it does not get moved by mistake, or prevent the linked model from being selected.

- To pin the linked model in place, select it and in the *Modify* tab>Modify panel, click ⚲ (Pin).

- To prevent pinned elements from being selected, in the Status Bar, click 🗝 (Select Pinned Elements).

- To toggle off the ability to select links, in the Status Bar, click 🗝 (Select Links).

If a linked file is moved, you can reposition it to the Project Base Point or Internal Origin. Right-click on it and select the option, as shown in Figure 3–4.

Figure 3–4

Multiple Copies of Linked Models

Copied instances of a linked model are typically used when creating a master project with the same building placed in multiple locations, such as a university campus with six identical student residence halls.

- Linked models can be moved, copied, rotated, arrayed, and mirrored. There is only one linked model, and any copies are additional instances of the link.

- Copies are numbered automatically. You can change their names in Properties when the instance is selected.

- When you have placed a link in a project, you can drag and drop additional copies of the link into the project from the Project Browser>**Revit Links** node, as shown in Figure 3–5.

Figure 3–5

Managing Links

The Manage Links dialog box (shown in Figure 3–6) enables you to reload, unload, add, and remove links, and also provides access to set other options. To open the Manage Links dialog box, in the *Insert* tab>Link, panel click  (Manage Links) or select the link and, in the *Modify | RVT Links* tab> Link panel, click (Manage Links)

Figure 3–6

The options available in the Manage Links dialog box include the following:

- **Reload From:** Opens the Add Link dialog box, which enables you to select the file you want to reload. Use this if the linked file location or name has changed.

- **Reload:** Reloads the file without additional prompts.

- **Unload:** Unloads the file so that the link is kept, but the file is not displayed or calculated in the project. Use **Reload** to restore it.

- **Add:** Opens the Import/Link RVT dialog box, which enables you to link additional models into the host project.

- **Remove:** Deletes the link from the file.

Links can be nested into one another. How a link responds when the host project is linked into another project depends on the option in the *Reference Type* column:

- **Overlay:** The nested linked model is not referenced in the new host project.

- **Attach:** The nested linked model displays in the new host project.

*Reload is also available in the Project Browser. Expand the **Revit Links** node. Right-click on the Revit Link and select **Reload** or **Reload From…***

The option in the *Path Type* column controls how the location of the link is remembered:

- **Relative**
  - Searches the root folder of the current project.
  - If the file is moved, the software will still search for it.
- **Absolute**
  - Searches only the folder where the file was originally saved.
  - If the original file is moved, the software will not be able to find it.
- Other options control how the linked file interfaces with Worksets and Shared Positioning.

Hint: Visibility Graphics and Linked Files

When you open the Visibility/Graphics dialog box (type **VV** or **VG**), you can modify the graphic overrides for Revit links as shown in Figure 3–7. This can help you clean up the view, or assign a view to build on.

Figure 3–7

The *Display Settings* include:

- **By host view:** The display of the Revit link is based on the view properties of the current view in the host model.

- **By linked view:** The appearance of the Revit link is based on the view properties of the selected linked view and ignores the view properties of the current view.

- **Custom:** You can override all of the graphical elements.

Practice 3a

Link Revit Models

Practice Objectives

- Start a new project from a template.
- Link architectural models into a new project.

Estimated time for completion: 10 minutes

In this practice, you will link a site model with topography created in the Autodesk Revit software into a new landscape project and pin the linked model into place. You will then link in two other architectural models: the base of the tower and the tower, as shown in Figure 3–8.

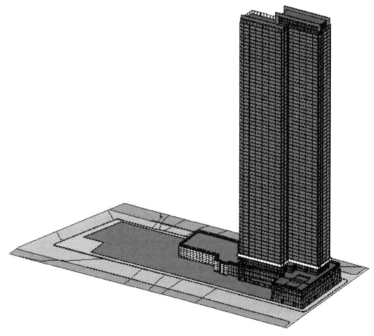

Figure 3–8

Task 1 - Link models into a landscape project.

1. In the *File* tab, expand ☐ (New) and click ☐ (Project).

2. In the New Project dialog box, expand the *Template file* list and select **Architectural Template**.Click **OK**.

3. Save the project as **Urban Garden <your initials>.rvt**.

4. In the Quick Access Toolbar, click 🔹 (Default 3D View).

5. In the *Insert* tab>Link panel, click 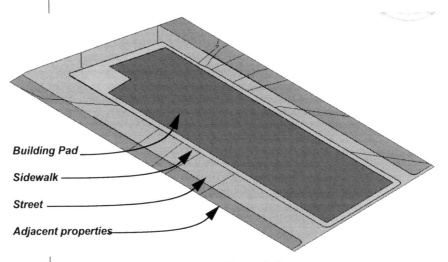 (Link Revit).

6. In the Import/Link RVT dialog box, navigate to the practice files folder and select **Building-Site.rvt**. Set the *Positioning: is set* to **Auto - Origin to Origin** and then click **Open**.

7. Zoom to fit the view (**Hint:** Type **ZF**) to see the entire linked model. In the View Control Bar, set the *Visual Style* to **Consistent Colors** so you can see the various parts of the topography, as shown in Figure 3–9.

Building Pad

Sidewalk

Street

Adjacent properties

Figure 3–9

8. Select the linked model in the view.

9. In the *Modify | RVT Links* tab>Modify panel, click (Pin). This will ensure that the linked model will not be accidentally moved in the view.

10. Repeat the **Link Revit** command, select **Building-Base.rvt** and click **Open**. This is the base of the tower where most of the work on this project will be completed.

11. Repeat the command again and link in **Building-Tower.rvt**.

12. Zoom out to display the entire tower, as shown in Figure 3–10.

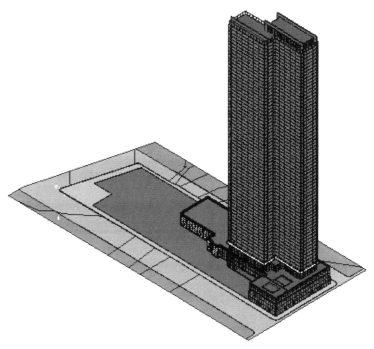

Figure 3–10

13. Pin the building links in place.

14. Save the project.

3.2 Setting Up Levels

Levels define stories and other vertical heights, as shown in Figure 3–11. Templates typically include two or more default levels, but you can define as many levels in a project as required. They can go down as well as up. Floor levels are set by the architect and need to be copied and monitored into the landscape model if you are designing directly on a building for a green roof. You can also draw levels directly in a project, as required.

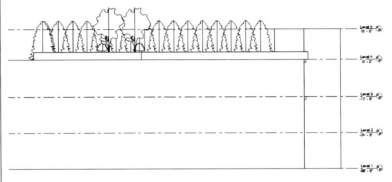

Figure 3–11

- You must be in an elevation or section view to define levels.

- Once you constrain an element to a level it moves with the level when the level is changed.

How To: Create Levels

1. Open an elevation or section view.

2. In the *Architecture* tab>Datum panel, click (Level), or type **LL**.

3. In the Type Selector, set the Level Head type, if required.

4. In the Options Bar, select or clear **Make Plan View**, as required. You can also click **Plan View Types...** to select the types of views to create when you place the level.

5. In the *Modify | Place Level* tab>Draw panel, click:

   - (Line) to draw a level.

   - (Pick Lines) to select an element using an offset.

- When using **Pick Lines**, ensure that you do not place levels on top of each other or other elements by mistake.

6. Continue adding levels, as required.

- Level names are automatically incremented as you place them so it is helpful to name them in simply (i.e., Floor 1, Floor 2, etc., rather than First Floor, Second Floor, etc.). This also makes it easier to find the view in the Project Browser.

- A fast way to create multiple levels is to use the 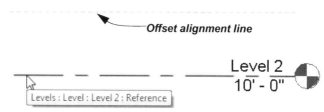 (Pick Lines) option using an offset. In the Options Bar, specify an *Offset,* select an existing level, and then pick above or below to place the new level, as shown in Figure 3–12.

You specify above or below the offset by hovering the mouse on the required side.

Figure 3–12

- When using the ✏ (Line) option, alignments and temporary dimensions help you place the line correctly, as shown in Figure 3–13.

You can sketch the level lines from left to right or right to left. However, ensure that they are all sketched in the same direction.

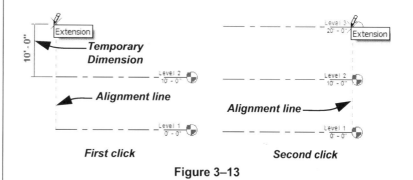

Figure 3–13

- You can also use (Copy) to duplicate level lines. The level names are incremented but a plan view is not created.

Modifying Levels

You can change levels using standard controls and temporary dimensions, as shown in Figure 3–14. You can also make changes in the Properties palette.

Figure 3–14

- ☑ ☐ (Hide / Show Bubble) displays on either end of the level line and toggles the level head symbol and level information on or off.

- 2D 3D (Switch to 3d / 2d extents) controls whether any movement or adjustment to the level line is reflected in other views (3D) or only affects the current view (2D).

- ↬ (Modify the level by dragging its model end) at each end of the line enables you to drag the level head to a new location.

- 🔒 🔓 (Create or remove a length or alignment constraint) controls whether the level is locked in alignment with the other levels. If it is locked and the level line is stretched, all of the other level lines stretch as well. If it is unlocked, the level line stretches independent of the other levels.

- Click ⌇ (Add Elbow) to add a jog to the level line, as shown in Figure 3–15. Drag the shape handles to new locations, as required. This is a view-specific change.

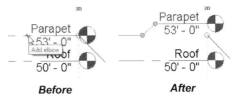

Before   **After**

Figure 3–15

- To change the level name or elevation, double-click on the information next to the level head, or select the level and modify the *Name* or *Elevation* fields in Properties, as shown in Figure 3–16.

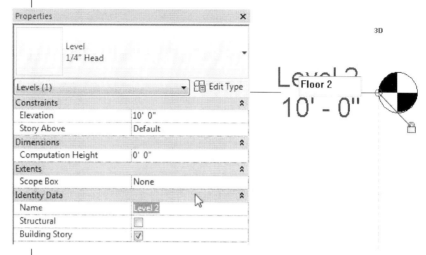

Figure 3–16

- When you rename a Level, an alert box opens, prompting you to rename the corresponding views as shown in Figure 3–17.

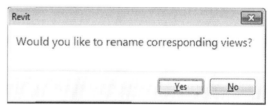

Figure 3–17

- The view is also renamed in the Project Browser.

Hint: Copying Levels and Grids from other projects

Levels and grid lines can be added by drawing over existing levels or grids in an imported or linked CAD file. They can also be copied and monitored from a linked Autodesk Revit file. Some projects might require both methods.

Creating Plan Views

By default, when you place a level, plan views for that level are automatically created. If **Make Plan View** was toggled off in the Options Bar when adding the level, or if the level was copied, you can create plan views to match the levels.

- Level heads with views are blue and level heads without views are black, as shown in Figure 3–18.

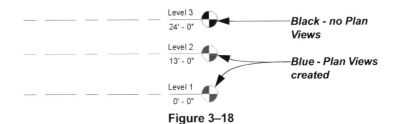

Figure 3–18

Typically, you do not need to create plan views for levels that specify data, such as the top of a foundation wall or the truss bearing height.

How To: Create Plan Views

1. In the *View* tab>Create panel, expand ⬚ (Plan Views) and select the type of plan view you want to create, as shown in Figure 3–19.
2. In the New Plan dialog box (shown in Figure 3–20), select the levels for which you want to create plan views.

Hold <Ctrl> or <Shift> to select more than one level.

Figure 3–19

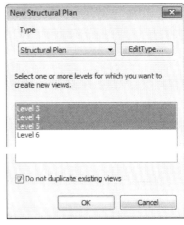

Figure 3–20

3. Click **OK**.

- When **Do not duplicate existing views** is selected, views without the selected plan type display in the list.

3.3 Copying and Monitoring Elements

Once a linked architectural model is in place, the next step is to copy and/or monitor elements that you need from the linked file into the current project. These elements most often include grids, levels, columns, walls, and floors. A monitoring system keeps track of the copied elements and prompts for updates if something is changed. In the example shown in Figure 3–21, grids have been linked from an architectural model and the

⌐Λ⌐ (Monitor) icon indicates the monitored elements.

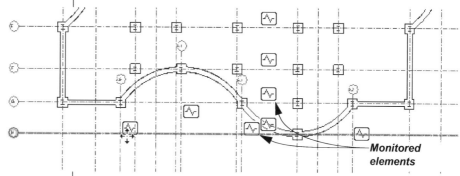

Figure 3–21

- **Copy:** Creates a duplicate of a selected element in the current project and monitors it to a selected element in the linked model or current project.

- **Monitor:** Compares two elements of the same type against each other, either from a linked model to the current project (as shown in Figure 3–22) or in the current project.

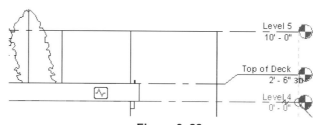

Figure 3–22

How To: Copy and Monitor Elements from a Linked File

1. In the *Collaborate* tab>Coordinate panel, expand 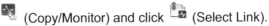 (Copy/Monitor) and click (Select Link).

2. Select the link.

3. In the *Copy/Monitor* tab>Tools panel, click (Copy) or (Monitor).

4. If copying from the linked file, select each element that you want to copy. Alternatively, use **Multiple**:

   • In the Options Bar, select **Multiple**, as shown in Figure 3–23.

Figure 3–23

   • Hold <Ctrl> and select the elements that you want to copy into your model individually, or use a pick and drag the window around multiple elements.

   • In the Options Bar, click **Finish**.

   If monitoring elements in the current project with elements in the linked model, first select the element in the current project and then select the element in the linked model.

5. Click (Finish) to end the Copy/Monitor session.

How To: Copy and Monitor Elements in the Current Project.

1. In the *Collaborate* tab>Coordinate panel, expand  (Copy/Monitor) and click (Use Current Project).

2. In the *Copy/Monitor* tab>Tools panel, click (Copy) or (Monitor).

3. Select the two elements that you want to monitor.

4. Repeat the process for any additional elements.

5. Click (Finish) to end the command.

   • The elements do not have to be at the same elevation or location for the software to monitor them.

Warnings about duplicated or renamed types might display.

Copy/Monitor Settings

Before starting the copy/monitor process, you can modify settings for the types of elements.

- In the *Copy/Monitor* tab>Tools panel, click 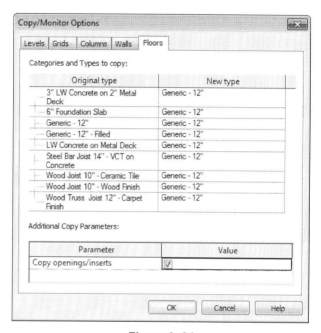 (Options). In the Copy/Monitor Options dialog box, select the tab for the type of element that you want to copy: *Levels*, *Grids*, *Columns*, *Walls*, or *Floors*, as shown in Figure 3–24.

Tabs display for the categories that exist in the linked project.

Copy/Monitor Options

| Levels | Grids | Columns | Walls | Floors |

Categories and Types to copy:

Original type	New type
3" LW Concrete on 2" Metal Deck	Generic - 12"
6" Foundation Slab	Generic - 12"
Generic - 12"	Generic - 12"
Generic - 12" - Filled	Generic - 12"
LW Concrete on Metal Deck	Generic - 12"
Steel Bar Joist 14" - VCT on Concrete	Generic - 12"
Wood Joist 10" - Ceramic Tile	Generic - 12"
Wood Joist 10" - Wood Finish	Generic - 12"
Wood Truss Joist 12" - Carpet Finish	Generic - 12"

Additional Copy Parameters:

Parameter	Value
Copy openings/inserts	☑

OK   Cancel   Help

Figure 3–24

Practice 3b

Copy and Monitor Elements

Practice Objectives

- Copy and monitor elements from the linked model into the current project.
- Create plan views.

Estimated time for completion: 10 minutes

In this practice, you will remove the tower link that is not required in the landscape project and setup a view for working with levels. You will then monitor existing levels and copy additional levels from a linked architectural model into the current project, as shown in Figure 3–25.

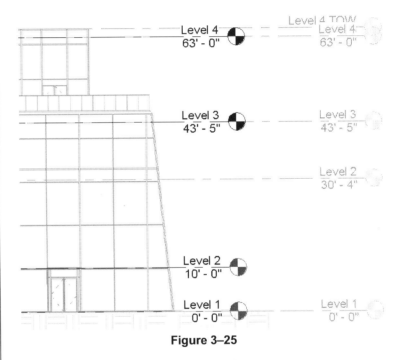

Figure 3–25

Task 1 - Setup a view for working with levels.

1. Open the project **Urban-Garden-Monitor.rvt** from the practice files folder.

2. In the Project Browser, open the **Elevations (Building Elevation): South** view. There are many levels in the linked file that you do not need for this project. Most of them are in the tower part of the design.

3. Select the tower link, as shown in Figure 3–26.

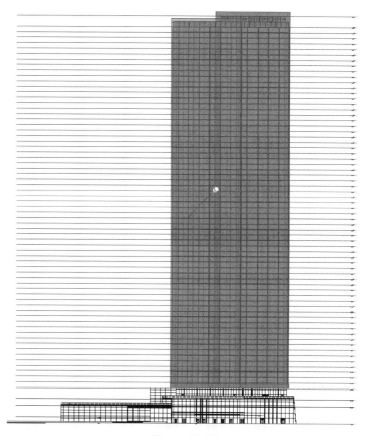

Figure 3–26

4. In the *Modify | RVT Links* tab>Link panel, click (Manage Links).

5. In the Manage Links dialog box, select **Building-Tower.rvt** and click **Remove**.

6. When the warning dialog box comes up, click **OK** and then click **OK** again to exit the dialog box.

7. Right-click on the tower base link and select **Override graphics in View>By Category**.

8. In the View-Specific Category Graphics dialog box, select **Halftone**, as shown in Figure 3–27. Then, click **OK**.

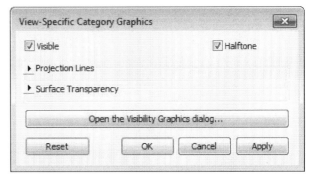

Figure 3–27

9. In the View Control Bar, change the *Scale* to **1/16"=1'-0"**. This increases the size of the level annotation information.

10. Zoom in on the right side of the building where you should see all of the levels as shown in Figure 3–28.

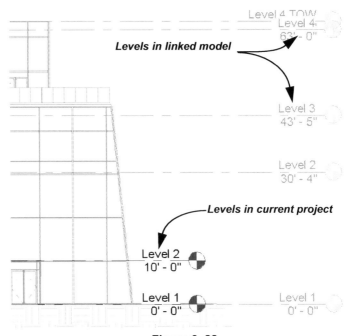

Figure 3–28

11. Save the project.

Task 2 - Copy and monitor levels.

1. In the *Collaborate* tab>Coordinate panel, expand (Copy/Monitor) and click (Select Link).

2. Select the linked model.

3. In the *Copy/Monitor* tab>Tools panel, click (Monitor).

4. Select **Level 1** in the current project and then the corresponding level in the linked model. Ensure that you select the link where it highlights, not the level name, as shown in Figure 3–29.

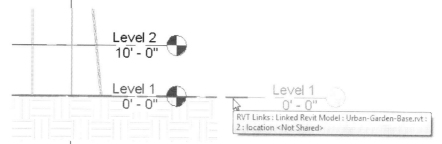

Figure 3–29

5. Repeat the process and monitor **Level 2** in the current project with **Level 2** in the linked model (although they are not at the same location).

6. In the *Copy/Monitor* tab>Tools panel, click (Copy).

7. Select both **Level 3** and **Level 4**. These levels from the linked model are now copied into the host project.

8. In the Copy/Monitor panel, click (Finish).

9. Select one of the two new levels and drag the extents, as shown in Figure 3–30, so it aligns with the other two levels in the project.

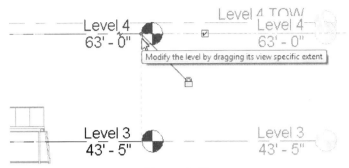

Figure 3–30

10. Select all of the new levels and zoom out so you can see that they are monitored as shown in Figure 3–31.

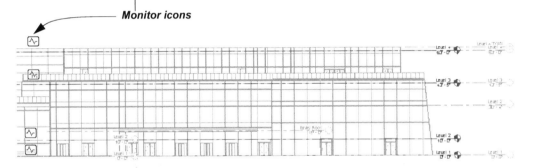

Figure 3–31

11. Save the project.

Task 3 - Set up plan views.

1. In the Project Browser, note that the floor plans of the new levels do not display, as shown in Figure 3–32.

Figure 3–32

2. In the *View* tab>Create panel, expand 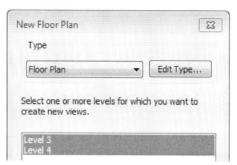 (Plan Views) and click (Floor Plan).

3. In the New Floor Plan dialog box, select Levels 3 and 4, as shown in Figure 3–33, and click **OK**.

Figure 3–33

4. The new views display in the Project Browser as shown in Figure 3–34. **Level 4** (the last plan created) is automatically opened.

Figure 3–34

5. Open a 3D view.

6. Save and close the project.

3.4 Coordinating Linked Models

Monitoring elements identifies changes in the data as well as changes in placement. For example, if you move a grid line, a Coordination Monitor alert displays, as shown in Figure 3–35. You can run a Coordination Review to correct or accept these changes.

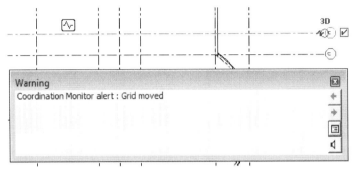

Figure 3–35

- If you open a project with a linked file, which contains elements that have been modified and monitored, the Warning shown in Figure 3–36 displays.

Figure 3–36

- Warnings alert you that the element is being monitored and needs further coordination. They do not prevent you from making a change.

- If you no longer want an element to be monitored, select it and in the associated *Modify* tab>Monitor panel, click (Stop Monitoring).

How To: Run a Coordination Review

1. In the *Collaborate* tab>Coordinate panel, expand (Coordination Review) and click (Use Current Project) or (Select Link). The Coordination Review dialog box lists any conflicts detected, as shown in Figure 3–37.

    • If there are no conflicts, the *Message* area is empty.

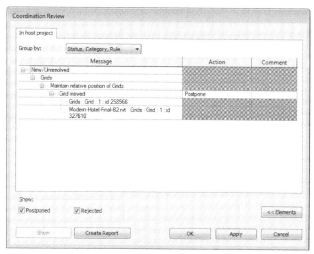

Figure 3–37

2. Use the Group by: drop-down list to group the information by **Status**, **Category**, and **Rule** in a variety of different ways. This is important if you have many elements to review.

3. Select an *Action* for each conflict related to the elements involved, as shown in Figure 3–38.

Figure 3–38

- **Postpone** - Do nothing and leave it to be handled later.
- **Reject** - Do not accept the change. The change needs to be made in the other model.
- **Accept Difference** - Make no change to the monitored element in the current project but accept the change (such as a distance between the elements) in the monitor status.

- **Rename/Modify/Move** - Apply the change to the monitored element.
- Other options display when special cases occur. See the Autodesk Revit help files for more information.

4. Click **Add comment** to add a comment in the column to the right. This enables you to make a note about the change, such as the date of the modification.
5. Select the element names or click **Show** to display any items in conflict. Clicking **Show** changes the view to center the elements in your screen. Selecting the name does not change the view.
6. Click **Create Report** to create an HTML report that you can share with other users, as shown in Figure 3–39.

Revit Coordination Report

In host project

New/Unresolved	Levels	Maintain Position	Level moved by 1' - 0"	Levels : Level : TOS-14 ROOF : id 518290 Syracuse-Suites-Architectural-TEST.rvt : Levels : Level : 14 ROOF : id 199895

Figure 3–39

Hint: Trouble Shooting

When working with various elements, Warnings (such as the one shown in Figure 3–40) display to alert you that something is wrong. In many cases, you can close the dialog box and fix the issue, or wait and do fix them later.

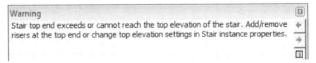

Warning
Stair top end exceeds or cannot reach the top elevation of the stair. Add/remove risers at the top end or change top elevation settings in Stair instance properties.

Figure 3–40

Sometimes Errors display where you must take action. These force you to stop and fix the situation.

When you select an element for which there has been a warning, ⚠ (Show Related Warnings) displays in the ribbon. It opens a dialog box in which you can review the warning(s) related to the selected element. You can also display a list of all of the warnings in the project by clicking ⚠ (Review Warnings) in the *Manage* tab>Inquiry panel.

Practice 3c

Coordinate Linked Models

Practice Objectives

- Make modifications to levels in a copy/monitored project.
- Run a Coordination Review.

In this practice, you will make changes to level names and locations in the host project and read the warnings created when those changes are made, as shown in Figure 3–41. You will then run a Coordination Review and accept the differences between the host project and linked project.

Estimated time for completion: 10 minutes

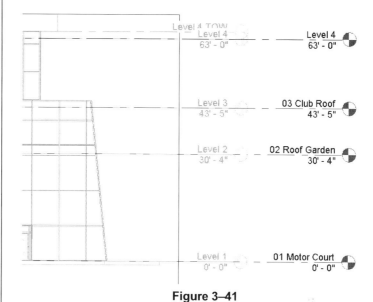

Figure 3–41

Task 1 - Modify Levels in the host project that are copy/monitored to the linked project.

1. Open the project **Urban-Garden-Coordinate.rvt** from your practice files folder.

2. Open the **Elevations: South** view.

3. Zoom in on the right side of the building so you can see the level heads.

4. In the current project, click on the **Level 1** name and rename the level to **01 Motor Court**, as shown in Figure 3–42.

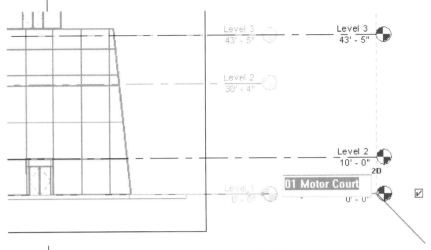

Figure 3–42

5. When prompted, click **Yes** to rename the corresponding views.

6. Because the level was monitored, a Warning displays as shown in Figure 3–43. Close the Warning dialog box.

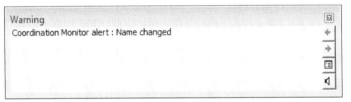

Figure 3–43

7. In the Project Browser, the former **Level 1** view has been renamed **01 Motor Court** and the related Ceiling Plan has been changed as well, as shown in Figure 3–44.

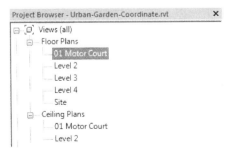

Figure 3–44

8. You do not need to work with ceilings plans, therefore, hold <Ctrl> and select both ceiling plan views.

9. Right-click and select **Delete**. The ceiling plan views are removed from the project.

10. In the *Modify* tab>Modify panel, click 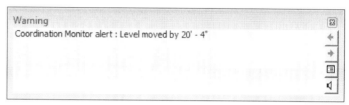 (Align).

11. Select **Level 2** in the linked model and then **Level 2** in the host project.

12. **Level 2** is moved and another Warning displays as shown in Figure 3–45.

Warning	⊠
Coordination Monitor alert : Level moved by 20' - 4"	← → ▤ ◁

Figure 3–45

13. Close the Warning dialog box.

14. Click **Modify** and rename *Level 2* to **02 Roof Garden** and *Level 3* to **03 Club Roof**. In both cases, rename the corresponding views and ignore the warnings.

15. Move the level markers over so the level name does not overlap the building.

16. Save the project.

Task 2 - Coordinate the changes.

1. Select the linked model and in the *Modify RVT Links* tab> Monitor panel, click (Coordination Review).

2. In the Coordination Review dialog box, review the changes, as shown in Figure 3–46.

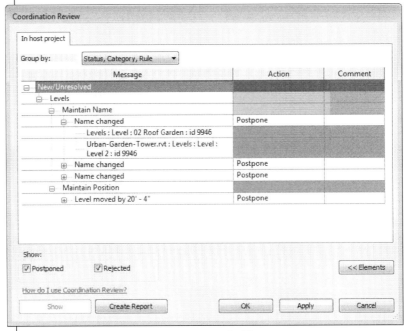

Figure 3–46

3. In the *Action* column, select **Accept difference** for each of the changes, as shown in Figure 3–47. Click **OK**.

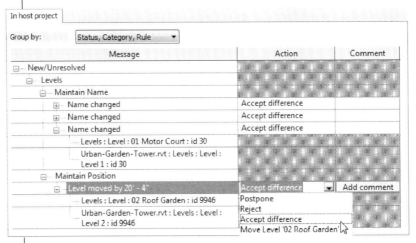

Figure 3–47

4. Zoom out to see the entire elevation.

5. Save and close the project.

Chapter Review Questions

1. What type of view do you need to be in to add a level to your project?

   a. Any non-plan view.

   b. As this is done using a dialog box, the view does not matter.

   c. Any view except for 3D.

   d. Any section or elevation view.

2. Which of the following elements can be copied and monitored? (Select all that apply.)

   a. Grids

   b. Levels

   c. Beams

   d. Braces

3. On which of the following element types can a coordination review with the host project be performed?

   a. CAD link

   b. CAD import

   c. Revit link

   d. Revit import

4. When linking an architectural model into a landscape project which of the positioning methods, as shown in Figure 3–48, keeps the model in the same place if the extents of the linked model changes in size?

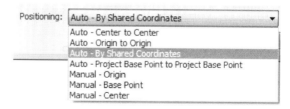

Figure 3–48

   a. Auto - Center-to-Center

   b. Auto - Origin-to-Origin

   c. Manual - Basepoint

   d. Manual - Center

5. How many times can one project file be linked into another project?

    a. Once

    b. It is limited by the size of the link.

    c. As many as you want.

Command Summary

Button	Command	Location
General Tools		
	Level	• **Ribbon:** *Architecture* tab>Datum panel • **Shortcut:** LL
	Override By Category	• **Ribbon:** *Modify* tab>View panel, expand Override Graphics in View • **Shortcut Menu:** Override Graphics in View>By Category...
	Override By Element	• **Ribbon:** *Modify* tab>View panel, expand Override Graphics in View • **Shortcut Menu:** Override Graphics in View>By Element...
	Pin	• **Ribbon:** *Modify* tab>Modify Panel
	Select Links	• **Status Bar**
	Select Pinned Elements	• **Status Bar**
Linked Revit Files		
	Coordination Review	• **Ribbon:** *Collaborate* tab>Coordinate panel
	Copy (from linked file)	• **Ribbon:** *Copy/Monitor* tab>Tools panel
	Copy/Monitor> Select Link	• **Ribbon:** *Collaborate* tab>Coordinate panel, expand Copy/Monitor
	Copy/Monitor> Use Current Project	• **Ribbon:** *Collaborate* tab>Coordinate panel, expand Copy/Monitor
	Link Revit	• **Ribbon:** *Insert* tab>Link panel
	Manage Links	• **Ribbon:** *Manage* tab>Manage Projects panel or *Insert* tab>Link panel
	Monitor	• **Ribbon:** *Copy/Monitor* tab>Tools panel
	Options (Copy/Monitor)	• **Ribbon:** *Copy/Monitor* tab>Tools panel

Creating Revit Site Elements

Many urban landscape designs are constructed on existing structures, such as plazas or roofs. However, most landscape design also modifies the soft structure, the topography, of the site. The Autodesk® Revit® software enables you to create and make basic modifications to toposurfaces, which are frequently created from a linked CAD file. The CAD file often includes important coordinate information that can be imported into the project using Shared Coordinates. Basic modifications to toposurfaces include editing points, splitting the surface, and creating graded regions. Additional toposurface tools include property lines, building pads, and manual grading techniques.

Learning Objectives in this Chapter

- Link CAD files with contour information into an Autodesk Revit project.
- Understand the Autodesk Revit project coordinates, including Project Base Point, Survey Point, and True North.
- Acquire coordinates from a linked CAD file.
- Create toposurfaces from a linked CAD file.
- Split and join the surfaces of a toposurface.
- Name toposurfaces.
- Modify the phasing of toposurfaces.
- Manually grade toposurfaces.

4.1 Starting CAD-based Projects

You can print a hybrid drawing - part Autodesk Revit project and part imported/linked drawing.

Many firms have legacy drawings from vector-based CAD programs, or could be working with consultants that use these programs. In cases like this, you may want to link a DWG plan into your project (as shown in the Link CAD Formats dialog box in Figure 4–1), which you would then trace over using the Autodesk Revit tools. You can also link 3D contour information created in CAD files into an Autodesk Revit project, and then transform the contours into Autodesk Revit toposurfaces.

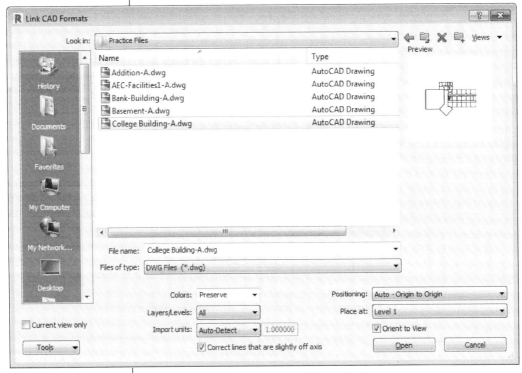

Figure 4–1

CAD Files can be either linked or imported into a project.

- **Link:** A connection to the original file is maintained, and the link updates if the original file is updated.
- **Import:** There is no connection to the original file. The CAD project becomes a separate element in the Autodesk Revit model.

- CAD file formats that can be imported or linked include: AutoCAD® (DWG and DXF), MicroStation® (DGN), Trimble® SketchUp® (SKP and DWG), Standard ACIS Text format (SAT), and Rhinoceros® (3DM).

How To: Import or Link a CAD File

1. Proceed as follows:

To...	Then...
Import a CAD file	On the *Insert* tab>Import panel, click (Import CAD).
Link a CAD file	On the *Insert* tab>Link panel, click (Link CAD).

2. Complete the Import CAD (or Link CAD) dialog box. The top area of the dialog box contains the standard select file options. The bottom area outlines the options for importing or linking, as shown in Figure 4–2.

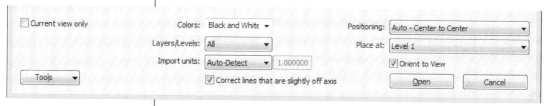

Figure 4–2

3. Click **Open**.
4. Depending on the Positioning option you selected, the file is automatically placed or you can place it with the cursor.

Import/Link Options

Current view only	If selected, the file is imported/linked into the current view and not into other views. You might want to enable this option if you are working on a floor plan and do not want the objects to display in 3D or other views.
Colors	The Autodesk Revit software works mainly with black lines of different weights on a white background to describe elements, but both AutoCAD and MicroStation use a variety of colors. When importing into the Autodesk Revit software easier, you can select to turn all colors to **Black and White**, **Preserve colors**, or **Invert** colors.
Layers	You can select which layers from the original drawing are imported/linked. The options are **All**, **Visible** (those that are not off or frozen), and **Select**. Using the **Select** option displays a list of layers or levels that you can select when you import the drawing file.

Import units	The Autodesk Revit software can automatically detect the units that are used in the imported/linked file. You can also specify the units that you want to use from a list of typical Imperial and Metric units, or set a Custom scale factor.
Correct lines that are slightly off axis	Corrects lines that are less than 0.1 degree off axis so that any elements based on those lines are created correctly. This option is on by default. Toggle the option off if you are working with site plans.
Positioning	Select one of the methods to place the imported/linked file in the Autodesk Revit host project. Positioning: Auto - Origin to Origin Place at: Auto - Center to Center Auto - Origin to Origin Auto - By Shared Coordinates Manual - Origin Manual - Base Point Manual - Center
Place at:	Select a level in the drop-down list to specify the vertical positioning for the file. This option is grayed out if you have selected the **Current view only** option.
Orient to View	Places the file at the same orientation as the current view.

- The default positioning is **Auto - Origin to Origin**. The software remembers the most recently used positioning type as long as you are in the same session of the Autodesk Revit software.

- If you are working in a 3D view, the file is automatically positioned using the **Auto-Origin to Origin** option and placed at the lowest level in the project.

- If you are linking a file, an additional Positioning option, **Auto-By Shared Coordinates**, is available. It is typically used with linked Autodesk Revit files. If you use it with a CAD file, an alert box opens that contains information about the coordinate systems and what the Autodesk Revit software does, as shown in Figure 4–3.

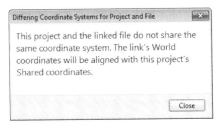

Figure 4–3

- When you link a DWG file that includes reference files (XREFS) (as shown in the AutoCAD software in Figure 4–4) the software only displays files whose *Type* is set to **Attach**. Files whose *Type* is set to **Overlay** do not display.

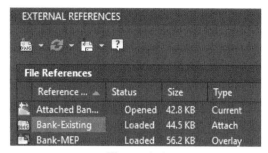

Figure 4–4

- When you import a DWG file, all XREFS display no matter how they are set up in the DWG file.

- When a file is positioned using the **Auto-Origin to Origin** option, it is pinned in place and cannot be moved. To move the file, click on the pin to unpin it, as shown in Figure 4–5.

To pin a file that is not automatically pinned, select it and in the Modify tab>Modify panel, click ⚲ (Pin).

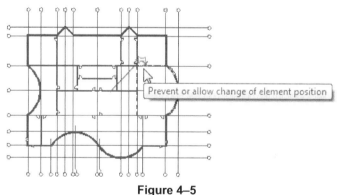

Figure 4–5

4.2 Preparing a Project for Site Design

Coordinate Systems in Autodesk Revit

All Autodesk Revit projects have an internal coordinate system based on N/S (Y-axis), E/W (X-axis) and Elevation (Z-axis). There are primary and secondary coordinates systems specified by the Project Base Point and Survey Point. These points can be at the same location, causing the icons to overlap.

- The **Project Base Point** defines the origin of the project. It is helpful to have the Project Base Point at a useful place in the project (such as the intersection of principle grid lines or the corner of the building), as shown in Figure 4–6.

- The **Survey Point** defines the secondary coordinate system. It is typically a specific point in the physical environment, such as a survey marker, as shown in Figure 4–6. You can specify the Survey Point coordinates directly, or you can acquire this survey point from a linked file (such as a DWG) from which the topography information is gathered.

The Autodesk Revit software has a high level of accuracy of up to 20 miles from the project origin.

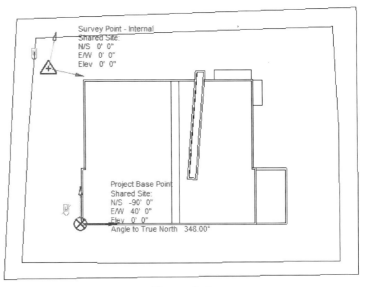

Figure 4–6

- The Project Base Point impacts absolute elevations, as well as what is reported using the **Spot Elevation** and **Spot Coordinate** commands.

- The icons typically display in site plan views. To display the icons in other views, in the Visibility Graphics dialog box, in the *Model Categories* tab, expand *Site* and select **Project Base Point** and **Survey Point**.

Sharing Coordinates

If you are working in a project with linked models and want to use the coordinates from one of the linked models (rather than from the host project), you can acquire the coordinates, as shown in Figure 4–7. For example, you might have a drawing site plan that was created in the AutoCAD software linked to a project created in the Autodesk Revit Architecture software and want to use the coordinates from the DWG file

- If you are working with a linked site, before acquiring the coordinates, ensure that you move, rotate, and align the site into place.

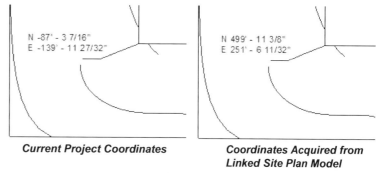

Current Project Coordinates **Coordinates Acquired from Linked Site Plan Model**

Figure 4–7

- Shared coordinates are typically acquired from a site plan. This could be a CAD file or a linked Autodesk Revit model.

- If you are working in a site plan, you can also publish the shared coordinates to linked Autodesk Revit models.

- You can only acquire coordinates once.

New
in **2018**

To maintain a consistent geographic location between models you can use the GIS coordinates stored in a linked DWG file that includes a Geographic Marker, as shown in the AutoCAD software in Figure 4–8. When you acquire the coordinates from the linked DWG files, these are shared with the Autodesk Revit project.

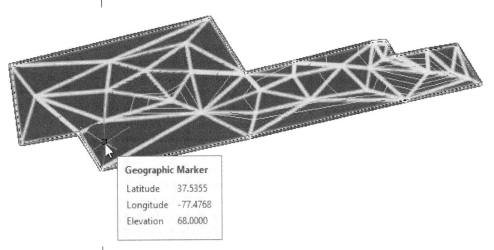

Figure 4–8

When you acquire coordinates from a Geographic Marker (as shown in Figure 4–9), this updates the Autodesk Revit model with the real-world position of the model, which improves energy analysis.

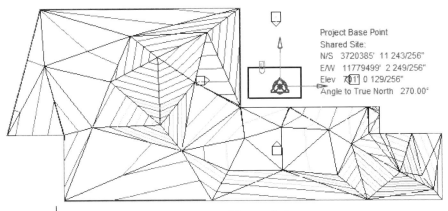

Figure 4–9

How To: Acquire Coordinates from a Linked Project

1. In the *Manage* tab>Project Location panel, expand

    (Coordinates), and click   (Acquire Coordinates).

2. Select a linked model from which to acquire the shared coordinate system. The current project now uses the new coordinates.

• Alternately, you can select the linked file first and, in Properties, in the *Other* group, beside *Shared Site,* click **<Not Shared>**. Then, in the Share Coordinates dialog box, select the **Acquire** option and then click **Reconcile**, as shown in Figure 4–10.

Figure 4–10

• If you move or rotate a linked instance after it has been shared and saved, a Warning box displays, as shown in Figure 4–11. You can click **Save Now** to save the position, or click **OK** to continue working in the project. You can save the linked model later using the Manage Links dialog box.

Figure 4–11

Hint: Project North and True North

When you acquire coordinates, they include the orientation of the site. When you are working on a building or site layout, it is easier to work with standard horizontal and vertical axes, as shown in Figure 4–12. This is called Project North. You can also display a view at True North, as shown in Figure 4–13.

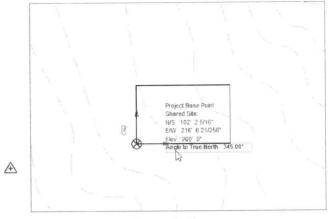

Figure 4–12

Figure 4–13

- To change the orientation, activate the view where you want to change the orientation. With no elements selected, in Properties, in the *Graphics* group, set the *Orientation* to **True North**.

Modifying Coordinates Individually

If you are not working with shared coordinates from a linked file, you can modify each of the coordinate systems independently.

- To modify the Project Base Point and Survey Points, click on the icon and modify *N/S*, *E/W*, *Elev*, and *Angle to True North* as required, as shown in Figure 4–14. Alternatively, you can set up the values in Properties, as shown in Figure 4–15.

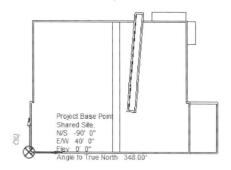

Figure 4–14

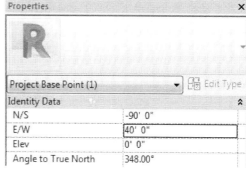

Figure 4–15

- If the Project Base Point or Survey Point is clipped ( ) and you move them, the coordinates do not change but the model elements move. If they are unclipped ( ), the project coordinates change and the model elements do not move.

Hint: Spot Elevations and Spot Coordinates

Two types of dimensions reference the Project Base Point:
Spot Elevation gathers the elevation information from a
selected point, while **Spot Coordinate** gathers the coordinate
information for a point, as shown in Figure 4–16.

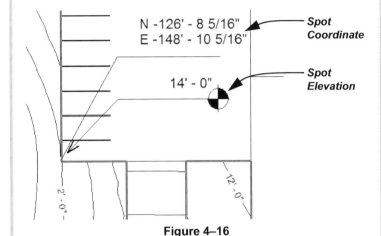

Figure 4–16

Spot dimensions can be added to any type of model element.

How To: Add Spot Elevations/Coordinates

1. In the *Annotate* tab>Dimension panel, click ⬩ (Spot
   Elevation) or ⬩ (Spot Coordinate).
2. In the Type Selector, select the type that you want to use
   from the list.
3. In the Options Bar, select **Leader** and **Shoulder**. The Spot
   Coordinate also includes a list of **Display Elevations**, as
   shown in Figure 4–17.

Figure 4–17

4. Select a point that you want to dimension and place the
   leader line and target or text. The software automatically
   gathers the information from the selected point.
5. Select another point, as required. The value of the spot
   dimension displays as you move the cursor over the site.

Practice 4a

Start a CAD-based Project

Practice Objectives

- Link a CAD File.
- Move, Rotate, and Align a linked CAD file with the Autodesk Revit model.
- Acquire shared coordinates from the CAD file.
- Set a view to True North.

Estimated time for completion: 10 minutes

In this practice you will link a CAD file with contour information into an Autodesk Revit project. You will then move and rotate the CAD file to match the appropriate location in the model. You will also align one of the contours to a level in the model so that the site is at the correct elevation. You will then acquire coordinates from the CAD file and set up a view that displays True North, as shown in Figure 4–18.

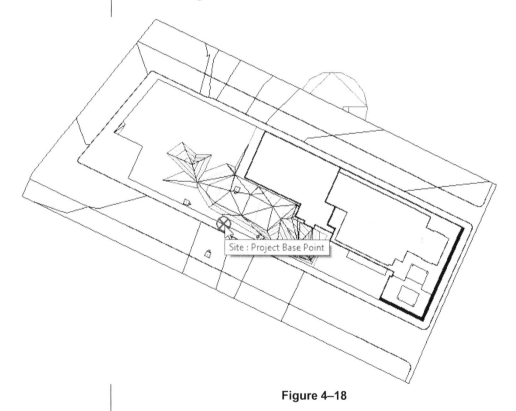

Figure 4–18

Task 1 - Link a CAD File and move it into place.

1. Open the **Urban-Garden-CAD.rvt** project.

2. In the *Insert* tab>Link panel, click ⬚ (Link CAD).

By preserving the colors, the colors of the contour lines display, and you will be able to use the contour line that matches the ground level.

3. In the Link CAD Formats dialog box, navigate to the practice files folder and select **CAD-Site-Contours.dwg**. Ensure that *Colors* is set to **Preserve**, and then click **Open**.
   - Note that the rest of the options are not available because you are working in a 3D view.

4. Type **ZE** to zoom to the extents of the view. Note that the site contours are far away from the main model, as shown in Figure 4–19

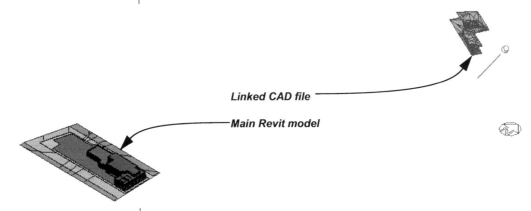

Linked CAD file

Main Revit model

Figure 4–19

5. Open the **Floor Plans: Site** view.

6. Select the linked CAD file and click on the pin so that you can move it.

7. Start the **Move** command and move the CAD file to the location shown in Figure 4–20.

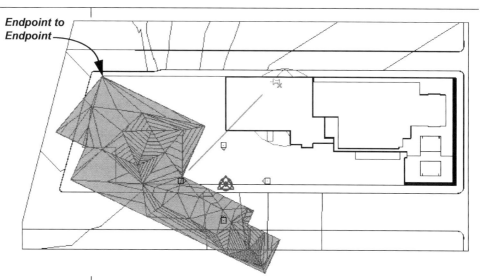

Endpoint to Endpoint

Figure 4–20

8. Start the **Rotate** command.

9. Drag the center of rotation to the point shown in Figure 4–21.

10. Set the start and end rays to the points shown in Figure 4–21.

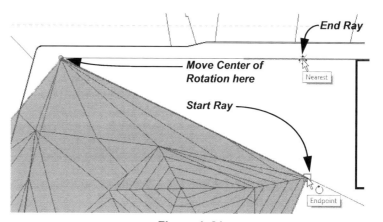

End Ray

Move Center of Rotation here

Start Ray

Figure 4–21

11. Open the **Elevations (Building Elevation): South** view and zoom out so that the linked CAD file displays. Note that you might need to cut off the crop region to display the linked CAD file.

12. Start the **Align** command.

13. Select the 01 Motor Court level line from the Autodesk Revit model.

14. Zoom in on the CAD file and select the red contour line.

15. Open the 3D view and note that the contours of the linked CAD file now align with the building location, as shown in Figure 4–22.

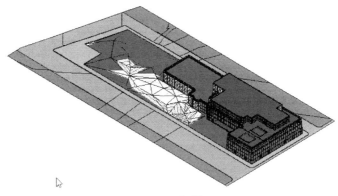

Figure 4–22

16. Save the project.

Task 2 - Acquire Coordinates from the linked CAD file.

---

1. Open the **Floor Plans: Site** view and notice the location of the Project Base Point and Survey Point markers as shown in Figure 4–23. You can also see the North Arrow that displays with the CAD file elements.

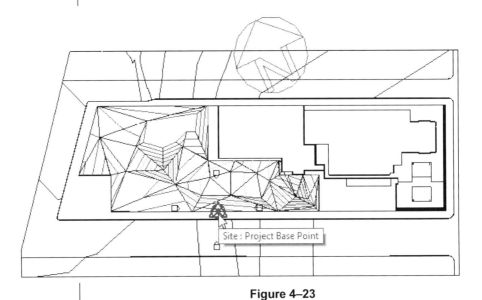

Site : Project Base Point

Figure 4–23

2. Select the linked CAD file.

3. In Properties, in the *Other* group, beside *Shared Site,* select **<Not Shared>**.

4. In the Share Coordinates dialog box, select **Acquire the shared coordinate system** (as shown in Figure 4–24), and then click **Reconcile**.

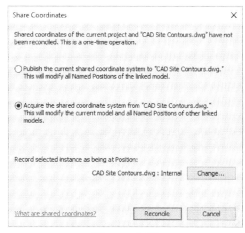

Figure 4–24

5. Zoom out and select the Survey Point marker, as shown in Figure 4–25. The survey point is set at the 0,0,0 of the shared site coordinates.

6. Select the Project Base Point marker, as shown in Figure 4–26. The project base point is set a specific distance from the shared site coordinates.

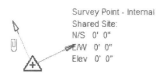

Figure 4–25

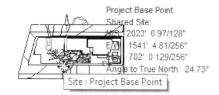

Figure 4–26

7. Zoom in on the site.

8. With no elements selected, in Properties in the Graphics group, set the *Orientation* to **True North**.

9. The elements in the view rotate to true north.

10. Save the project.

4.3 Creating Topographical Surfaces

Once you have set up the project with the Survey Point, Project Base Point, Elevation, and True North, you can create topographical surfaces (toposurfaces), as shown in Figure 4–27. The primary method you will use create toposurfaces is to link a CAD file that includes the 3D contour information. Once you have the toposurface in place, you can modify the Site Settings to change the display of the contours and section graphics.

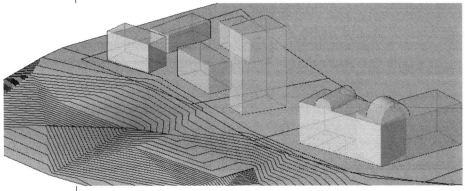

Figure 4–27

- You can specify points directly in the project, or import a points file (.TXT or .CVS) developed by a survey.

- You can edit toposurfaces by modifying individual points, but you should use the Site Designer tools to make large scale changes to the site.

How To: Create a Toposurface Using an Imported File

1. In a site or 3D view, link a CAD file (DWG, DXF, or DGN) that holds the site information.
   - When linking, do not use the **Current view only** option. You need the 3D information stored in the CAD file.
2. If you are working in a project with existing model elements, move the CAD file into place.
3. Acquire the coordinates from the linked CAD file.
4. In the *Massing & Site* tab>Model Site panel, click

   (Toposurface).

5. In the *Modify | Edit Surface* tab>Tools panel, expand 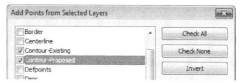 (Create from Import), and click (Select Import Instance).
6. Select the imported file by clicking on the edge of the file.
7. In the Add Points from Selected Layers dialog box, select the layers that hold the points, as shown in Figure 4–28. Note that the layer names vary according to the original drawing file standard.

Figure 4–28

8. Click **OK**. The new toposurface is created with points at the same elevations as the imported information.

9. Click (Finish Surface) to end the command.
10. If you do not need the CAD file for other information, delete it.

• If the CAD file is going to be updated with information (such as the footprint of the building or roads and parking areas), it is important to link the CAD file. This way, when the up-to-date information is provided, it is included in the project.

Site Settings

In the *Massing & Site* tab>Model Site panel, click in the panel title. The Site Settings dialog box opens, which enables you to set how contours display in the plan and section views of a toposurface, as shown in Figure 4–29.

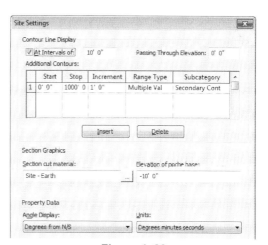

Figure 4–29

Site Setting Options

Contour Line Display

At Intervals of	Set the distance for the primary contour lines. These display with a heavy line and are not necessarily the places at which you added the points.
Passing Through Elevation	The starting elevation for contour lines.

Additional Contours

Start/Stop	**Start** is the location for a single additional contour or the first of a series of contours.
	Stop is the end of a series of additional contour lines.
Increment	The distance between sub-contours when the *Range type* is set to **Multiple Values**. The style is set according to the *Subcategory* specification.
Range Type	**Multiple Values:** Enables you to specify the start/stop and the increment.
	Single Value: Enables you to specify the location of the single contour in the **Start Value**. Increments are grayed out.
Subcategory	Select from a list of object styles that define how to display the additional contours. For example, **Secondary Contours** display with a thin line, while **Primary Contours** display with a wide line. You can create additional options in **Object Styles** under **Topography**.
Insert / Delete	Insert or delete additional contour descriptions.

Section Graphics

Section cut material	The default material is set to **Earth**. To select a different material, click ⬚ (Browse) to open the Material Browser. Additional site-related materials can be found in the *AEC Materials: Misc* area at the bottom of the Material Browser. The following shows a section cut using the **Earth** material.
Elevation of poche base	The height of the poche (or hatching) that displays below the bottom contour line in a section view. It is usually negative.

Property Data	
Angle Display	Select the type of angles to display: **Degrees from N/S** or **Degrees**.
Units	Select the type of units to display: **Degrees Minutes Seconds** or **Decimal Degrees**.

Additional Toposurface Options

In most cases, you create toposurfaces using information from linked CAD files and then make major changes to the surfaces using the Site Designer add-in app tools. But, you can also create a toposurface from scratch by specifying points or by using a points file supplied by a surveyor. You can also modify individual points in a toposurface.

How To: Create a Toposurface By Specifying Points

1. Open a site or 3D view. In the *Massing & Site* tab>Model Site panel, click 🖾 (Toposurface).
2. In the *Modify | Edit Surface* tab>Tools panel, click ⬡ (Place Point).
3. In the Options Bar, set the *Elevation* for the point, as shown in Figure 4–30. By default, you are only able to select **Absolute Elevation**. After you create a surface of three points, you can also select **Relative to Surface**.

Figure 4–30

4. Click in the drawing area to place the point.
5. Continue placing points. You can vary the elevation, as required. After you have placed three points, a boundary displays, connecting them. When you add a point at a different elevation, you see the contour lines forming, as shown in Figure 4–31.

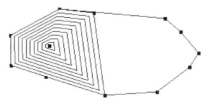

Figure 4–31

6. When you have finished selecting points, in the Surface panel, click ✓ (Finish Surface).

- You can add points in plan and 3D views.

- To create a clean outer boundary for a toposurface, draw reference planes and then select points at the intersections of the planes.

How To: Create a Toposurface from a Points File

1. Open a site or 3D view.
2. In the *Massing & Site* tab>Model Site panel, click

   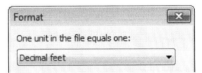 (Toposurface).
3. In the *Modify | Edit Surface* tab>Tools panel, expand

   (Create from Import) and click (Specify Points File).
4. In the Select File dialog box, select the CSV or comma delimited text file (TXT) that contains the list of points and click **Open**.
5. In the Format dialog box, select the unit format required (as shown in Figure 4–32) and click **OK**.

   - The units available include **Decimal feet**, **Decimal inches**, **Meters**, **Centimeters**, and **Millimeters**.

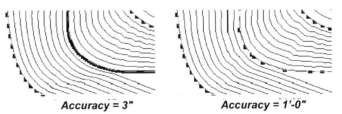

Figure 4–32

6. The points create a toposurface in the project. Add additional points as required and then click (Finish Surface).

- Having too many points on a surface can slow down your system's performance. While still in the *Modify | Edit Surface* tab>Tools panel, click (Simplify Surface) to reduce the number of points. Set the required accuracy, as shown in Figure 4–33, and click **OK**.

Accuracy = 3"   *Accuracy = 1'-0"*

Figure 4–33

Practice 4b

Create Topographical Surfaces

Practice Objectives

- Create a Toposurface from an imported file.
- Create views where you can see the toposurface features.

Estimated time for completion: 10 minutes

In this practice, you will create a toposurface from a linked CAD file, modify the Site Settings, and modify views to display the contours, as shown in Figure 4–34.

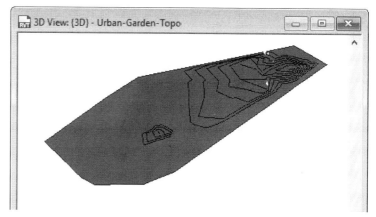

Figure 4–34

Task 1 - Create a Toposurface from a Linked CAD file.

1. Open the project **Urban-Garden-Topo.rvt**.

2. In the **Floor Plans:Site** view, select the linked Revit building model.

3. In the *Modify | RVT Links* tab> Link panel, click (Manage Links).

4. In the Manage Links dialog box, in the *Revit* tab, hold <Ctrl> and select **Building-Site.rvt** and **Building-Base.rvt**. With both projects selected, click **Unload** and then click **OK**. This frees you to focus on the toposurface.

5. In the *Massing & Site* tab>Model Site panel, click (Toposurface).

6. In the *Modify | Edit Surface* tab>Tools panel, expand 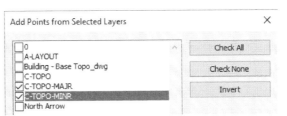 (Create from Import) and click (Select Import Instance).

7. Select the linked CAD file.

8. In the Add Points from Selected Layers dialog box, click **Check None**. Select **C-TOPO-MAJR** and **C-TOPO-MINR**, as shown in Figure 4–35. Click **OK**.

Figure 4–35

9. The new toposurface is created with points applied along the contour lines from the CAD file, as shown in Figure 4–36.

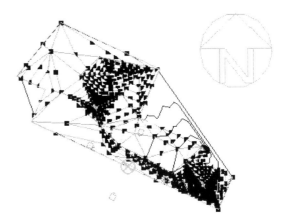

Figure 4–36

10. In the *Modify | Edit Surface* tab>Tools panel, click 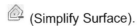 (Simplify Surface).

11. In the Simplify Surface dialog box, set the *Accuracy* to **1'-0"**, as shown in Figure 4–37. Click **OK**.

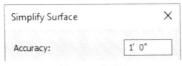

Figure 4–37

12. Note that fewer points are placed in the toposurface, but that the actual contour location is not compromised. Click

     (Finish Surface).

13. Save the project.

Task 2 - View the Toposurface

1. Open the **Elevations (Building Elevation): South** view and set the *Visual Style* to **Shaded**.

2. Select the linked CAD file and type **VH** to hide it in the view. You can now see the ups and downs of the site, as shown in Figure 4–38.

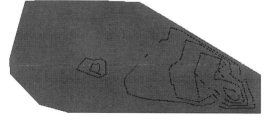

Figure 4–38

3. Open the default 3D view, set the *Visual Style* to **Shaded,** and hide the CAD file. Rotate the view so that you can see the layout of the site.

4. Open the **Floor Plans: Site** view.

5. Clean up the view by hiding everything but the toposurface and setting the *Visual Style* to **Shaded**. The model displays as shown in Figure 4–39.

6. In the *Massing & Site* tab>Model Site panel, in the title bar, click (Site Settings).

7. In the Site Settings dialog box, in the *Additional Contours* area, set the *Increment* to **6"**, and then click **OK**. The distance between the contours changes, as shown in Figure 4–40.

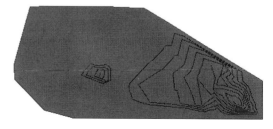

Figure 4–39   **Figure 4–40**

8. Save the project.

4.4 Modifying Topographical Surfaces

While this learning guide focuses on using the Site Designer for most large-scale changes, there are a number of other tools available in the Autodesk Revit software that can be used to modify toposurfaces. You can edit toposurfaces and modify points, split surfaces into smaller sections, and grade the site by manually modifying points, as shown in Figure 4–41. You can also modify the Properties of a toposurface, including material and phasing information.

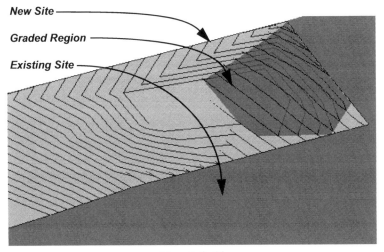

New Site

Graded Region

Existing Site

Figure 4–41

• To name a toposurface, first select the surface. Then, in Properties, in the *Identity Data* group, type in the *Name*. Naming your toposurfaces is important when you are working with multiple toposurfaces and making changes to them through Site Designer.

Editing Toposurfaces

You can make changes to a toposurface by adding points or editing existing point locations and elevations, as shown in Figure 4–42. These changes can be made independently or with the **Graded Region** command.

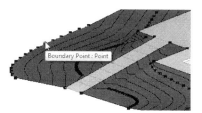

Figure 4–42

How To: Edit a Toposurface

1. Select the toposurface that you want to edit.
2. In the *Modify | Topography* tab>Surface panel, click (Edit Surface).
3. In the *Modify | Edit Surface* tab>Tools panel, click (Place Point), and then add more points to the surface.
4. To edit existing points, select one or more points.
5. In the *Interior (or Boundary) Points* tab, you can use various modification tools. You can change the elevation of the points in the Options Bar, as shown in Figure 4–43.

When adding points, it helps to be in a 3D shaded view so that you can see the effects of your new points.

Figure 4–43

6. Select another point or click in an empty space to finish editing the points.
7. In the *Modify | Edit Surface* tab>Surface panel, click

   (Finish Surface) to end the command.

Splitting Surfaces

You can split toposurfaces into separate pieces. Each surface can be edited individually and be assigned different materials, as shown in Figure 4–44. For example, you can break the topography into sections that will become parking lots, grassy areas, roadways, and sidewalks. You can also delete sections that you do not need in the project.

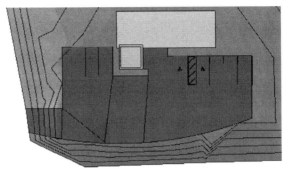

Figure 4–44

How To: Split a Surface

1. In the *Massing & Site* tab>Modify Site panel, click (Split Surface).
2. Select the toposurface to split.
3. In the *Modify | Split Surface* tab>Draw panel, use the Draw tools to create a splitting boundary.
4. In Properties, modify the *Material* for the surface, as required.
5. Click (Finish Edit Mode).

- The boundary does not need to be a closed object, but it must split the surface into two pieces.

How To: Join Surfaces

1. In the *Massing & Site* tab>Modify Site panel, click (Merge Surfaces).
2. Select two adjacent surfaces that you want to merge.

- If materials are applied to the surfaces, the new merged surface uses the material of the surface that you select first.

How To: Change the Material of a Toposurface

1. Select the subregion or other toposurface element. In Properties, in the *Materials and Finishes* group, beside *Material*, click in the text box and then click **...** (Browse).
2. In the Material Browser (shown in Figure 4–45), select the material you want to use, and then click **OK**.

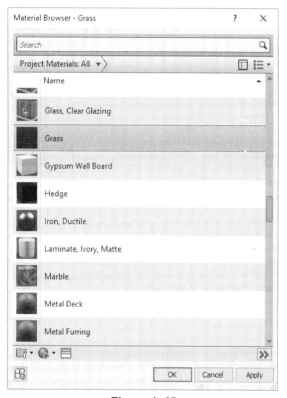

Figure 4–45

Hint: Labeling Contours

Labeling contours (as shown in Figure 4–46) can help you when you are working with topography surfaces by displaying the level of the contour lines in the region in which you are working.

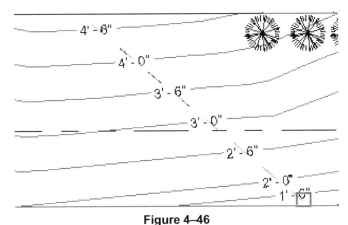

Figure 4–46

- **Label Contours** only works with toposurfaces.

How To: Label Contours

1. In the *Massing & Site* tab>Modify Site panel, click

   50 (Label Contours).
2. Draw a line across the contours that you want to label.
3. Continue drawing as many lines as required.

Working with Phases

Phases show distinct stages in a project's life. For building design, phases are typically used with renovations and additions or when a project involves several phases for its completion. For topography, phases help to distinguish between Existing and New Construction before you start modifying the toposurfaces, as shown in Figure 4–47.

Phases are applied to elements. The phases that display are controlled by views.

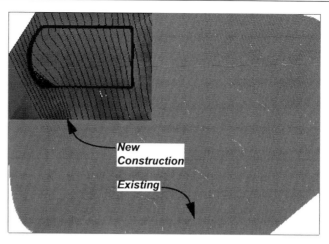

Figure 4–47

- There are two default phases included in the template files: **Existing** and **New Construction**. Many projects can be completed just using these two options, but you can create additional phases for more complex projects.

- When you add new elements in a view, they are assigned to the phase set in the current view. To set the phase of a view, in Properties, under the *Phasing* group, select the *Phase* from the list, as shown in Figure 4–48.

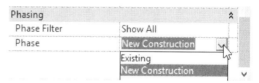

Figure 4–48

- To move elements to a different phase, select the element(s) and, in Properties, change the *Phase Created*, as shown in Figure 4–49.

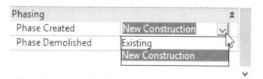

Figure 4–49

- Toposurfaces are typically placed on New Construction by default. You can change it to Existing before making changes

Viewing Phases

In a view, the *Phase Filter* determines which phases are displayed in the view relative to the current phase. For example, when you set the *Phase Filter* to **Show All**, it includes existing, new, and cut and fill from a graded region, as shown in Figure 4–50. When you set the *Phase Filter* to **Show Complete**, all of the changes display, as shown in Figure 4–51.

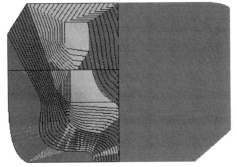

Figure 4–50

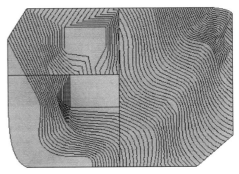

Figure 4–51

- The Phase Filter options are as follows:
    - **None:** All elements regardless of the current phase.
    - **Show All:** All phases up to the current phase, with all except the current phase grayed out.
    - **Show Complete:** All construction up to the current phase.
    - **Show Demo + New:** The current phase and any demolished elements.
    - **Show New:** Only elements created in the current view.
    - **Show Previous + Demo:** Elements created in previous phases and any demolished elements from the current phase.
    - **Show Previous + New:** Elements created in the previous phase and any new elements created in the current phase.
    - **Show Previous Phase:** Elements created in any previous phases.

Grading a Site

Graded regions are not compatible with Site Designer Elements.

The most time-consuming task in site work is deciding how to grade a site, and then adjusting the contours as required. You can make sections of the site flatter or steeper, and you must ensure that the drainage pattern flows away from the building and towards storm drains. To make this process easier, use the

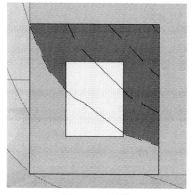 (Graded Region) command to modify the location of points and then automatically demolish and add contours, as shown in Figure 4–52.

Figure 4–52

- Graded regions change the phase of the toposurface. Before starting the **Graded Region** command, in Properties, set the *Phase* of the original toposurface to **Existing**.

- When you modify topography with the **Graded Region** command, the Autodesk Revit software automatically calculates the *Cut* and *Fill* for the surface. This information displays in Properties (as shown in Figure 4–53) and can be added to a schedule.

Phasing		☆
Phase Created	New Construction	
Phase Demolished	None	
Other		☆
Net cut/fill	-14782.56 CF	
Fill	8143.94 CF	
Cut	22926.49 CF	

Figure 4–53

How To: Grade a Site

1. Ensure that the *Phase* of the toposurface is set to **Existing**.
2. In the *Massing & Site* tab>Modify Site panel, click

   ⚐ (Graded Region).
3. The Edit Graded Region dialog box displays, as shown in Figure 4–54. Select how you want the new toposurface to be copied: either as a replica of the original, or as an outline of the points.

The existing toposurface is automatically demolished and a new copy is created in its place.

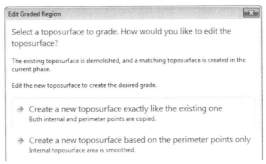

Figure 4–54

4. Select the toposurface that you want to grade.
5. Modify the points in the surface:
   - To add new points, in the *Modify | Edit Surface* tab>Tools panel, click ⌂ (Place Point).
   - Select a point and in the Options Bar, change its *Elevation*.
   - Delete points that are no longer required.

6. Click ✓ (Finish Surface).

- If the surface is open or if there is a conflict, an alert box opens.

- If you are in a shaded view, the demolished area displays in red, as shown in Figure 4–55. Set the *Visual Style* to **Hidden** to display the contours and points more clearly.

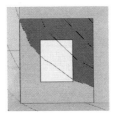

Figure 4–55

Practice 4c

Modify Topographical Surfaces

Practice Objectives

- Split toposurfaces.
- Name toposurfaces.
- Modify the phasing of toposurfaces.
- Grade toposurfaces.
- Set the material of toposurfaces.

Estimated time for completion: 40 minutes

In this practice you will split a toposurface and delete part of it. You will then prepare the toposurfaces for grading by naming them, changing the phasing, and creating model lines as guidelines for the grading location. You will then use the Graded Region command on several surfaces and specify materials to create a reflecting pool, as shown in Figure 4–56.

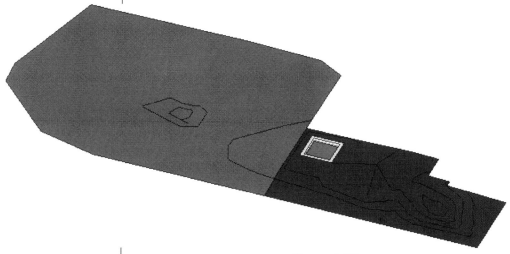

Figure 4–56

Task 1 - Split a toposurface.

1. Open the **Urban-Garden-Topo-Modify.rvt** project.

2. Work in the **Floor Plans: Site** view.

3. In the *Manage* tab>Manage Project panel, click ▣ (Manage Links).

4. In the Manage Links dialog box, select **Building-Base.rvt**, and then click **Reload**.
   - Ignore the Coordination Review alert.

*If the file is unavailable, click **Reload From...** and select the file from the practice files folder.*

5. Click **OK**. Note that part of the toposurface is under the building.

6. In the *Massing & Site* tab>Modify Site panel, click ⬚ (Split Surface).

7. Select the toposurface element.

8. Using the Draw tools, sketch a line similar to that shown in Figure 4–57 to separate the unnecessary boundary region.

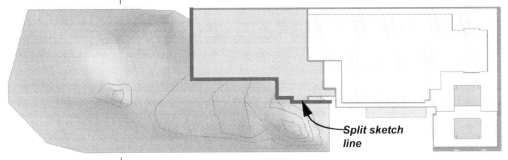

Split sketch line

Figure 4–57

9. Click ✓ (Finish Edit Mode).

10. Start the **Split Surface** command again and split the toposurface as shown in Figure 4–58.

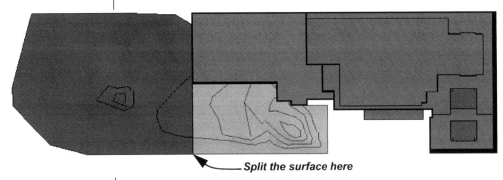

Split the surface here

Figure 4–58

11. In the *Manage* tab>Manage Project panel, click ⬚ (Manage Links).

12. In the Manage Links dialog box, select **Building-Base.rvt**, and then click **Unload**.

13. Select and delete the toposurface that was under the building.

14. Save the project.

Task 2 - Prepare surfaces for grading.

1. Select the two toposurfaces.

2. In the Properties palette, in the *Phasing* group, change *Phase Created* to **Existing**, as shown in Figure 4–59.

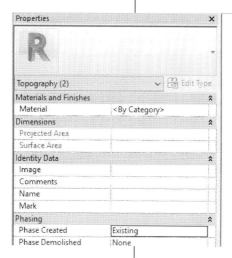

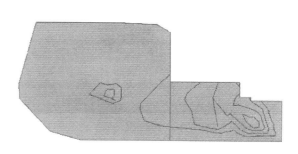

Figure 4–59

3. Click **Apply**. Note that the toposurface changes from brown (the material Earth) to gray to indicate that it is existing.

4. Select the larger toposurface on the left. In Properties, in the *Identity Data* group beside *Name*, type **Existing Topo West**.

5. Name the smaller toposurface on the right **Existing Topo East**.

6. Zoom in on the **Existing Topo East** surface.

7. In the View Control Panel, change the *Visual Style* to **Wireframe**. The wireframe style makes it easier to see the elements you will create next.

8. In the *Architecture* tab>Model panel, click (Model Line).

9. Draw two squares, one inside the other, similar to those shown in Figure 4–60. These surfaces will become a reflecting pool.

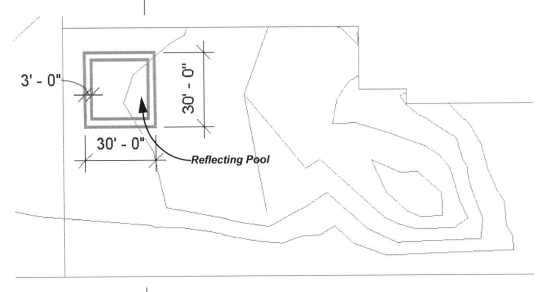

Figure 4–60

10. Use **Split Surface** to divide the outer square from the toposurface, and then again to divide the inner square from the outer square.

11. Save the project.

Task 3 - Grade regions of the toposurfaces.

1. Zoom in on the reflecting pool surfaces.

2. In the *Massing & Site* tab>Modify Site panel, click ☝ (Graded Region).

3. In the Edit Graded Region dialog box select **Create a new toposurface based on the perimeter points only**.

4. Select the edge of the reflecting pool. The points display as shown in Figure 4–61.

To select more than one point at a time, draw a window around them.

5. Delete all of the points except for those on the corners of the outer and inner edge of the pool, as shown in Figure 4–62. This flattens the edge surface.

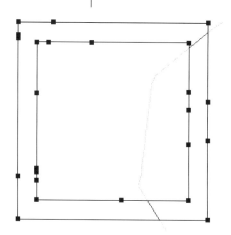

Figure 4–61

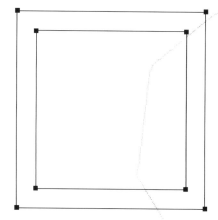

Figure 4–62

6. Select all of the remaining points. In the Options Bar, set the *Elevation* to **2'-0"**.

7. In the *Modify | Edit Surface* tab>Surface panel, click

   (Finish Surface).

8. Start the **Graded Region** command again.

9. In the Edit Graded Region dialog box, select **Create a new toposurface based on the perimeter points only**.

10. Select the inner pool surface.

11. Delete all of the point except the corner points, change the *Elevation* of the points to (negative) **-1'-0"**, and click

   (Finish Surface).

12. In the View Control Bar, change the *Visual Style* to **Shaded**. The cut area displays in red, as shown in Figure 4–63.

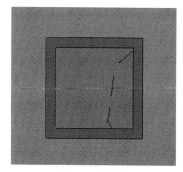

Figure 4–63

13. Start the **Graded Region** command again.

14. In the Edit Graded Region dialog box, select **Create a new toposurface exactly like the existing one** and select the surrounding toposurface.

15. In the area around the reflecting pool, delete all but the corner points and set the *Elevation* of the corner points of the pool to **2'-0"**.

16. Click 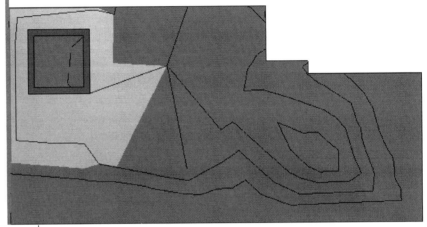 (Finish Surface). The new cut and fill displays as shown in Figure 4–64.

Figure 4–64

17. Select the newly graded site and, in Properties, in the *Other* group, review the *Cut* and *Fill* information, as shown in Figure 4–65.

Name	Existing Topo East
Mark	
Phasing	
Phase Created	New Construction
Phase Demolished	None
Other	
Net cut/fill	1676.02 CF
Fill	1676.02 CF
Cut	0.00 CF

Figure 4–65

18. Save the project.

Task 4 - Set the Materials of the Toposurfaces.

1. Open the default 3D view.

2. In Properties, set the *Phase Filter* to **Show Complete**.

Press <Tab> to help you select the correct surface, if required.

3. Select the inner pool toposurface. In Properties, in the *Materials and Finishes* group, beside *Material*, click **<By Category>** and then click the **...** (Browse) button.

4. In the Material Browser, start typing **Water**. When the **Water** material displays (as shown in Figure 4–66), select it and click **OK**.

*The material does not display because the Phase of surfaces is set to **Existing**.*

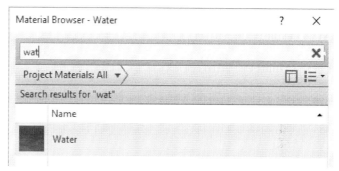

Figure 4–66

5. Select the outer edge toposurface and set the *Material* to **Marble**.

6. Select the toposurface around these elements and set the *Material* to **Grass**.

7. View the changed toposurfaces.

8. Save the project.

Chapter Review Questions

1. You have linked a CAD File with contour information into a project that includes a building model. Before you acquire the shared coordinate system, what should you do first?

   a. Move the CAD file to the building model.

   b. Move the building model to the CAD file.

   c. Nothing needs to be done.

   d. Change the elevation of the building model.

2. Which of the following values typically update when you acquire the shared coordinate system from a linked CAD file? (Select all that apply.)

   a. True North

   b. Project Base Point

   c. Origin

   d. Survey Point

3. Which of the following defines the origin of the project coordinate system and impacts absolute elevations?

   a. Project Origin

   b. Survey Point

   c. Project Base Point

   d. Survey Base Point

4. Which of the following methods can be used to create a topographical surface, such as the one shown in Figure 4–67? (Select all that apply.)

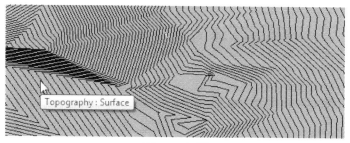

Figure 4–67

a. Importing a drawing created in the AutoCAD® software.

b. Sketching.

c. Importing a drawing created in the AutoCAD® Civil 3D® software.

d. Using a points file.

5. Which of the following commands enables you to modify a toposurface so that you can delete sections or change various parts of the surface to different materials (as shown in Figure 4–68)?

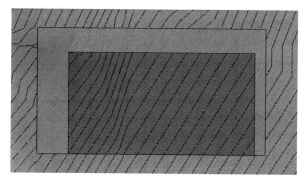

Figure 4–68

a. Edit Surface

b. Graded Region

c. Merge Surface

d. Split Surface

6. Before you start editing a toposurface, you should change the *Phase* to **Existing**.

a. True

b. False

Command Summary

Button	Command	Location
Import and Link CAD Files		
	Acquire Coordinates	• **Ribbon:** *Manage* tab> Project Location panel> expand Coordinates
	Import CAD	• **Ribbon:** *Insert* tab>Import panel
	Link CAD	• **Ribbon:** *Insert* tab>Link panel
	Manage Links	• **Ribbon:** *Manage* tab>Manage Project panel
Primary Toposurface Tools		
	Merge Surfaces	• **Ribbon:** *Massing & Site* tab>Modify Site panel
	Select Import Instance	• **Ribbon:** *Modify	Edit Surface* tab> Tools panel>Create from Import drop-down list
	Simplify Surface	• **Ribbon:** *Modify	Edit Surface* tab> Tools panel
	Split Surface	• **Ribbon:** *Massing & Site* tab>Modify Site panel
	Toposurface	• **Ribbon:** *Massing & Site* tab>Model Site panel
Other Site Related Tools		
	Label Contours	• **Ribbon:** *Massing & Site* tab>Modify Site panel
	Site Settings	• **Ribbon:** *Massing & Site* tab>Model Site panel title
	Spot Coordinate	• **Ribbon:** *Annotate* tab> Dimension panel
	Spot Elevation	• **Ribbon:** *Annotate* tab> Dimension panel
Additional Toposurface Tools		
	Edit Surface	• **Ribbon:** (*select toposurface*) *Modify	Topography* tab>Surface panel
	Graded Region	• **Ribbon:** *Massing & Site* tab>Modify Site panel
	Place Point	• **Ribbon:** *Modify	Edit Surface* tab> Tools panel
	Specify Points File	• **Ribbon:** *Modify	Edit Surface* tab> Tools panel>Create from Import drop-down list

Working with Site Designer

The Autodesk® Site Designer Extension for Autodesk® Revit® software is a plug-in that enables you to modify toposurfaces. Using this tool, you can quickly create features including mass grading, building pads, swales, berms, sidewalks, roads, and retaining walls.

Learning Objectives in this Chapter

- Import LandXML files from the AutoCAD Civil 3D software as a base toposurface.
- Prepare a toposurface to be used in the Site Designer.
- Create soft terrain features, including building pads, berms, swales, and mass grading
- Create hardscape features, such as sidewalks, curbs, retaining walls, and parking lots.
- Modify Site Designer features.

5.1 Preparing a Project for Site Designer

Before using the Site Designer tools, you need to create a toposurface, as shown in Figure 5–1. You can do this from:

- an imported DWG file,
- the Autodesk Revit toposurface command,
- a points file, or
- by importing a LandXML file in Site Designer from the AutoCAD Civil 3D software.

Then, you can set the base toposurface you want to modify using the Site Designer tools.

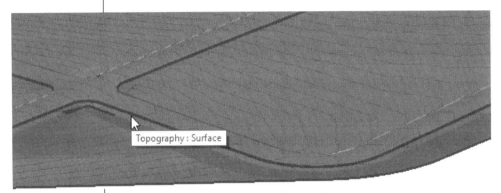

Figure 5–1

- Ensure that the toposurface is large enough to cover all of the area you want to modify. Enlarging the surface after you have applied elements can cause significant problems.

Importing LandXML Files

(Site Designer Only)

Topographical surfaces created in Civil 3D can be saved as LandXML files and then imported into the Autodesk Revit software, as shown in Figure 5–2. You can also export toposurfaces to LandXML so that they can be imported back into the AutoCAD Civil 3D software for more extensive modification.

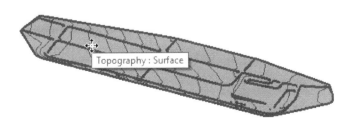

Figure 5–2

How To: Import a LandXML file

1. In the *Site Designer* tab>Import/Export panel, click

    (Import LandXML).

2. In the Import Land XML dialog box, click (Browse), navigate to the folder where the XML file is located, select the file, and then click **Open**.

3. Specify the import options as shown in Figure 5–3. Click **OK**.

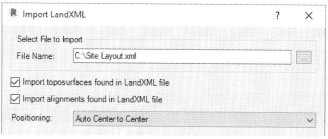

Figure 5–3

4. In the Toposurface Selection dialog box, highlight the toposurface(s) you want to import and click **OK**.

5. In the Toposurface User Information dialog box, select how you want to use the toposurface, as shown in Figure 5–4. Click **OK**.

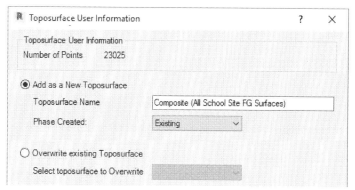

Figure 5–4

- This process creates the full toposurface required for the next stages of modification in Site Designer.

- Move the toposurface into place and acquire the correct coordinates before modifying the surface further.

- Once you have made changes to a toposurface, you can export the project to LandXML so it can be opened in the AutoCAD Civil 3D software.

Setting Up Toposurfaces for Editing in Site Designer

Instead of modifying the original toposurface, Site Designer works on a copy of the toposurface. Ensure that the original toposurface *Phase* is set to **Existing** before you create the new toposurface. The new toposurface will be placed on the **New Construction** phase by default, as shown in Figure 5–5.

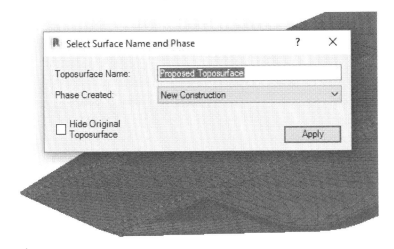

Figure 5–5

How To: Set up a Toposurface for Editing

1. Either create a toposurface using the Autodesk Revit Toposurface commands, or import a LandXML file.
2. Select the toposurface. In Properties, set *Phase Created* to **Existing**. If desired, name the existing toposurface.
3. In the *Site Designer* tab>Convert panel, click ▧ (Set Base Toposurface).
4. In the Set Base Toposurface dialog box, select the name of the toposurface, as shown in Figure 5–6. This is the surface you want to copy and modify using the Site Designer tools.

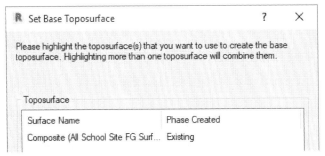

Figure 5–6

- If there are several surfaces in the project, you can select more than one. The surfaces are combined in the new toposurface.

- To select a surface in the view, in the Set Base Toposurface dialog box, click **Pick**, and then select the toposurface. To return to the dialog box, right-click and select **Cancel**.

5. Click **OK**.

6. In the Select Surface Name and Phase dialog box (shown in Figure 5–7), type a name for the new toposurface, specify the Phase Created, and select **Hide Original Toposurface**, if required. Click **Apply**.

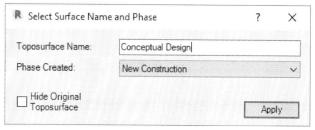

Figure 5–7

- Hiding the original toposurface keeps the surface in the project, but prevents it from displaying in the view so that it does not compete with the new toposurface.

- Alternately, you can change the view *Phase Filter* to **Show New**.

7. The new toposurface is ready to be modified using the Site Designer tools.

5.2 Adding Site Designer Features

Site Designer shapes the terrain of a toposurface using sketched model (or detail) lines to define the area to be graded. Site Designer includes both softscape and hardscape tools, some of which are shown in Figure 5–8. The Soft Terrain, Feature Line, and Point Wipeout commands modify the toposurface, while Street, Sidewalk, Parking Lot, and Curb Retaining Wall adds elements and modifies the toposurface.

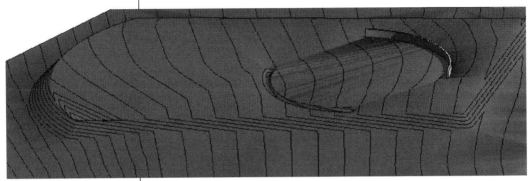

Figure 5–8

	Soft Terrain	Modifies the selected topography to create elements using a preset family and type (e.g., berms, building pads, swales).
	Feature Line	Adds contours, lines, and edges that modify the toposurface.
	Point Wipeout	Removes points in a selected area to smooth out the toposurface.
	Street	Creates road elements separate from the toposurface. Some street types include associated gutters, curbs, and other options.
	Retaining Wall	Adds a retaining wall element and modifies the adjacent toposurfaces.
	Sidewalk	Creates a road element separate from the toposurface that acts as a sidewalk.
	Parking Lot	Creates a separate topography element with specified materials. Parking lots can be modified to include catch basins and other drainage patterns.
	Curb	Creates a road element that acts as a curb. If the curb is closed, a new toposurface is created inside the curb.

- Most Site Designer elements are based on model or detail lines. Either method works, but model lines display in 3D views, as shown in Figure 5–9. The completed site element follows the lines, as shown for a berm in Figure 5–10.

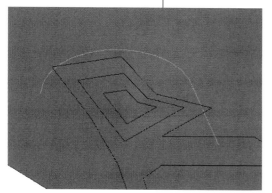

Figure 5–9

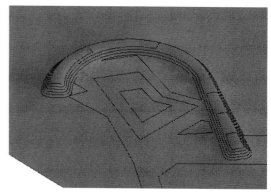

Figure 5–10

How To: Add Site Designer Features

1. Sketch model lines or detail lines to signify the centerline of soft terrain, feature lines, streets, retaining walls, and sidewalks, the edge of a curb, or the outline of a parking lot or closed curb such as an island.
   - All of the Draw tools (except Splines) are supported.
2. In the *Site Designer* tab>Locate panel, select the type of element that you want to create.

3. The related Locate dialog box displays, as shown in Figure 5–11. Set the following options:

- Set the *Family* and *Type* using the drop-down lists.
- Type a *Name* for the feature.
- Select either **Relative Elevation from Toposurface** or **Constant Elevation**, and then specify the related *Elevation*.
- Select either **Segment** (the feature is applied to the selected segment only) or **Chain** (the feature is applied to any connected segments).
- Select **Create A Copy** if you want to keep a copy of the sketched lines.
- Select either **Use an Existing Host Line** if you already sketched lines (as recommended) or **Draw Host Line** to create a sketch.

Feature Lines have additional options for setting the elevation, while Parking Lots and Curbs do not have options for elevation.

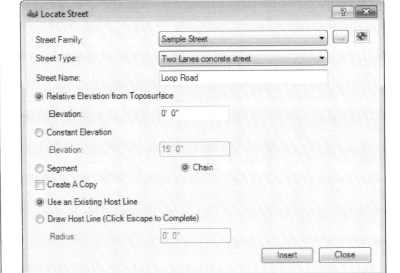

Figure 5–11

4. Click **Insert**
5. Select an existing host line or sketch a new host line, as required.
6. If you are creating a curb, click the side for the face of the curb and then, in the Toposurface Association dialog box, select the associated toposurface, as shown in Figure 5–12, and click **OK**.

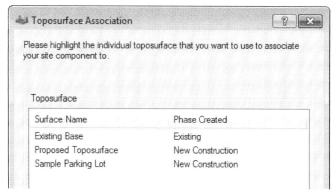

Figure 5–12

7. The Locate dialog box displays. Create another feature or click **Close**.

• Parking lots and curbs that are based on a closed host line create a new toposurface using the material assigned by the selected type. Note that toposurfaces do not support surface patterns and you might get a warning about this.

• Once Parking Lots are in place, you can modify them with more precise information.

• Sketched lines that are used to create features must be inside the toposurface boundary. If there are any sketched lines outside the boundary, an error occurs, as shown in Figure 5–13.

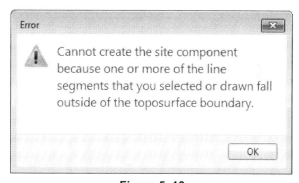

Figure 5–13

Hint: Reports and Schedules from Site Designer

There are two different types of reports you can gather from Site Designer elements. The first is a standard Autodesk Revit schedule that shows the cut and fill created by the changes, as shown in Figure 5–14

<Cut and Fill Schedule>			
A	B	C	D
Name	Cut	Fill	Net cut/fill
Sample Curb - 1	81.34 CF	2286.62 CF	2205.28 CF
South East New	0.15 CF	193167.31 CF	193167.16 CF
Sample Curb - 2	0.00 CF	37162.30 CF	37162.30 CF

Figure 5–14

The other report covers site components, such as curbs and sidewalks. It is exported out to a text file. In the *Site Designer* tab>Reports panel, click (Reports). In the Site Component Reports dialog box, review the component information, specify the *Export Options* (as shown in Figure 5–15), and click **Export**.

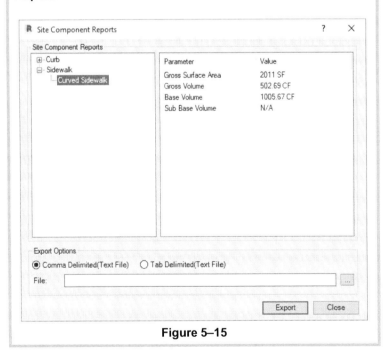

Figure 5–15

Practice 5a

Add Site Designer Features

Practice Objectives

- Split toposurfaces.
- Set a base toposurface.
- Draw model lines as the basis of new topography elements.
- Use the Soft Terrain Site Designer tool to add mass grading and a berm.
- Add Sidewalk and curb elements
- Modify the material of toposurfaces.

Estimated time for completion: 30 minutes

In this practice you will draw model lines and use them to define Site Designer features. You will name and set the base toposurface and create new soft terrain features for a mass surface. You will also create a soft terrain berm feature, a sidewalk and a curb that defines a planting area, as shown in Figure 5–16.

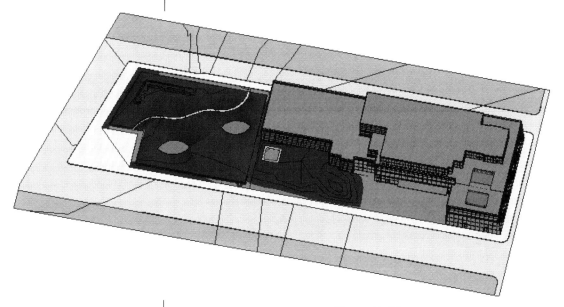

Figure 5–16

Task 1 - Set up a Base Toposurface.

1. Open the **Urban-Garden-Park.rvt** project.

2. View the existing features, including the overall site toposurface with roads and sidewalks, the reflecting pool toposurface, and the building base, which are linked into the current project. Note that there is also a toposurface in the current project for you to modify, as shown in Figure 5–17.

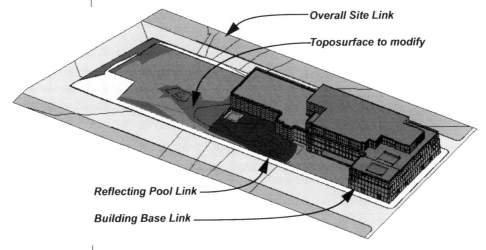

Figure 5–17

3. In the *Manage* tab>Manage Project panel, click ⬛ (Manage Links).

4. In the Manage Links dialog box, select **Building-Base.rvt** and **Site-Pool.rvt** (but not **Building-Site.rvt**). Click **Unload**, and then click **OK**.

5. Open the **Floor Plans: Site** view.

6. Select the toposurface. Note that it overlaps some of the site, as shown in Figure 5–18.

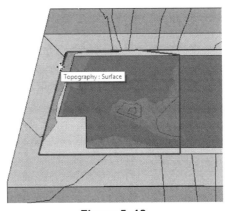

Figure 5–18

7. While still in Properties, set the *Name* to **Existing Topo West** and the *Phase Created* to **Existing**.

8. Save the project.

Task 2 - Add model lines to define Site Designer features.

---

1. In the View Control Bar, set the *Visual Style* to **Wireframe** so that the model lines display even if the toposurface is covering them.

2. In the *Architecture* tab>Model panel, click 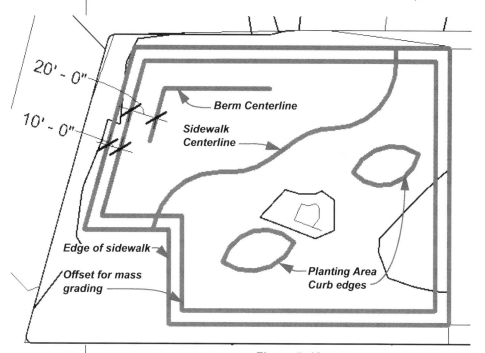 (Model Line).

3. In the *Modify | Place Lines* tab>Draw panel, click ✎ (Line).

4. in the Options Bar, ensure that the *Placement Plane* is set to **Level: 01 Motor Court**.

The lines shown in Figure 5–19 are heavier for clarity.

5. Sketch lines around the outside edge of the sidewalk, and then offset lines as shown in Figure 5–19. Create additional sketches similar to the other elements shown in Figure 5–19. Use modify tools as required to create a closed loop.

20' - 0"

10' - 0"

Berm Centerline

Sidewalk
Centerline

Edge of sidewalk

Offset for mass
grading

Planting Area
Curb edges

Figure 5–19

• Other than the mass grading line, the exact design of each feature is up to you.

- To create the curved sidewalk, draw straight lines and then use the 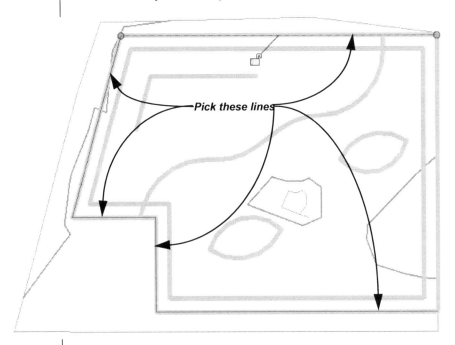 (Fillet Arc) tool with a wide radius to smooth them out. Note that the Spline tool and Ellipse tools do not work with Site Designer.

6. Select the **Building-Site.rvt** link and unload it.

7. In the *Massing & Site* tab>Modify Site panel, click (Split Surface.

8. Select the toposurface.

9. In the *Modify |Split Surface* tab>Draw panel, click (Pick Lines) and select the lines that follow the edge of the sidewalk, as shown in Figure 5–20. Use the **Drag End Line** control on the horizontal lines on the right to ensure that they extend beyond the toposurface.

Pick these lines

Figure 5–20

10. Click (Finish Edit Mode).

11. Select and delete the outside toposurface. Delete the outside model lines. The final toposurface should display similar to Figure 5–21.

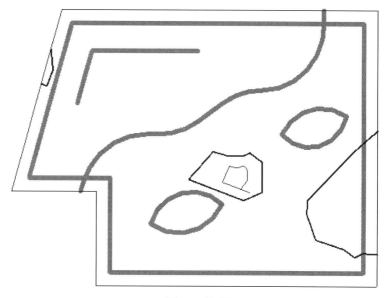

Figure 5–21

12. Select the toposurface and name it **Existing Park Toposurface**.

13. Save the project.

Task 3 - Create a proposed mass grading toposurface.

---

1. In the *Site Designer* tab>Convert panel, click (Set Base Toposurface).

2. In the Set Base Toposurface dialog box, highlight **Existing Park Toposurface** (as shown in Figure 5–22) and click **OK**.

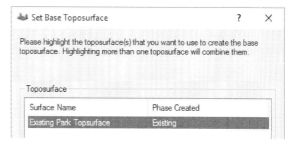

Figure 5–22

3. In Select Surface Name and Phase dialog box, set the *Toposurface Name* to **Proposed Park Toposurface** and the *Phase Created* to **New Construction**, as shown in Figure 5–23. Select **Hide Original Toposurface** and then click **Apply**.

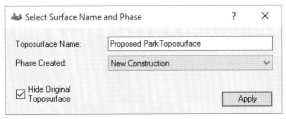

Figure 5–23

4. In the *Site Designer* tab>Locate panel, click (Soft Terrain).
   - If a warning box displays about no Soft Terrain Families, select **Always Load Default Families** and click **OK**.

5. In the Locate Soft Terrain dialog box, beside *Soft Terrain Family,* click (Load Family).

6. In the Please select Site Designer Soft Terrain Family File dialog box, select **Mass Grading.rfa** and click **Open**.

7. In the Locate Soft Terrain dialog box, set the values shown in Figure 5–24.

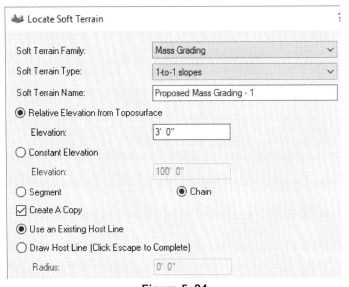

Figure 5–24

8. Click **Insert**. Select a segment of the model line that is offset from the edge of the toposurface.

9. When the Warning box about a closed chain displays, click **No**.

10. Close the Locate Soft Terrain dialog box.

11. Review the Proposed Mass Grading surface in 3D View, as shown in Figure 5–25.

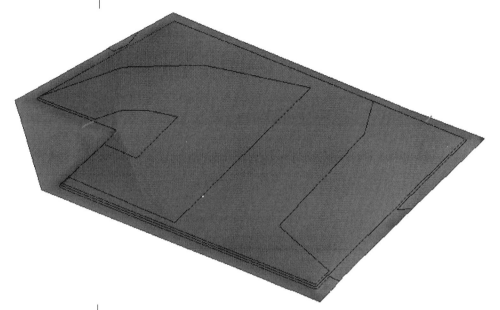

Figure 5–25

12. Save the project.

Task 4 - Create a berm using the Soft Terrain tool.

1. Return to the **Floor Plans: Site** view.

2. In the *Site Designer* tab>Locate panel, click ✎ (Soft Terrain).

3. In the Locate Soft Terrain dialog box, beside *Soft Terrain Family*, click 🔲 (Load Family).

4. In the Please select Site Designer Soft Terrain Family File. dialog box, select **Berms.rfa,** and then click **Open**.

5. In the Locate Soft Terrain dialog box, set the values shown in Figure 5–26.

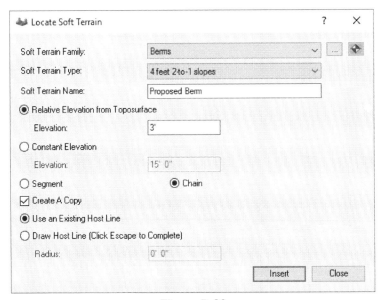

Figure 5–26

6. Click **Insert**.

7. Select the model line and close the dialog box. The new berm is created, as shown in Figure 5–27.

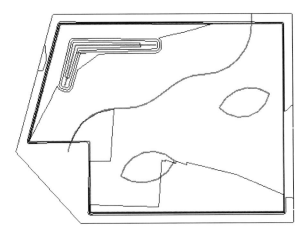

Figure 5–27

8. Review the surfaces in 3D view.

9. Save the project.

Task 5 - Add a sidewalk and curbs.

1. In the *Site Designer* tab>Locate panel, click 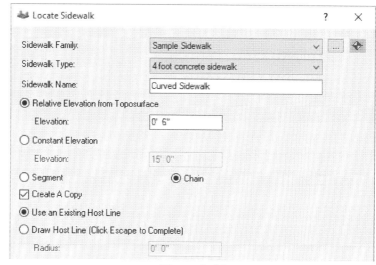 (Sidewalk).

2. In the Locate Sidewalk dialog box, name the sidewalk **Curved Sidewalk** and set the *Elevation* and other information as shown in Figure 5–28. Click **Insert** and select the curved sidewalk line you created earlier. Click **Close**.

Figure 5–28

3. Review the new sidewalk in a 3D view, as shown in Figure 5–29.

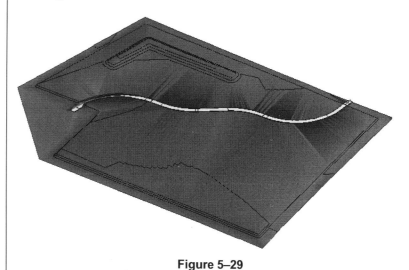

Figure 5–29

4. Return to the **Floor Plans>Site** view.

5. In the *Site Designer* tab>Locate panel, click (Curb).

6. In the Locate Curb dialog box:
   - Name the curb **Planting Bed 1**.
   - Select **Chain**, **Create a Copy**, and **Use an Existing Host Line**.
   - Click **Insert.**

7. Select one of the planting bed model lines.

8. In the Toposurface Association dialog box, select **Proposed Park Toposurface** and click **OK**.

9. In the Locate Curb dialog box, change the *Curb Name* to **Planting Bed 2** and click **Insert**.

10. Select the other planting bed model lines. In the Toposurface Association dialog box, select **Proposed Park Toposurface** and click **OK**.

11. Close the Locate Curb dialog box.

12. Review the new planting beds in a 3D view.

13. Save the project.

Task 6 - Set the materials of the toposurfaces.

1. Select the large toposurface.

2. In Properties, set the *Material* to **Grass**.

3. Select the two toposurfaces that form the planting beds.

4. In Properties, set the *Material* to **Plant**. The new materials display as shown in Figure 5–30.

Figure 5–30

5. In the *Manage* tab>Manage Project panel, click (Manage Links).

6. Reload all of the Autodesk Revit links.

7. Review the full project in the 3D view.

8. Save the project.

5.3 Modifying Site Designer Features

You can modify Site Designer features, as shown in Figure 5–31. You can adjust the location and the elevation of points and the slope between points. You can also add and delete vertices, change the type of element, and delete features.

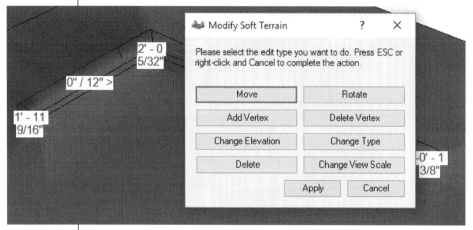

Figure 5–31

The commands are found in the *Site Designer* tab>Modify panel, as shown in Figure 5–32.

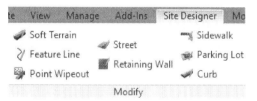

Figure 5–32

- Do not attempt to delete or otherwise modify Site Designer features using the standard Autodesk Revit tools. Use the specific modify command related to the type of feature.

How To: Modify Site Designer Features

1. In the *Site Designer* tab>Modify panel select the appropriate modify tool.
2. Select the related host line. (Press <tab>as needed to select the correct element.)
3. In the Modify dialog box (as shown for Soft Terrain in Figure 5–33), select the appropriate modify command.

To see the host lines you can set the Visual Style to Wireframe.

Figure 5–33

4. Follow the prompts for the command.

   • When required, green circles display around vertices (as shown in Figure 5–34) and slopes. Select the edge of the circle to make the modification.

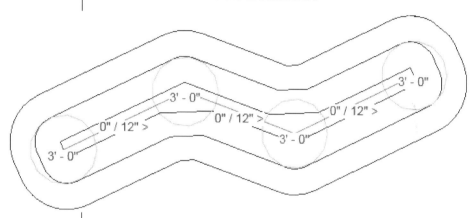

Figure 5–34

5. Right-click and select **Cancel** to return to the dialog box.
6. Click **Apply**.

Hint: Annotating Site Components

You can add grades and elevation text notes to Site Designer elements. In the *Site Designer* tab> Reports panel click

⚟ (Annotate). In the Annotate Site Components dialog box (shown in Figure 5–35), specify the Text Type and types of notes to add.

Figure 5–35

Modify Command Prompts

Move	Select a start point to move from, and then select an end point to move to. The entire feature moves.
Rotate	First, select a rotation base point Then, select a point to define the rotation base (i.e., along the existing line), and then select a second point to define the rotation base (another point that defines the new angle).

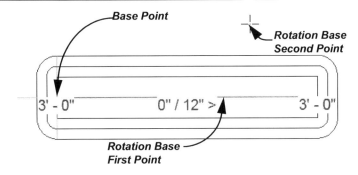

Add Vertex	Select a point or points where you want to add vertices.
Delete Vertex	Select the circle around the vertex to delete the point.
Change Elevation	**Vertex:** Pick the circle around the vertex you want to change. In the Change Elevation dialog box, enter a new elevation and click **OK**.

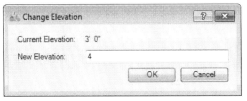

Grade: Pick the circle around the grade (slope) you want to change. Select the arrow of the direction in which you want to change the grade. In the Change Grade dialog box, enter a new elevation or slope and click **OK**.

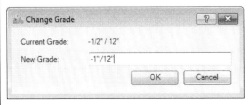

Change Interval	(Feature Line only) Change the distance between points on the toposurface.

Change Type	In the Change Family Type dialog box, specify a *New Family* and *New Type* from the drop-down list and click **OK**. 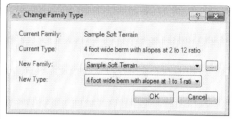
Delete	When you are prompted if you are sure you want to delete the site component, click **Yes**. This deletes the entire element.
Change View Scale	If you are already in the command and the text is not readable, you can change the view scale using the Change View Scale dialog box. 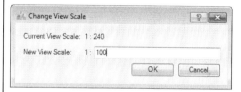
Add Breakline	(Parking Lot only). Breaklines create hard breaks in a parking lot surface. Use them to create high and low points, grading planes, and catch basin areas. In the Add Breakline dialog box, specify the *Linear Point Interval* (distance between new topography points), **Relative Elevations**, **Constant Elevations**, or **Grade**, and how you want to create the line. Click **OK** 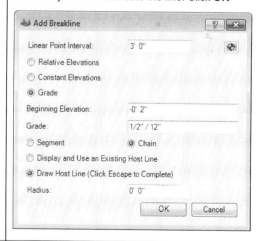
Delete Breakline	(Parking Lot only). Select the breakline to remove.

Hint: Site Designer Families

Site Designer features have families and types just like other Autodesk Revit elements. These families are created through special Family Managers. You can load custom families that have been created.

How To: Load a Site Designer Family

1. In the *Site Designer* tab>Family Managers panel, expand Family Managers (as shown in Figure 5–36), and select the type of family you want to load.

Figure 5–36

2. In the Family Manager dialog box, click **Load**.
3. Navigate to the folder where the family file is located and select the file. (It will have a .rfa extension.) Click **Open**.
4. The new family with a list of types displays, as shown for a Sidewalk family in Figure 5–37. Click **OK**.

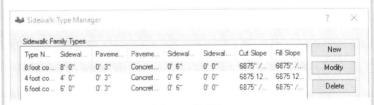

Figure 5–37

5. In the main Family Manager dialog box, click **Save**. The new family will be available when you create and edit Site Designer features of that type.

Practice 5b | Modify Site Designer Features

Practice Objectives

Estimated time for completion: 15 minutes

- Modify soft terrain features by changing the elevation of individual points.
- Modify a berm by adding vertices.
- Change the type of a sidewalk.

In this practice you will modify a soft terrain mass grading element by changing the elevation of points. You will then modify a berm element by adding vertices and change the width of the sidewalk by changing its type as shown in Figure 5–38. If you have time, you can modify other existing features.

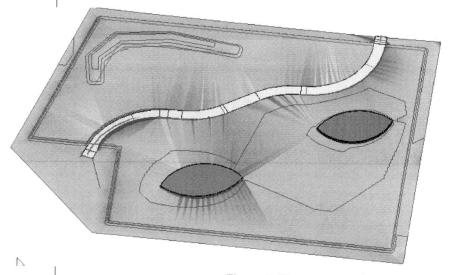

Figure 5–38

Task 1 - Modify the Mass Grading element.

1. Open the **Urban-Garden-Park-Modify.rvt** project.

2. Unload all of the linked Autodesk Revit files.

3. In the View Control Bar, change the *Visual Style* to **Wireframe** so that the model lines used to create the Site Designer features display.

Press <tab> as required to highlight the line.

4. In the *Site Designer* tab>Modify panel, select ✎ (Soft Terrain). Select one of the model lines (host line) used to create the Proposed Mass Grading surface.

5. In the Modify Soft Terrain dialog box, click **Change View Scale**.

6. In the Change View Scale dialog box, set the *New View Scale* to **1:200** (as shown in Figure 5–39) and click **OK**.

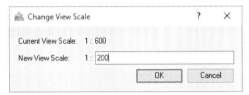

Figure 5–39

7. In the Modify Soft Terrain dialog box, select **Change Elevation**.

8. In the model, change the elevations of each corner point to **2'-6"** as shown in Figure 5–40.

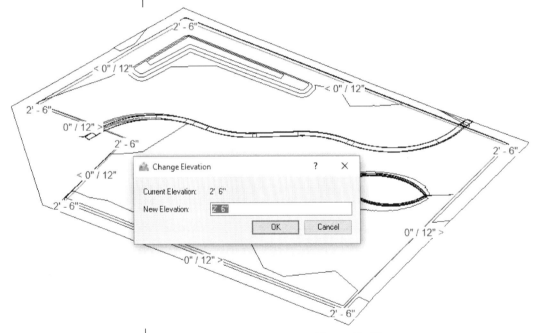

Figure 5–40

9. Right click and select **Cancel**.

10. In the Modify Soft Terrain dialog box, click **Apply**.

11. Set the *Visual Style* to **Shaded** and review the updated surface.

12. Save the project.

Task 2 - Add Vertices to the Berm.

1. Open the **Floor Plans: Site** view.

2. Zoom in on the Berm and set the *Visual Style* to **Wireframe**, if required.

3. In the *Site Designer* tab>Modify panel, click (Soft Terrain).

4. Select one of the model lines that defines the berm.

5. In the Modify Soft Terrain dialog box, click **Change View Scale** and set it to **1:100**.

6. Click **Add Vertex** and pick two points similar to those shown in Figure 5–41.

If you want to be more precise about placing the points, add reference planes or model or detail lines before you start the command.

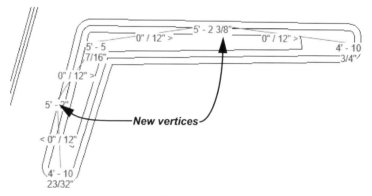

Figure 5–41

7. Right-click and select **Cancel**.

8. In the Modify Soft Terrain dialog box, click **Apply**. The new berm shape displays as shown in Figure 5–42.

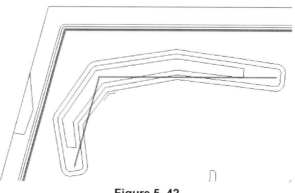

Figure 5–42

9. Review the modified feature in a 3D view.

10. Save the project.

Task 3 - Load a Sidewalk Family and change the Type of the Sidewalk.

1. Open the **Floor Plans: Site** view.

2. In the *Site Designer* tab>Family Managers panel, expand (Family Managers) and select (Sidewalk).

3. In the Sidewalk Family Manager, click **Load**.

4. In the Open dialog box, navigate to the practice files folder, select **Urban-Garden-Sidewalks.rfa**, and click **Open**. This is a family file that includes additional sidewalk widths.

5. Click **OK** and then **Save**. The sidewalk family is ready to use.

6. In the *Site Designer* tab>Modify panel, click (Sidewalk).

7. Select one of the model lines that defines the sidewalk.

8. In the Modify Sidewalk dialog box, click **Change Type**.

9. In the Change Family Type dialog box, set the *New Family* to **Urban-Garden-Sidewalks** and the *New Type* to **8 foot concrete sidewalk**, as shown in Figure 5–43.

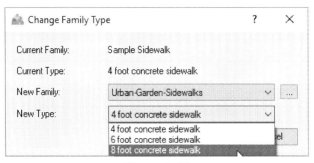

Figure 5–43

10. Click **OK**.

11. In the Modify Sidewalk dialog box, click **Apply**. The sidewalk widens and the toposurface is modified to match the new width, as shown in Figure 5–44.

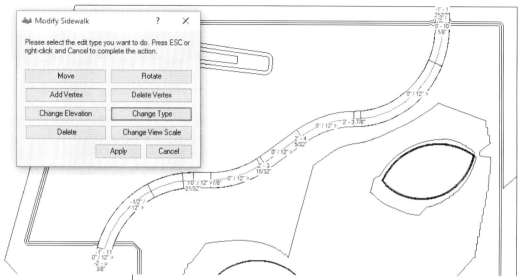

Figure 5–44

12. Review the changes in the 3D view.

13. Save the project.

14. If you have time, modify the other Site Designer features as desired.

Chapter Review Questions

1. Which of the following must be completed before you create a Site Designer feature? (Select all that apply.)

   a. A toposurface must be in the project.

   b. All Site Designer families must be pre-loaded.

   c. Set the Base Toposurface.

   d. The phase of all elements must be set to *Existing*.

2. Which of the following commands would you use to create a berm?

   a. Soft Terrain

   b. Feature Line

   c. Point Wipeout

   d. Berm

3. What type of element is created when you add a sidewalk?

   a. Toposurface

   b. Floor

   c. Sidewalk

   d. Road

4. To modify a Site Designer feature you must select...

   a. The feature element.

   b. The related toposurface.

   c. The host line.

   d. The feature line.

Command Summary

Button	Command	Location
General Site Designer Tools		
	Annotate	• **Ribbon:** *Site Designer* tab>Reports panel
	Import LandXML	• **Ribbon:** *Site Designer* tab>Import/Export panel
	Export LandXML	• **Ribbon:** *Site Designer* tab>Import/Export panel
	Family Managers	• **Ribbon:** *Site Designer* tab>Family Managers panel
	Reports	• **Ribbon:** *Site Designer* tab>Reports panel
Site Designer Locate Tools		
	Locate Curb	• **Ribbon:** *Site Designer* tab>Locate panel
	Locate Feature Line	• **Ribbon:** *Site Designer* tab>Locate panel
	Locate Parking Lot	• **Ribbon:** *Site Designer* tab>Locate panel
	Locate Point Wipeout	• **Ribbon:** *Site Designer* tab>Locate panel
	Locate Retaining Wall	• **Ribbon:** *Site Designer* tab>Locate panel
	Locate Sidewalk	• **Ribbon:** *Site Designer* tab>Locate panel
	Locate Soft Terrain	• **Ribbon:** *Site Designer* tab>Locate panel
	Locate Street	• **Ribbon:** *Site Designer* tab>Locate panel
Site Designer Modify Tools		
	Modify Curb	• **Ribbon:** *Site Designer* tab>Modify panel
	Modify Feature Line	• **Ribbon:** *Site Designer* tab>Modify panel
	Modify Parking Lot	• **Ribbon:** *Site Designer* tab>Modify panel
	Modify Point Wipeout	• **Ribbon:** *Site Designer* tab>Modify panel
	Modify Retaining Wall	• **Ribbon:** *Site Designer* tab>Modify panel
	Modify Sidewalk	• **Ribbon:** *Site Designer* tab>Modify panel

	Modify Soft Terrain	• **Ribbon**: *Site Designer* tab>Modify panel
	Modify Street	• **Ribbon**: *Site Designer* tab>Modify panel

Working with Views

Views are the cornerstone of working with Autodesk® Revit® models as they enable you to see the model in both 2D and 3D. As you are working, you can duplicate and change views to display different information based on the same view of the model. Callouts, elevations, and sections are especially important views for construction documents.

Learning Objectives in this Chapter

- Change the way elements display in different views to show required information and set views for construction documents.
- Duplicate views so that you can modify the display as you are creating the model and for construction documents.
- Create callout views of parts of plans, sections, or elevations for detailing.
- Add building and interior elevations that can be used to demonstrate how a building will be built.
- Create building and wall sections to help you create the model and to include in construction documents.

6.1 Setting the View Display

Views are a powerful tool that they enable you to create multiple versions of a model without having to recreate building elements. For example, you can have views that are specifically used for planting layout (as shown in Figure 6–1), while other views are annotated and used for construction documents, as shown in Figure 6–2.

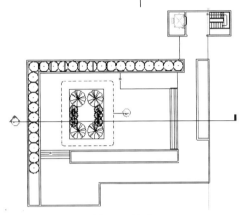

Figure 6–1

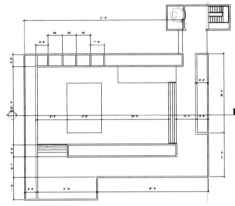

Figure 6–2

The view display can be modified in the following locations:

- View Control Bar

- Properties

- Shortcut menu

- Visibility/Graphic Overrides dialog box

Hiding and Overriding Graphics

Two common ways to customize a view are to:

- Hide individual elements or categories.

- Modify how graphics display for elements or categories (e.g., altering lineweight, color, or pattern).

An element is an individual item such as a wall in a view, while a category includes all instances of a selected element, such as all walls in a view.

In the example shown in Figure 6–3, a planting plan has been created by toggling off some categories and setting other categories halftone.

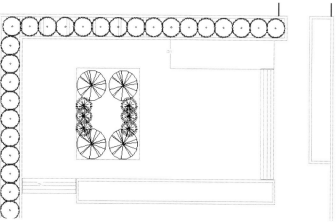

Figure 6–3

How To: Hide Elements or Categories in a view

1. Select the elements or categories that you want to hide.
2. Right-click and select **Hide in View>Elements** or **Hide in View>Category**, as shown in Figure 6–4.

   • The elements or categories are hidden in current view only.

*A quick way to hide an entire category is to select an element(s) and type **VH**.*

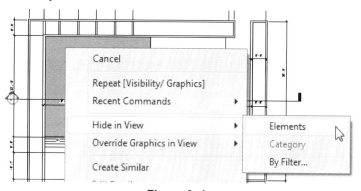

Figure 6–4

How To: Override Graphics of Elements or Categories in a View

1. Select the element(s) that you want to modify.
2. Right-click and select **Override Graphics in View>By Element** or **By Category**. The View-Specific Element (or Category) Graphics dialog box opens, as shown in Figure 6–5.

The exact options in the dialog box vary depending on the type of elements selected.

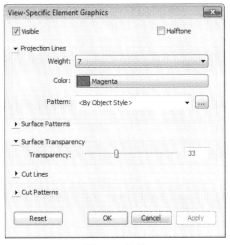

Figure 6–5

3. Select the changes that you want to make and click **OK**.

View-Specific Options

- Clearing the **Visible** option is the same as hiding the elements or categories.

- Selecting the **Halftone** option grays out the elements or categories.

- The options for Projection Lines, Surface Patterns, Cut Lines, and Cut Patterns include **Weight**, **Color**, and **Pattern**, as shown in Figure 6–5.

- The **Surface Transparency** option can be set by moving the slider bar, as shown in Figure 6–6.

Figure 6–6

- The View-Specific Category dialog box includes **Open the Visibility Graphics dialog...**, which opens the full dialog box of options.

The Visibility/Graphic Overrides dialog box

The options in the Visibility/Graphic Overrides dialog box (shown in Figure 6–7) control how every category and sub-category of elements displays per view.

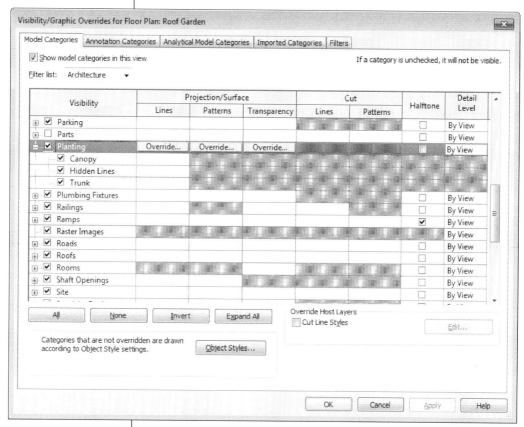

Figure 6–7

To open the Visibility/Graphic Overrides dialog box, type **VV** or **VG**. It is also available in Properties: in the *Graphics* area, beside *Visibility/Graphic Overrides*, click **Edit...**.

- The Visibility/Graphic Overrides are divided into *Model*, *Annotation*, *Analytical Model*, *Imported,* and *Filters* categories.

- Other categories might be available if specific data has been included in the project. These include *Design Options*, *Linked Files*, and *Worksets*.

- To limit the number of categories showing in the dialog box, select a discipline from the *Filter list,* as shown in Figure 6–8.

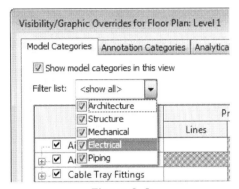

Figure 6–8

- To help you select categories, use **All**, **None**, and **Invert**. The **Expand All** button displays all of the sub-categories.

Hint: Restoring Hidden Elements or Categories

You can display any hidden categories using the Visibility/Graphic Overrides dialog box. However, to display hidden elements, you must temporarily reveal the elements first.

1. In the View Control Bar, click 🔲 (Reveal Hidden Elements). The border and all hidden elements display in magenta, while visible elements in the view are grayed out, as shown in Figure 6–9.

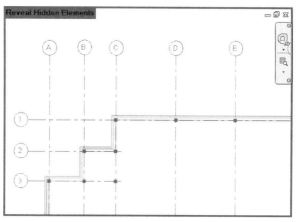

Figure 6–9

2. Select the hidden elements that you want to restore, right-click, and select **Unhide in View>Elements** or **Unhide in View>Category**. Alternatively, in the *Modify |* contextual tab>Reveal Hidden Elements panel, click 🖘 (Unhide Element) or 🔲 (Unhide Category).

3. When you are finished, in the View Control Bar, click 🔲 (Close Reveal Hidden Elements), or in the *Modify |* contextual tab>Reveal Hidden Elements panel, click ⊠ (Toggle Reveal Hidden Elements Mode).

View Properties

The most basic properties of a view are accessed using the View Control Bar, shown in Figure 6–10. These include **Scale**, **Detail Level,** and **Visual Style**. Additional tools include temporary overrides and other advanced settings.

Figure 6–10

Other modifications to views are available in Properties, as shown in Figure 6–11. These properties include *Underlays*, *View Range*, and *Crop Regions*.

The options in Properties vary according to the type of view. A plan view has different properties than a 3D view.

Figure 6–11

Setting an Underlay

Setting an *Underlay* is helpful if you need to display elements on a different level, such as the basement plan shown with an underlay of the first floor plan in Figure 6–12. You can then use the elements to trace over or even copy to the current level of the view.

Underlays are only available in Floor Plan and Ceiling Plan views.

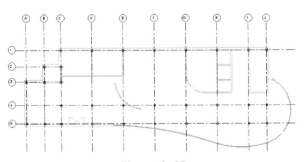

Figure 6–12

In Properties, in the *Underlay* area, specify the *Range: Base Level* and the *Range: Top Level*. You can also set the *Underlay Orientation* to **Look down** or **Look up**, as shown in Figure 6–13.

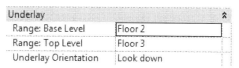

Underlay	☆
Range: Base Level	Floor 2
Range: Top Level	Floor 3
Underlay Orientation	Look down

Figure 6–13

- To prevent from accidentally moving elements in the underlay, in the Select panel, expand the panel title and clear **Select underlay elements**. You can also toggle this on/off using 🔲 (Select Underlay Elements) in the Status Bar.

How To: Set the View Range

1. In Properties, in the *Extents* area, beside *View Range*, select **Edit...** or type **VR**.
2. In the View Range dialog box, as shown in Figure 6–14, modify the levels and offsets for the *Primary Range* and *View Depth*.
   - Click **Show>>** to display the Sample View Range graphics and key to the various options.
3. Click **OK**.

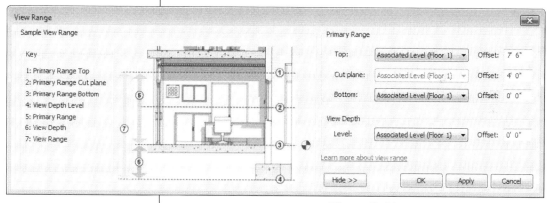

Figure 6–14

- If the settings used cannot be represented graphically, a warning displays stating the inconsistency.

- A Reflected Ceiling Plan (RCP) is created as if the ceiling is reflected by a mirror on the floor, so that the ceiling is the same orientation as the floor plan. The cutline is placed just below the ceiling to ensure that any windows and doors below it do not display.

Plan Regions

When you have a plan view with multiple levels of floors or ceilings, you can create plan regions that enable you to set a different view range for part of a view, as shown in Figure 6–15 for a set of clerestory windows.

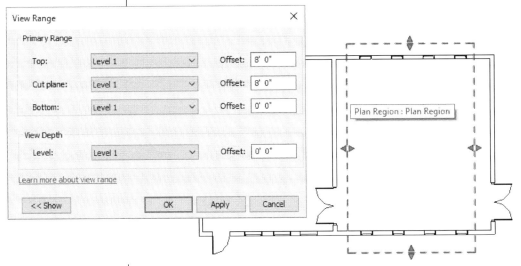

Figure 6–15

How To: Create Plan Regions

1. In a plan view, in the *View* tab>Create panel, expand 🗗 (Plan Views) and select 🗗 (Plan Region).
2. In the *Modify | Create Plan Region Boundary* tab>Draw panel, select a draw tool and create the boundary for the plan region.
   - The boundary must be closed and cannot overlap other plan region boundaries, but the boundaries can be side by side.
3. Click ✔ (Finish Edit Mode).
4. In the *Modify | Plan Region t*ab>Region panel, click 🗄 (View Range).
5. In the View Range dialog box, specify the offsets for the plan region and click **OK**. The plan region is applied to the selected area.

   - Plan regions can be copied to the clipboard and then pasted into other plan views.

- You can use shape handles to resize plan region boundaries without having to edit the boundary.

- If a plan region is above a door, the door swing displays, but the door opening does not display. as shown in Figure 6–16.

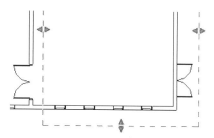

Figure 6–16

- Plan Regions can be toggled on and off in the Visibility/ Graphic Overrides dialog box on the *Annotation Categories* tab. If they are displayed, the plan regions are included when printing and exporting.

Hint: Depth Clipping and Far Clipping

Depth Clipping, shown in Figure 6–17, is a viewing option which sets how sloped walls are displayed if the *View Range* of a plan is set to a limited view.

Far Clipping (shown in Figure 6–18) is available for section and elevation views.

Figure 6–17   **Figure 6–18**

- An additional Graphic Display Option enables you to specify *Depth Cueing*, so that items that are in the distance will be made lighter.

Crop Regions

Plans, sections, and elevations can all be modified by changing how much of the model displays in a view. One way to do this is to set the Crop Region. If there are dimensions, tags, or text near the required crop region, you can also use the Annotation Crop Region to include these, as shown in Figure 6–19.

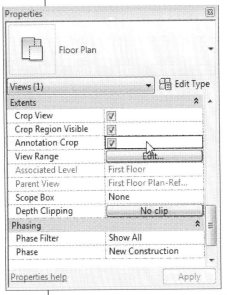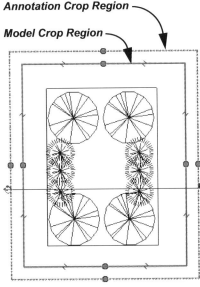

Annotation Crop Region
Model Crop Region

Figure 6–19

Zoom out if you do not see the crop region when you set it to be displayed.

- The crop region must display to modify the size of the view. In the View Control Bar, click (Show Crop Region). Alternatively, in Properties, in the *Extents* area, select **Crop Region Visible**. The **Annotation Crop** option is also available in this area.

- Resize the crop region using the ⊙ control on each side of the region.

Breaking the crop region is typically used with sections or details.

- Click (Break Line) control to split the view into two regions, horizontally or vertically. Each part of the view can then be modified to display what is required and allowed to be moved independently.

- You can also resize the Crop Region and the Annotation Crop Region using the Crop Region Size dialog box, as shown in Figure 6–20. In the *Modify | Views* tab>Crop panel, click 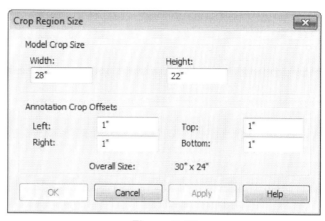 (Size Crop) to open the dialog box.

Figure 6–20

- It is a best practice to hide a crop region before placing a view on a sheet. In the View Control Bar, click (Hide Crop Region).

Using View Templates

A powerful way to use views effectively is to set up a view and then save it as a View Template. You can apply view templates to views individually, or though the Properties palette. Setting the View Template using the Properties palette helps ensure that you do not accidentally modify the view while interacting with it.

How To: Create a View Template from a View

1. Setup a view, as required.
2. In the Project Browser, right-click on the view and select **Create View Template from View...**.
3. In the New View Template dialog box, type in a name and click **OK**.
4. The new view template is now added in the View Templates dialog box. Make any other required modifications here.
5. Click **OK**.

How To: Specify a View Template for a View

1. In the Project Browser, select the view or views to which you want to apply a view template.
2. In Properties, scroll down to the *Identity Data* section and click the button beside *View Template*.
3. In the Apply View Template dialog box, select the view template from the list, as shown in Figure 6–21.

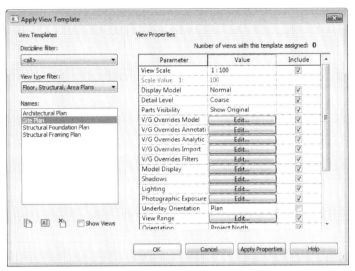

Figure 6–21

4. Click **OK**.

• In the View Control Bar, use (Temporary View Properties) to temporarily apply a view template to a view.

6.2 Duplicating Views

Once you have created a model, you do not have to recreate the elements at different scales or copy them so that they can be used on more than one sheet. Instead, you can duplicate the required views and modify them to suit your needs.

Duplication Types

Duplicate creates a copy of the view that only includes the building elements, as shown in Figure 6–22. Annotation and detailing are not copied into the new view. Building model elements automatically change in all views, but view-specific changes made to the new view are not reflected in the original one.

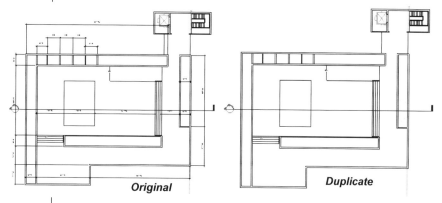

Original   Duplicate

Figure 6–22

Duplicate with Detailing creates a copy of the view and includes all annotation and detail elements (such as tags), as shown in Figure 6–23. Any annotation or view-specific elements created in the new view are not reflected in the original view.

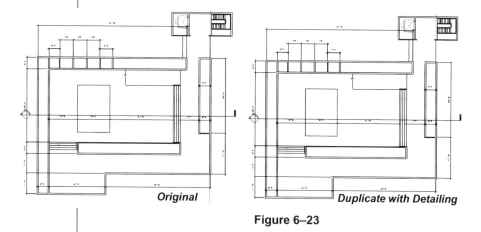

Original   Duplicate with Detailing

Figure 6–23

Duplicate as a Dependent creates a copy of the view and links it to the original (parent) view, as shown in the Project Browser in Figure 6–24. View-specific changes made to the overall view, such as changing the *Scale*, are also reflected in the dependent (child) views and vice-versa.

Figure 6–24

- Use dependent views when the building model large enough that you need to split the building onto separate sheets, while ensuring that the views are all the same scale.

- If you want to separate a dependent view from the original view, right-click on the dependent view and select **Convert to independent view**.

How To: Create Duplicate Views

1. Open the view you want to duplicate.
2. In the *View* tab>Create panel, expand **Duplicate View** and select the type of duplicate view that you want to create, as shown in Figure 6–25.

Figure 6–25

- Alternatively, you can right-click on a view in the Project Browser and select the type of duplicate that you want to use, as shown in Figure 6–26.

Figure 6–26

- To rename a view, right-click on the new view in the Project Browser and select **Rename**. In the Project Browser, type in the new name.

Most types of views can be duplicated.

You can also press <F2> to start the **Rename** *command.*

Hint: Viewing a True North Site Plan

When you are ready to annotate and place a site plan on a sheet, you can create a view displaying the rotation to True North, as shown in Figure 6–27.

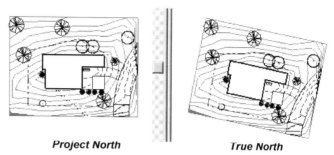

Project North   **True North**

Figure 6–27

1. Create a copy of the plan view that you want to rotate to true north. You can tile the views so that they both display.
2. In the Properties of the true north plan, set the *Orientation* to **True North**, as shown in Figure 6–28.

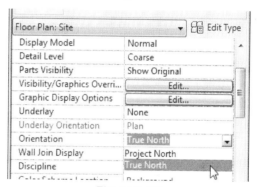

Figure 6–28

3. The view rotates to match the **True North** option specified in the Project Base Point.

Practice 6a

Duplicate Views and Set the View Display

Practice Objectives

- Modify crop regions.
- Duplicate views.
- Change the visibility and graphic display of elements in views.
- Create and apply View Templates.

Estimated time for completion: 20 minutes

In this practice, you will modify the crop region of plan views. You will then duplicate views and hide different element categories in each. One view will remain the primary working model with all categories of elements displaying. The others will show specific parts of the model required for construction documents. The finished views of the second floor are shown in Figure 6–29. You will also create view templates from the views and apply the view templates to similar views on other levels.

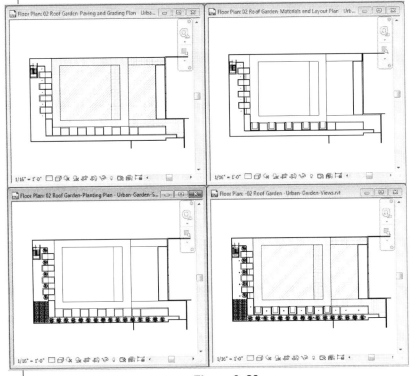

Figure 6–29

- The model includes some elements on the roof garden so you can see the differences in the views.

Task 1 - Modify the Crop Region of views.

1. Open the project **Urban-Garden-Views.rvt** from the practice files folder.

2. Open the **Floor Plans: 01 Motor Court** view.

3. In the View Control Bar, click ⏣ (Show Crop Region).

4. Select the crop region and use the controls to resize the view so that it only shows the motor court area, as shown in Figure 6–30.

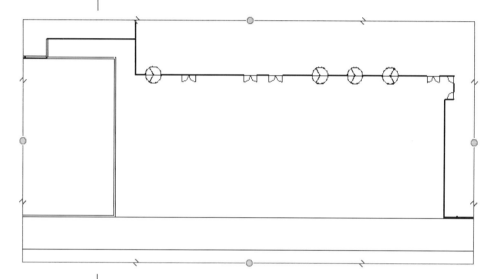

Figure 6–30

5. Type **ZF** to zoom to fit the view.

6. Note that one of the elevation markers that is not required still displays. In Properties (with nothing selected so the properties of the view are available), in the *Extents* section, select **Annotation Crop**, as shown in Figure 6–31.

7. Move the cursor into the view or click **Apply**. The annotation crop boundary displays as shown in Figure 6–32, and the marker is automatically removed from the view.

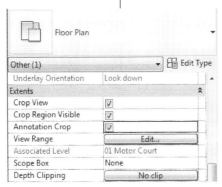

Figure 6–31

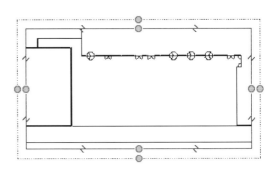

Figure 6–32

8. In the View Control Bar, click 🖼 (Hide Crop Region).

9. Zoom to fit the view.

10. Open the **Floor Plans: 02 Roof Garden** view. Modify the crop region and annotation crop of this view so only the roof garden area displays, as shown in Figure 6–33.

11. Open the **Floor Plans: 03 Club Roof** view. Modify the crop region of this view so only the club roof area displays, as shown in Figure 6–34.

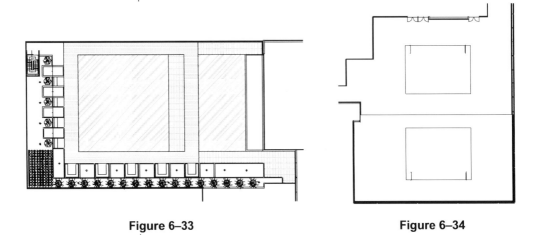

Figure 6–33

Figure 6–34

12. In the Project Browser, select the three floor plan views. (Hold <Ctrl> to select more than one.)

13. In Properties, change the *View Scale* to **1/8"=1'-0"**.

14. Save the project.

Task 2 - Duplicate Views.

1. In the Project Browser, right-click on the **Floor Plans: 01 Motor Court** view and select **Duplicate View>Duplicate**.

2. Right-click on the new view and click **Rename...**.

3. In the Project Browser, type **01 Motor Court-Materials and Layout Plan** and click **OK**.

4. Duplicate the view two more times and name the new views:
   - **01 Motor Court-Paving and Grading Plan**
   - **01 Motor Court-Planting Plan**

5. Repeat the process with the **02 Roof Garden** and **03 Club Roof** views using the same three extensions.

This is a standard where work is done in a model view and other views are setup for standard construction document views. Check with your BIM manager for your standard naming conventions.

6. To make the model views easy to access, rename each of them (do not rename levels and other views) and add a hyphen to the front of the name, as shown in Figure 6–35

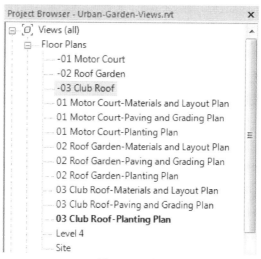

Figure 6–35

7. Save the project.

Task 3 - Override graphics in views.

1. Open the **Floor Plans: -02 Roof Garden** view.

2. In the Quick Access Toolbar, click (Close Hidden Windows) so only this view is open.

3. Open the other three **02 Roof Garden** views.

4. Type **WT** to tile the views and **ZA** to zoom them to fit the new view size, as shown in Figure 6–36.

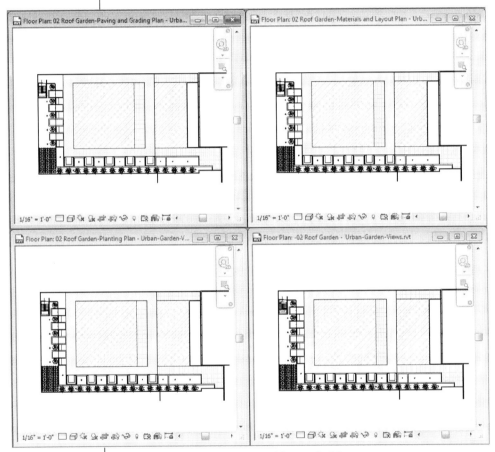

Figure 6–36

5. Click inside the **02 Roof Garden-Materials and Layout Plan** view.

6. Open the Visibility/Graphic Overrides dialog box by typing **VV**.

7. In the dialog box, set the *Filter list* to **Architecture** (by clearing the checkmarks for the other options). In the *Visibility* column, toggle off the visibility of the following and click **Apply**:

- **Lighting Fixtures**
- **Mechanical Equipment** (roof drains)

8. Expand the **Planting** category and toggle off the **Canopy** sub-category, as shown in Figure 6–37. Click **Apply**. The tree locations now display only a cross-mark, as shown in Figure 6–38. All other planting is toggled off.

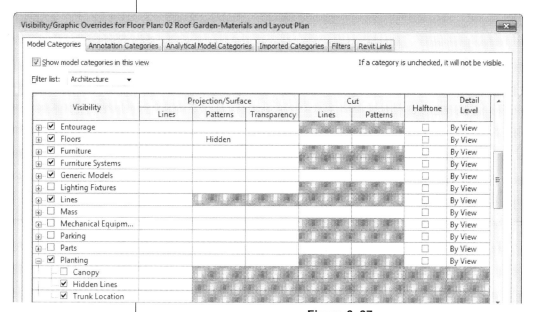

Figure 6–37

9. While still in the Visibility/Graphic Overrides dialog box, select the **Floor** category. In the *Projection/Surface> Patterns* column, click **Override...**

10. In the Fill Pattern Graphics dialog box, clear the checkmark from **Visible** and click **OK**. This leaves the floors in the view but removes the pattern, as shown in Figure 6–38.

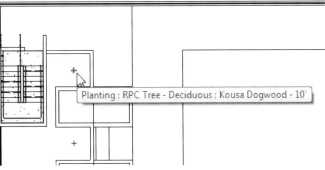

Figure 6–38

11. Click **OK**. The materials view should display as shown in Figure 6–39

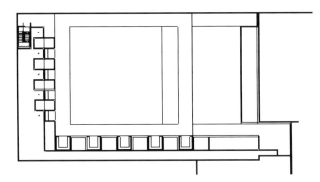

Figure 6–39

12. Click inside the **02 Roof Garden-Paving and Grading Plan** and toggle off the following visibilities:

- **Furniture**
- **Lighting Fixtures**
- **Mechanical Equipment**
- **Planting>Canopy** sub-category only
- Leave the floors as is because you will want to specify the patterns in this view.

13. Repeat the process with the **02 Roof Garden-Planting Plan** and toggle off or modify the following categories:

- **Furniture**
- **Lighting Fixtures**
- **Mechanical Equipment**
- **Floors** - Hide the surface pattern

14. Save the project.

Task 4 - Create and apply View Templates.

1. In the Project Browser, right-click on the **Floor Plans: 02 Roof Garden-Paving and Grading Plan** view and select **Create View Template from View...**.

2. In the New View Template dialog box, type **Paving and Grading Plan** and click **OK**. The View Templates dialog box displays as shown in Figure 6–40.

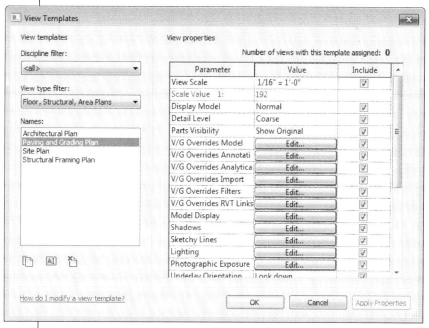

Figure 6–40

3. Review the parameters and values stored with the new paving and Grading Plan view template and click **OK**.

4. Repeat the process and create new view templates based on the **02 Roof Garden-Materials and Layout Plan** view and the **02 Roof Garden-Planting Plan** view.

5. In the Project Browser, select **01 Motor Court-Materials and Layout Plan** and **03 Club Roof-Material and Layout Plan**. (Hold <Ctrl> to select more than one.)

6. In Properties, under *Identity Data,* click the button beside *View Template.*

7. In the Apply View Template dialog box, select the **Materials and Layout Plan** view template, as shown in Figure 6–41. Then, click **OK**.

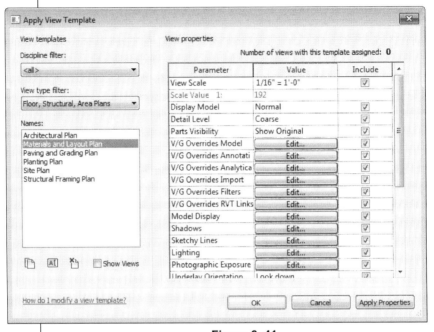

Figure 6–41

8. Review the properties of the view. Most of them will now be grayed out as they are set by the view template.

9. Repeat the process with the other Paving and Grading Plan views and then the Planting Plan views.

10. Take a look at the other views. You will not see much difference because the new landscape elements have not yet been placed in these areas.

11. Save the project.

6.3 Adding Callout Views

Callouts are details of plan, elevation, or section views. When you place a callout in a view, as shown in Figure 6–42, it automatically creates a new view clipped to the boundary of the callout, as shown in Figure 6–43. If you change the size of the callout box in the original view, it automatically updates the callout view and vice-versa. You can create rectangular or sketched callout boundaries.

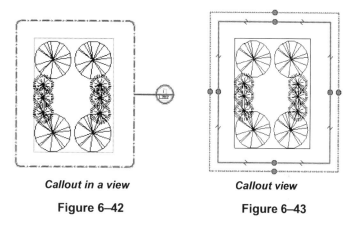

Callout in a view

Figure 6–42

Callout view

Figure 6–43

How To: Create a Rectangular Callout

1. In the *View* tab>Create panel, click ⌀ **(Callout)**.
2. Select points for two opposite corners to define the callout box around the area you want to detail.
3. Select the callout and use the shape handles to modify the location of the bubble and any other edges that might need changing.
4. In the Project Browser, rename the callout.

How To: Create a Sketched Callout

1. In the *View* tab>Create panel, expand ⌀ (Callout) and click ✎ (Sketch).

2. Sketch the shape of the callout using the tools in the *Modify | Edit Profile* tab>Draw panel, as shown in Figure 6–44.

Figure 6–44

3. Click (Finish) to complete the boundary.
4. Select the callout and use the shape handles to modify the location of the bubble and any other edges that might need to be changed.
5. In the Project Browser, rename the callout.

- To open the callout view, double-click on its name in the Project Browser or double-click on the callout bubble. (Verify that the callout itself is not selected before you double-click on it.)

Modifying Callouts

In the original view where the callout is created, you can use the shape handles to modify the callout boundary and bubble location, as shown in Figure 6–45.

The callout bubble displays numbers when the view is placed on a sheet.

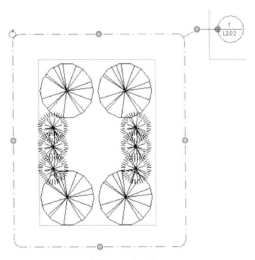

Figure 6–45

- You can rotate the callout box by dragging the ↻ (Rotate) control or by right-clicking on edge of callout and selecting **Rotate**.

In the callout view, you can modify the crop region with shape handles and view breaks, as shown in Figure 6–46.

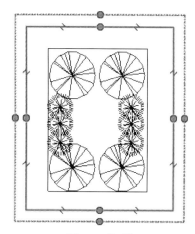

Figure 6–46

- If you want to edit the crop region to reshape the boundary of the view, select the crop region and in the *Modify | Views* tab>Mode panel, click ⬚ (Edit Crop).

- If you want to return a modified crop region to the original rectangular configuration, click ⬚ (Reset Crop).

6.4 Creating Elevations and Sections

Elevations and sections are critical elements of construction documents and can assist you as you are working on a model. Any changes made in one of these views (such as the section in Figure 6–47), changes the entire model and any changes made to the project model also display in the elevations and sections.

Figure 6–47

- In the Project Browser, elevations are separated by elevation type and sections are separated by section type, as shown in Figure 6–48.

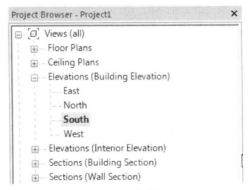

Figure 6–48

- To open an elevation or section view, double-click on the marker arrow or on its name in the Project Browser.

- To give the elevation or section a new name, right-click on it in the Project Browser and select **Rename...**.

Elevations

Elevations are *face-on* views of the interiors and exteriors of a building. Four Exterior Elevation views are defined in the default template: **North**, **South**, **East**, and **West**. You can create additional building elevation views at other angles or interior elevation views, such as the elevation shown in Figure 6–49.

When you add an elevation or section to a sheet, the detail number and sheet number are automatically added to the view title.

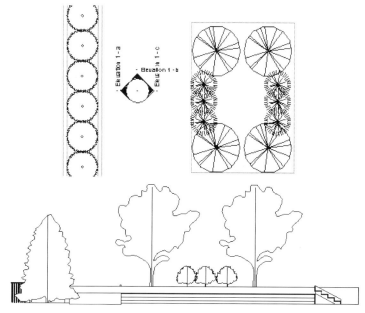

Figure 6–49

- Elevations must be created in plan views.

How To: Create an Elevation

The software remembers the last elevation type used, so if you want to use the same elevation command, you can click the top button.

1. In the *View* tab>Create panel, expand (Elevation) and click (Elevation).
2. In the Type Selector, select the elevation type. Two types come with the templates: **Building Elevation** and **Interior Elevation**.
3. Move the cursor near one of the walls that defines the elevation. The marker follows the angle of the wall.
4. Click to place the marker.

- The length, width, and height of an elevation are defined by the wall(s) and ceiling/floor at which the elevation marker is pointing.

- When creating interior elevations, ensure that the floor or ceiling above is in place before creating the elevation or you will need to modify the elevation crop region so that the elevation markers do not show on all floors.

Sections

Sections can be created in plan, elevation, and other section views.

Sections are slices through a model. You can create a section through an entire building, as shown in Figure 6–50, or through one wall for a detail.

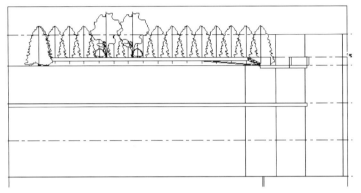

Figure 6–50

How To: Create a Section

1. In the *View* tab>Create panel or in the Quick Access Toolbar, click $\diamondsuit$ (Section).

2. In the Type Selector, select **Section: Building Section** or **Section: Wall Section**. If you want a section in a Drafting view, select **Detail View: Detail**.

3. In the view, select a point where you want to locate the bubble and arrowhead.

4. Select the other end point that describes the section.

5. The shape controls display. You can flip the arrow and change the size of the cutting plane, as well as the location of the bubble and flag.

Hint: Selection Box

You can modify a 3D view to display parts of a building, as shown in Figure 6–51.

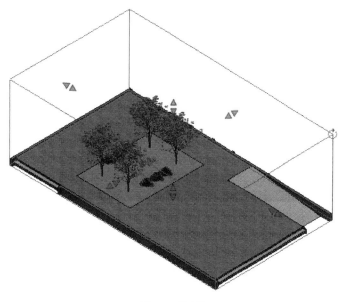

Figure 6–51

1. In a 3D view, select the elements that you want to isolate. In the example shown in Figure 6–51, the wood patio floor was selected.

2. In the *Modify* tab>View panel, click (Selection Box) or type **BX**.

3. The view is limited to a box around the selected item(s).

4. Use the controls of the Section Box to modify the size of the box to show exactly what you want.

- To toggle off a section box and restore the full model, in the view's Properties, in the *Extents* area, clear the checkmark from **Section Box**.

Modifying Elevations and Sections

There are two parts to modifying elevations and sections:

- To modify the view (as shown in Figure 6–52), use the controls to modify the size or create view breaks.

- To modify the markers (as shown in Figure 6–53), use the controls to change the length and depth of elevations and sections. There are other specific type options as well.

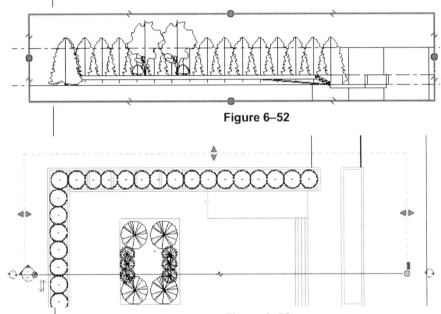

Figure 6–52

Figure 6–53

Modifying Elevation Markers

When you modify elevation markers, you can specify the length and depth of the clip plane, as shown in Figure 6–54.

- Select the arrowhead of the elevation marker, not the circle portion, to display the clip plane.

- Drag the round shape handles to lengthen or shorten the elevation.

- Drag the ▲▼ (Arrow) controls to adjust the depth of the elevation.

To display additional interior elevations from one marker, select the circle portion (not the arrowhead) and place a checkmark in the directions that you want to display, as shown in Figure 6–54.

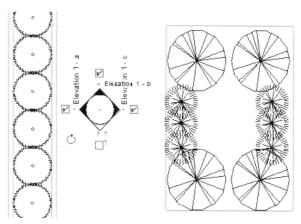

Figure 6–54

- Use the ↻ (Rotate) control to angle the marker (i.e., for a room with angled walls).

Modifying Section Markers

When you modify section markers, various shape handles and controls enable you to modify a section, as shown in Figure 6–55.

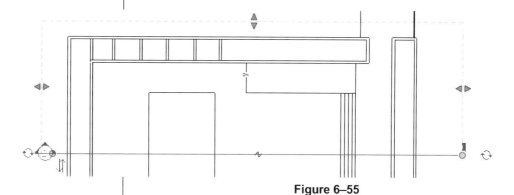

Figure 6–55

- Drag the ⬍ (Arrow) controls to change the length and depth of the cut plane.

- Drag the circular controls at either end of the section line to change the location of the arrow or flag without changing the cut boundary.

- Click ↔ (Flip) to change the direction of the arrowhead, which also flips the entire section.

- Click ↻ (Cycle Section Head/Tail) to switch between an arrowhead, flag, or nothing on each end of the section.

- Click ✂ (Gaps in Segments) to create an opening in section lines, as shown in Figure 6–56. Select it again to restore the full section cut.

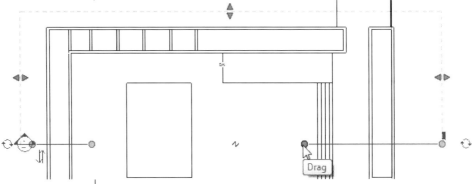

Figure 6–56

How To: Add a Jog to a Section Line

1. Select the section line that you want to modify.

2. In the *Modify | Views* tab>Section panel, click ⊟ (Split Segment).
3. Select the point along the line where you want to create the split, as shown in Figure 6–57.
4. Specify the location of the split line, as shown in Figure 6–58.

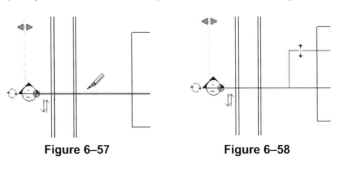

Figure 6–57   Figure 6–58

- If you need to adjust the location of any segment on the section line, modify it and drag the shape handles along each segment of the line, as shown in Figure 6–59.

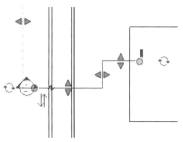

Figure 6–59

- To bring a split section line back into place, use a shape handle to drag the jogged line until it is at the same level with the rest of the line.

Hint: Using Thin Lines

The software automatically applies line weights to views, as shown for a section on the left in Figure 6–60. If a line weight seems heavy or obscures your work on the elements, toggle off the line weights. In the Quick Access Toolbar or in the *View* tab>Graphics panel, click ▦ (Thin Lines) or type **TL**. The lines display with the same weight, as shown on the right in Figure 6–60.

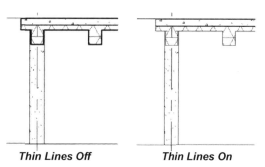

Thin Lines Off   *Thin Lines On*

Figure 6–60

- The **Thin Line** setting is remembered until you manually change it, even if you shut down and restart the software.

Practice 6b | Create Callouts, Elevations, and Sections

Practice Objectives

- Add callout views.
- Add building sections and wall sections.

Estimated time for completion: 15 minutes

In this practice, you will add callout views around typical planting areas, a detail section at a floor type change and two building sections, as shown in Figure 6–61.

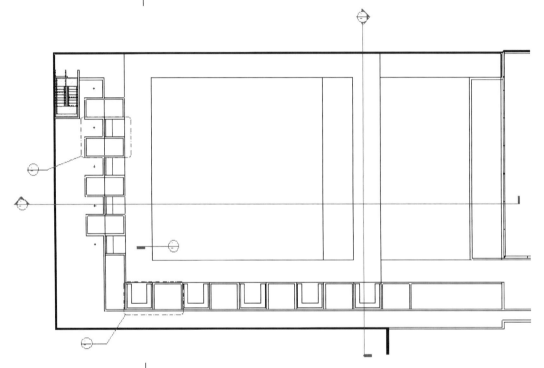

Figure 6–61

Task 1 - Add Callout Views.

1. Open the project **Urban-Garden-Sections.rvt** from the practice files folder.

2. Open the **Floor Plans: 02 Roof Garden-Materials and Layout Plan** view.

3. In the *View* tab>Create panel, click (Callout).

4. In the Type Selector, select **Detail View: Detail**.

5. Add a callout box around the planting beds shown in Figure 6–62. Click on the edge of the box and move the marker outside the building.

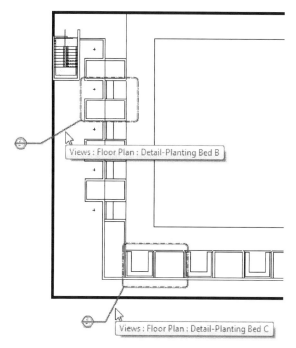

Figure 6–62

6. Create a second callout view around the other style of planting bed, as shown in Figure 6–62.

7. In the Project Browser, in the *Detail Views (Detail)* section, rename the new views to **Detail-Planting Bed B** and **Detail-Planting Bed C**.

8. Select both of the new detail views in the Project Browser.

9. In Properties, note that the *View Scale* of these views is automatically set to **1/4"=1'-0"**, double the scale of the view in which the callout is created. Set the *Detail Level* to **Fine**.

10. Open the views and note that these changes display in the View Control Bar of the view as shown in Figure 6–63.

Figure 6–63

11. If required, modify the size of the crop window so that only the selected part of the planting bed displays as shown in Figure 6–64

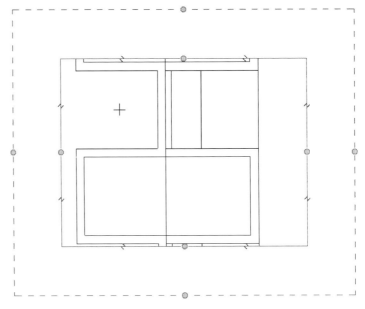

Figure 6–64

12. Save the project.

Task 2 - Add Detail and Building Sections.

1. Return to the **02 Roof Garden-Materials and Layout Plan** view.

2. In the Quick Access Toolbar or *View* tab>Create panel, click ◇ (Section).

3. In the Type Selector, select **Detail View: Detail**.

4. Draw a section across the edge of the floor, as shown in Figure 6–65.

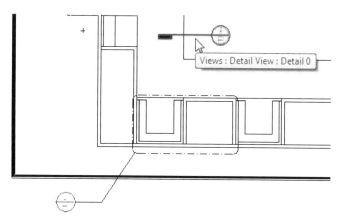

Figure 6–65

5. Click **Modify**.

6. Double-click on the section head to open the new view.

7. In the View Control Bar, change the *Detail Level* to **Fine**. The floors in the current project and the roof in the linked project both display as shown in Figure 6–66.

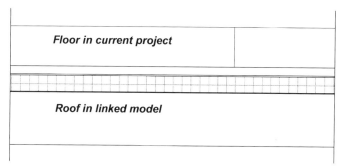

Floor in current project

Roof in linked model

Figure 6–66

8. Return to the **02 Roof Garden-Materials and Layout Plan** view.

9. Start the **Section** command again.

10. In the Type Selector, select **Section: Building Section**.

11. Draw a section horizontally across the entire area and then draw another one vertically across the building, as shown in Figure 6–67.

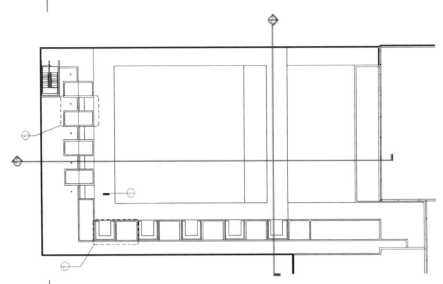

Figure 6–67

12. Open the section views and review the information, as shown in Figure 6–68.

Figure 6–68

13. Save the project.

Chapter Review Questions

1. Which of the following commands shown in Figure 6–69, creates a view that results in an independent view displaying the same model geometry and containing a copy of the annotation?

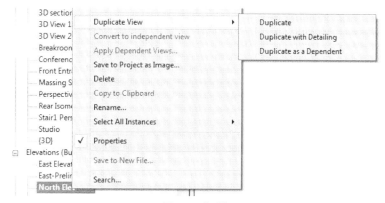

Figure 6–69

   a. Duplicate

   b. Duplicate with Detailing

   c. Duplicate as a Dependent

2. Which of the following is true about the Visibility Graphic Overrides dialog box?

   a. Changes made in the dialog box only affect the current view.

   b. It can only be used to toggle categories on and off.

   c. It can be used to toggle individual elements on and off.

   d. It can be used to change the color of individual elements.

3. The purpose of callouts is to create a...

   a. Boundary around part of the model that needs revising, similar to a revision cloud.

   b. View of part of the model for export to the AutoCAD® software for further detailing.

   c. View of part of the model that is linked to the main view from which it is taken.

   d. 2D view of part of the model.

4. You placed dimensions in a view and some of them display and others do not (as shown on the top in Figure 6–70) but you were expecting the view to display as shown on the bottom in Figure 6–70. To display the missing dimensions you need to modify the...

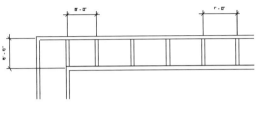

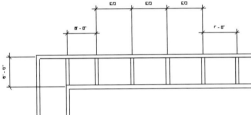

Figure 6–70

   a. Dimension Settings

   b. Dimension Type

   c. Visibility Graphic Overrides

   d. Annotation Crop Region

5. How do you create multiple interior elevations in one room?

   a. Using the **Interior Elevation** command, place the elevation marker.

   b. Using the **Elevation** command, place the first marker, select it and select the appropriate Show Arrow boxes.

   c. Using the **Interior Elevation** command, place an elevation marker for each wall of the room you want to display.

   d. Using the **Elevation** command, select a Multiple Elevation marker type, and place the elevation marker.

6. How do you create a jog in a building section, such as that shown in Figure 6–71?

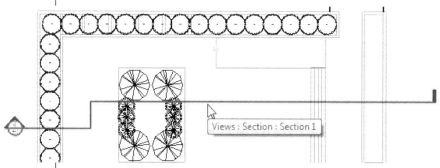

Figure 6–71

a. Use the **Split Element** tool in the *Modify* tab>Modify panel.

b. Select the building section and then click **Split Segment** in the contextual tab.

c. Select the building section and click the blue control in the middle of the section line.

d. Draw two separate sections, and use the **Section Jog** tool to combine them into a jogged section.

Command Summary

Button	Command	Location
Views		
	Elevation	• **Ribbon:** *View* tab>Create panel> expand Elevation
	Callout: Rectangle	• **Ribbon:** *View* tab>Create panel> expand Callout
	Callout: Sketch	• **Ribbon:** *View* tab>Create panel> expand Callout
	Duplicate	• **Ribbon:** *View* tab>Create panel> expand Duplicate View • **Right-click:** (*on a view in the Project Browser*) expand Duplicate View
	Duplicate as Dependent	• **Ribbon:** *View* tab>Create panel> expand Duplicate View • **Right-click:** (*on a view in the Project Browser*) expand Duplicate View
	Duplicate with Detailing	• **Ribbon:** *View* tab>Create panel> expand Duplicate View • **Right-click:** (*on a view in the Project Browser*) Duplicate View
	Section	• **Ribbon:** *View* tab>Create panel • **Quick Access Toolbar**
	Split Segment	• **Ribbon:** (*when the elevation or section marker is selected*) Modify | Views tab> Section panel
Crop Views		
	Crop View	• **View Control Bar** • **View Properties:** Crop View (*checkmark*)
	Do Not Crop View	• **View Control Bar** • **View Properties:** Crop View (*clear*)
	Edit Crop	• **Ribbon:** (*when the crop region of a callout, elevation, or section view is selected*) Modify | Views tab>Mode panel
	Hide Crop Region	• **View Control Bar** • **View Properties:** Crop Region Visible (*clear*)
	Reset Crop	• **Ribbon:** (*when the crop region of a callout, elevation or section view is selected*) Modify | Views tab>Mode panel

	Show Crop Region	• **View Control Bar** • **View Properties:** Crop Region Visible (*checkmark*)
	Size Crop	• **Ribbon:** (*when the crop region of a callout, elevation or section view is selected*) *Modify	Views* tab>Mode panel

View Display

	Hide in View	• **Ribbon:** *Modify* tab>View Graphics panel>Hide>Elements *or* By Category • **Right-click:** (*when an element is selected*) Hide in View>Elements *or* Category
	Override Graphics in View	• **Ribbon:** *Modify* tab>View Graphics panel>Hide>Elements *or* By Category • **Right-click:** (*when an element is selected*) Override Graphics in View> By Element *or* By Category • **Shortcut:** (*category only*) VV or VG
	Reveal Hidden Elements	• **View Control Bar**
	Temporary Hide/Isolate	• **View Control Bar**
	Temporary View Properties	• **View Control Bar**

Chapter 7

Modeling Hardscapes

Creating hardscapes in the Autodesk® Revit® software is primarily done by modeling walls and floors. Walls can be used for retaining walls, planters, and even curbs. You can modify the profile of a wall to change its shape above or below ground. Floors are used for most paving and some grassy areas. Floors can be sloped in one direction or in multiple directions to mimic topography or show drainage patterns. Other important parts of the hardscape that will also be discussed are stairs and ramps between level changes and railings.

Learning Objectives in this Chapter

- Model walls using specific wall types.
- Modify wall profiles.
- Sketch and modify floor boundaries.
- Modify floor faces to apply materials and align patterns.
- Slope a floor in one or more directions for drainage or topography.
- Add stairs and ramps.
- Add railings.

7.1 Modeling Hardscapes Using Walls

In the Autodesk Revit software, walls are more than just two lines on a plan. They are full 3D elements that store detailed information, including height, thickness, and materials. This means that walls are useful in both 2D and 3D views, When creating hardscapes in Autodesk Revit, you can add retaining walls, cast-in place planters, and square-cut curbs using the **Wall** command, as shown in Figure 7–1. You can also edit walls using common tools and modify the profile of a wall to change the shape of the wall.

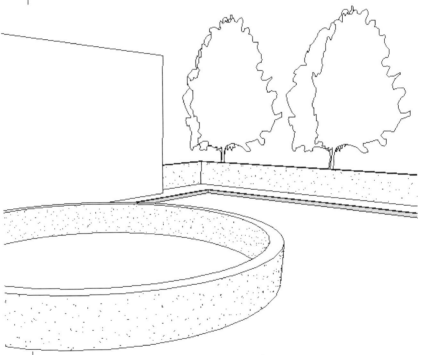

Figure 7–1

- Drawing aids such as reference planes, alignment lines, and temporary dimensions can help you sketch out and place the walls in the model.

How To: Model a Wall

1. In the *Architecture* tab>Build panel, click 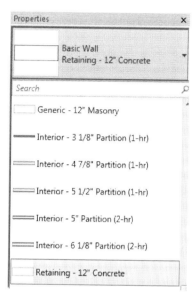 (Wall) or type the shortcut **WA**.
2. In the Type Selector, select a wall type, as shown in Figure 7–2.

You can use the Search box to quickly find specific types of walls.

Figure 7–2

3. In the Options Bar (shown in Figure 7–3), specify the following information about the wall before you start modeling:

Figure 7–3

- *Height:* Set the height of a wall to either **Unconnected** (with a specified height) or to a level.
- *Location Line:* Set the justification of the wall using the options shown in Figure 7–3.
- *Chain:* Enables you to model multiple connected walls.
- *Offset:* Enables you to enter the distance at which a new wall is created from an existing element.
- *Radius:* Adds a curve of a specified radius to connected walls as you model.
- *Join Status:* Allow or Disallow automatic wall joins.

4. In the *Modify | Place Wall* tab>Draw panel (shown in Figure 7–4), select one of the options to create the wall.

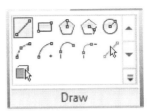

Figure 7–4

- Use alignment lines, temporary dimensions, and snaps to place the walls.
- As you are sketching you can press <Spacebar> to flip the orientation of compound walls.
- When using the *Chain* option, press <Esc> to finish the string of walls and remain in the Wall command.

Compound walls are a wall type that contain multiple layers (e.g., blocks, air space, bricks, etc.).

Hint: Creating Tree Lines

Tree lines are easily created using an open revision cloud as shown in Figure 7–5. In the *Annotate* tab> Detail panel, click

(Revision Cloud)). Use any of the Draw tools to sketch the

lines, then, in the Mode panel, click (Finish Edit Mode). The Spline tool makes the smoothest curves.

Figure 7–5

- Revision clouds are annotation tools and only display in the view in which they are created.

Modifying Walls

There are several methods of modifying walls. You can change the type of wall using the Type Selector, use controls and shape handles to modify the length and wall orientation, and use temporary and permanent dimensions to change the location or length of a wall in 2D and 3D, as shown in Figure 7–6. You can also modify the profile of a wall.

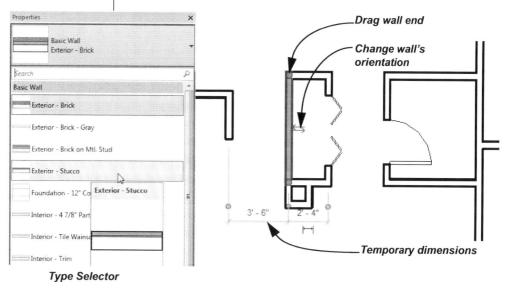

Type Selector

Figure 7–6

How To: Edit the Profile of a Wall

1. Open an elevation or section view in which you can see the face of the wall that you want to edit.
2. Select the wall (by highlighting the wall boundary).

You can also double-click on a wall to edit the profile.

3. In the *Modify | Walls* tab>Mode panel, click 🖊 (Edit Profile). The wall is outlined in magenta indicating the profile of the wall.
4. In the *Modify | Walls>Edit Profile* tab>Draw panel, use the tools to modify the profile sketch of the wall, as shown on the top in Figure 7–7.

5. Once the profile is complete, click ✓ (Finish Edit Mode). The wall now follows the new profile, as shown on the bottom in Figure 7–7.

The sketch must form a continuous loop. Verify that the lines are clean without any gaps or overlaps. Use any of the tools in the Modify panel to clean up the sketch.

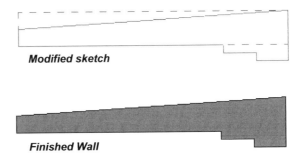

Modified sketch

Finished Wall

Figure 7–7

Hint: Using Dimensions to Model

When modeling, adding permanent dimensions to elements as you are working help to provide you with additional temporary dimensions. The most basic dimension method is ✕ (Aligned Dimension), which is found on the Quick Access Toolbar.

To add the dimensions, select the elements in order and then pick a final point not on an element at the location where you want to place dimension string, as shown in Figure 7–8.

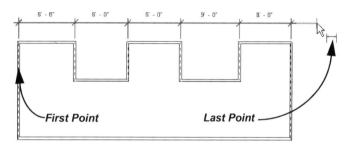

Figure 7–8

- In the Options Bar, specify set the preference for where the dimensions attach, as shown in Figure 7–9.

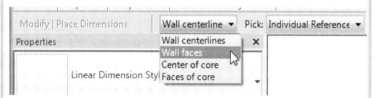

Figure 7–9

- To make dimensions equal, click the **EQ** control after placing the dimension string.

- For more information on dimensioning, see the chapter on annotating construction documents.

Practice 7a

Model Hardscapes Using Walls

Practice Objectives

- Add Reference Planes.
- Model walls.
- Use temporary dimensions and alignments to place the walls.
- Modify the profile of a wall.

Estimated time for completion: 15 minutes

In this practice, you will create walls that are used as curbs to outline the motor court drive and a planting bed. You will then use walls to create planters of different heights and modify the profile of one of the planter walls, as shown in Figure 7–10.

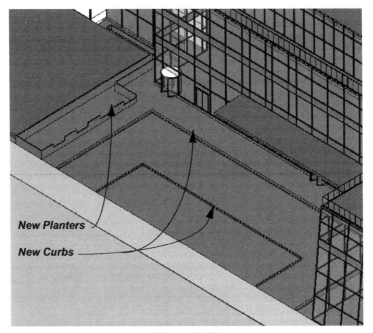

New Planters

New Curbs

Figure 7–10

Task 1 - Add curbs to the motor court area.

1. Open the project **Urban-Garden-Curbs.rvt** from the practice files folder.

2. Open the **Floor Plans:-01 Motor Court** view (the model view).

3. In the *Architecture* tab>Work Plane panel, click 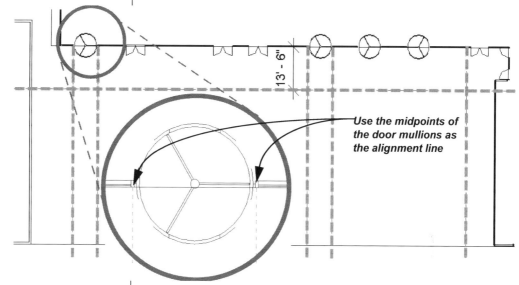 (Ref Plane).

4. Sketch the reference planes shown in Figure 7–11 to help you place the locations of the curbs. These are the main entrances.

13' - 6"

Use the midpoints of the door mullions as the alignment line

Figure 7–11

• To snap to the midpoints of the mullions, zoom in and if required, type **SM** to snap to the midpoint.

• Add a dimension from the outside face to the building to the horizontal reference plane. Then, you can select the reference plane and modify the temporary dimension to place the reference plane exactly. Delete the dimension.

5. In the *Architecture* tab>Build panel, click (Wall).

6. In the Type Selector, select **Basic Wall: Curb - Granite - 12"**.

7. In the Options Bar, set the *Height* to **Unconnected 0'-6"** and the *Location Line* to **Wall Centerline**. Verify that the **Chain** option is selected.

8. Sketch the walls shown in Figure 7–12.

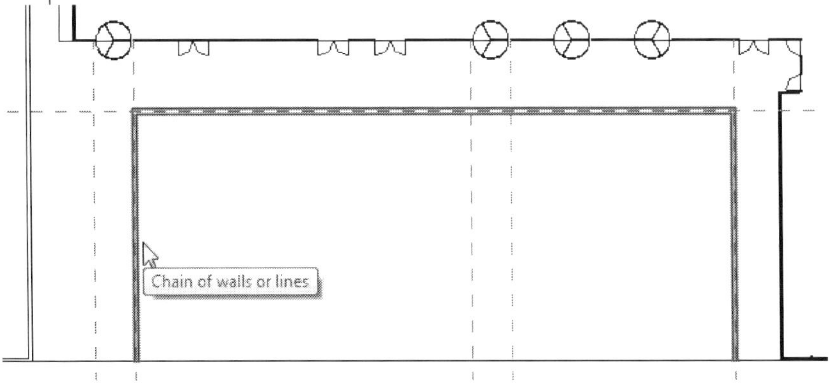

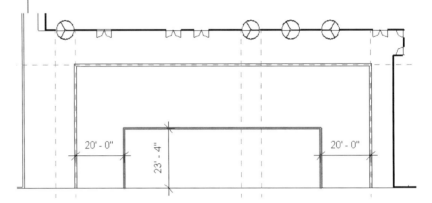

Figure 7–12

Dimensions are for information only.

9. In the Type Selector, change the type to **Basic Wall: Curb - Granite - 6"** and sketch walls as shown in Figure 7–13.

Figure 7–13

- When you first sketch them, do not worry about the right location. Once they are in, you can select them and use temporary dimensions to specify the exact location.

10. Save the project.

Task 2 - Add Planters.

1. Zoom in on the left side of the motor court, as shown in Figure 7–14.

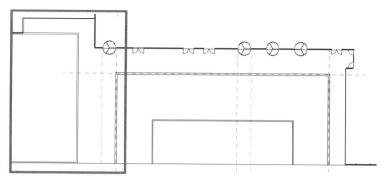

Figure 7–14

2. Start the **Wall** command and set the following properties:

   - *Type*: **Basic Wall: Curb - Granite - 4"**
   - *Height*: **Unconnected: 3'-0"**
   - *Location Line*: **Finish Face: Exterior**
   - Select **Chain**.

3. In the upper left corner, away from the main motor court, sketch the wall shown in Figure 7–15. Then, use the **Align** command and dimensions to get them in the correct place.

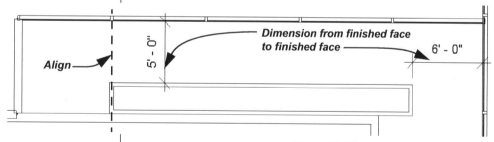

Figure 7–15

   - Press <Tab> to cycle through the wall alignment lines, as required.
   - After placing the dimensions, select the wall and modify the dimension to the correct distance. The wall moves with the change. Delete the dimensions.

4. Start the **Wall** command again and set the *Height* to **Unconnected: 3'-6"**. Draw the walls shown in Figure 7–16 using the reference planes to align the locations.

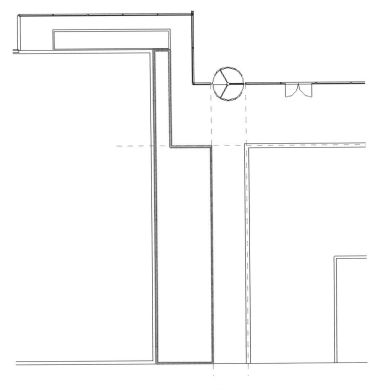

Figure 7–16

5. Save the project.

Task 3 - Modify the profile of a wall.

1. Continue working in the **-01 Motor Court** view.

2. In the Quick Access Toolbar or *View* tab>Create panel, click ⌖ (Section).

3. Add a section marker, as shown in Figure 7–17. (Sketch from bottom to top so that it faces in the right direction.)

4. In the *Modify | Views* tab>Section panel, click 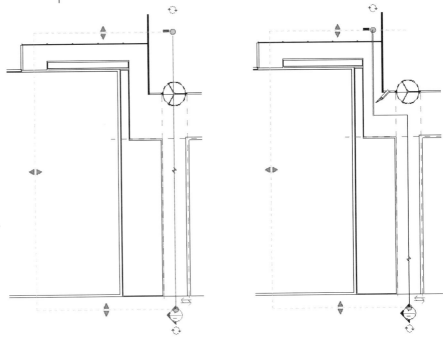 (Split Segment).

5. Click on the section line just below the revolving door and move part of the section line outside the building, as shown in Figure 7–18.

Figure 7–17   **Figure 7–18**

6. Click **Modify**.

7. Double-click on the section arrow head to open the new section view.

8. Select the wall shown in Figure 7–19 and in the *Modify |*

   Walls tab>Mode panel, click (Edit Profile). You can also double-click on the wall to edit the profile.

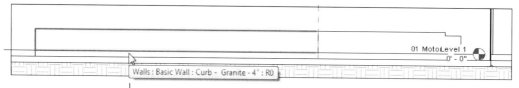

Figure 7–19

9. Delete the top sketch line and replace it with one that is similar to Figure 7–20.

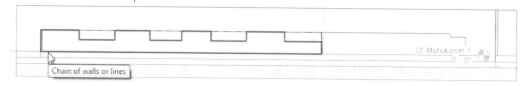

Figure 7–20

10. In the Quick Access Toolbar, click (Aligned Dimension) or type **DI**.

11. Select each vertical line and then pick a point away from any lines to place the dimension string.

12. Click the **EQ** control to make all of the distances the same as shown in Figure 7–21. Delete the dimension string.

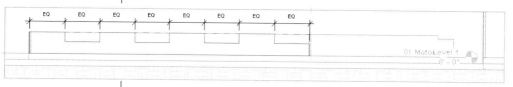

Figure 7–21

13. In the *Modify | Edit Profile* tab>Mode panel, click (Finish Edit Mode).

14. View the project in 3D and zoom in on the motor court area to see the new walls.

15. Save the project.

7.2 Modeling Hardscapes Using Floors

The **Floor** command can generate any flat or sloped surface, such as floors, balconies, sidewalks, decks, and patios, as shown in Figure 7–22. Typically created in a plan view, the floor can be based either on bounding walls or on a sketched outline. Floors can also be used for planting areas.

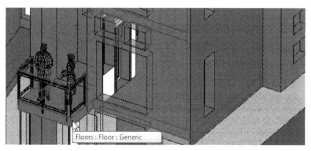

Floors : Floor : Generic

Figure 7–22

- The floor type controls the thickness and material of a floor.

How To: Add a Floor

1. In the *Architecture* tab>Build panel, expand ⬛ (Floor) and click ⬛ (Floor: Architectural). You are placed in sketch mode where other elements in the model are grayed out.
2. In the Type Selector, set the type of floor that you want to use. In Properties, set any other options you might require.
3. In the *Modify | Create Floor Boundary* tab>Draw panel, click ⌐ (Boundary Line).

   - Click ⬛ (Pick Walls) and select the walls, setting either the inside or outside edge. If you have selected a wall, you can click ↪ (Flip) to switch the inside/outside status of the boundary location, as shown in Figure 7–23.

   - Click ⟋ (Line) or one of the other Draw tools and sketch the boundary edges.

4. Click ⬛ (Slope Arrow) to define a slope for the entire floor.

The lines in the sketch must form a closed loop. Use tools in the Modify panel to adjust intersections.

The span direction is automatically placed on the first sketch line.

5. Click 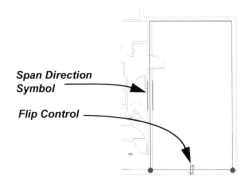 (Span Direction), as shown in Figure 7–23, to modify the direction of the structural elements in the floor.

Span Direction Symbol

Flip Control

Figure 7–23

6. Click (Finish Edit Mode) to create the floor.

- When using (Pick Walls), select **Extend into wall (to core)** in the Options Bar if you want the floor to cut into the wall. For example, the floor would cut through the gypsum wall board and the air space but stop at a core layer such as CMU.

This option is used primarily in architectural floors.

- If you select one or more of the boundary sketch lines, you can also set *Cantilevers* for *Concrete* or *Steel*, as shown in Figure 7–24.

Figure 7–24

- To create an opening inside the floor, create a separate closed loop inside the first one, as shown in Figure 7–25.

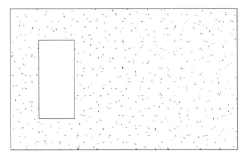

Figure 7–25

Hint: Sketched Arcs and Tangent Lock.

If you are adding arcs or ellipses to a sketch that are tangent to other lines, you can lock the geometry in place by clicking **Toggle Join Tangency**, as shown in Figure 7–26.

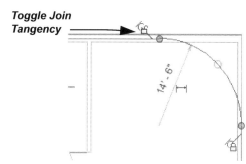

Figure 7–26

- This lock is available whenever you are in sketch mode.

- If you create a floor on an upper level, an alert box displays prompting if you want the walls below to be attached to the underside of the floor and its level. If you have a variety of wall heights, it is recommended to click **No** and attach the walls separately.

- Another alert box might open, as shown in Figure 7–27. You can automatically join the geometry or can do so at a later time.

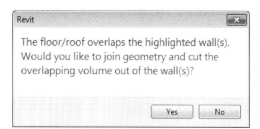

Figure 7–27

- Floors can be placed above other floors or roofs. For example, a floor or roof can have a finish floor of tile or brick placed on top of it, as shown in Figure 7–28. These floors can then be scheduled separately.

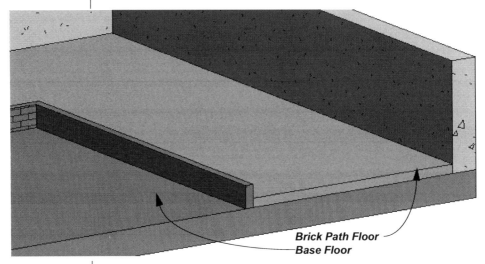

Brick Path Floor
Base Floor

Figure 7–28

Modifying Floors

You can change a floor to a different type using the Type Selector. In Properties, you can modify parameters including the *Height Offset From Level*, as shown in Figure 7–29. When you have a floor selected, you can also edit the boundaries.

Many of the parameters in Properties are used in schedules, including Elevation at Top (Bottom) and Elevation at Top (Bottom) Core for multi-layered floors.

Figure 7–29

How To: Modify the Floor Sketch

1. Select a floor. You might need to highlight an element near the floor and press <Tab> until the floor type displays in the Status Bar or in a tooltip, as shown in Figure 7–30.

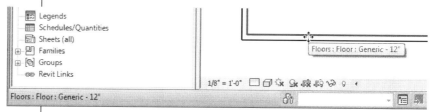

Figure 7–30

2. In the *Modify | Floors* tab>Mode panel, click (Edit Boundary). You are placed in sketch mode.
3. Modify the sketch lines using the draw tools, controls, and the various modify tools.

4. Click (Finish Edit Mode).

- Double-click on a floor to move directly to editing the boundary.

- Floor sketches can be edited in plan and 3D views, but not in elevations. If you try to edit in an elevation view, you are prompted to select another view in which to edit.

Hint: Selecting Floor Faces

If it is difficult to select the floor edges, toggle on the Selection

Option (Select Elements by Face). This enables you to select the floor face, not only the edges.

Hint: Matching Properties

You can select an existing element and use it to assign the type and instance properties to other elements of the same category by using the **Match Type** command.

1. In the *Modify* tab>Clipboard panel, click 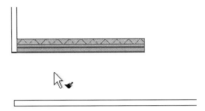 (Match Type) or type **MA**. The cursor changes to an arrow with a clean paintbrush.
2. Select the source element that you want all of the others to match. The paintbrush changes to look as if it has been dipped in black paint, as shown in Figure 7–31.

Figure 7–31

3. To select more than one element, in the *Modify | Match Type* tab>Multiple panel, click (Select Multiple). You can then use windows, crossings, <Ctrl>, and <Shift> to create a selection set of elements to change.
4. Select the elements that you want to change. For multiple selections, click (Finish) to apply the type to the selection.

- Click in an empty space in the project to empty the brush so that you can repeat the command with a different element.

- Elements to be matched must be of the same type (e.g., all walls, all floors, etc.).

Practice 7b

Model Hardscapes Using Floors

Practice Objectives

- Add floors.
- Change floor types.
- Modify floor boundaries.

Estimated time for completion: 10 minutes

In this practice, you will add two floors. You will then assign different floor types to the floor and change the boundary of one of the floors to match a new design, as shown in Figure 7–32.

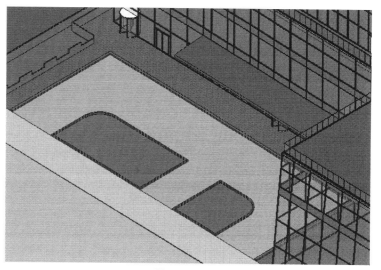

Figure 7–32

Task 1 - Sketch floor boundaries.

1. Open the project **Urban-Garden-Hardscape.rvt** from the practice files folder.

2. Open the **Floor Plans: -01 Motor Court** view.

3. In the *Architecture* tab>Build panel, click (Floor).

4. In the Type Selector, select **Floor: Generic - 12"**.

5. In the Draw panel, click ✎ (Line) and sketch the lines shown in Figure 7–33.

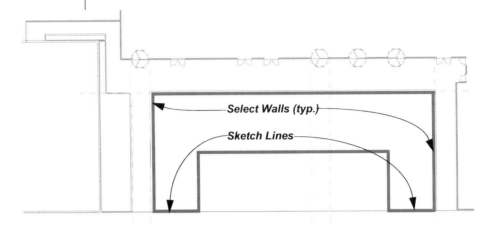

Figure 7–33

6. Click ✔ (Finish Edit Mode).

7. Create another floor following the footprint shown in Figure 7–34. Use any of the draw and modify tools to help you create a closed boundary.

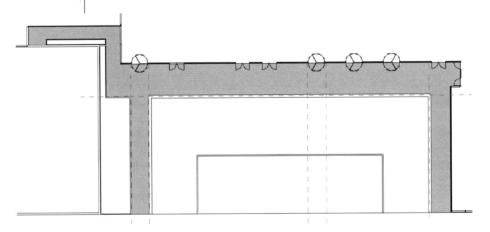

Figure 7–34

8. Save the project.

Task 2 - Modify the floor types and boundaries.

1. Select the floor that you just created.

2. In the Type Selector, change the type to **Floor: Pavers - 12"
   x 48"**. The floor type now displays a pattern, as shown in
   Figure 7–35.

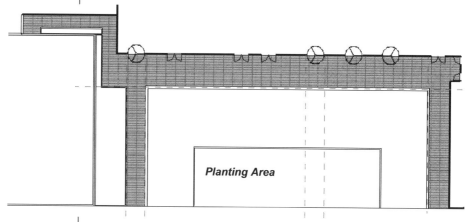

Planting Area

Figure 7–35

- The floor pattern is faint when the floor is not selected.
  Zoom in if required to see it. This material shows the
  actual size of the pavers.

3. Zoom in on the planting area in the center of the motor court
   shown in Figure 7–35.

4. Select one of the 6" Granite Curb walls. Right-click and select
   Create Similar.The **Wall** command starts with the type and
   other properties that match the selected wall.

5. In the *Modify | Place Wall* tab>Draw panel, click (Fillet
   Arc).

6. In the Options Bar, select **Radius** and set it to **7'-6"**.(**Hint:**
   You can type **7 6**. It automatically interprets this as **7'-6"**.)

7. Select the two edges of each corner to place the arc. Then, add the other walls shown in Figure 7–36.

8. In the *Modify* tab>Modify panel, click ⊲⊳ (Split Element) (or type **SL**) and split the top wall so there are two separate planting beds and then add walls, as shown in Figure 7–36.

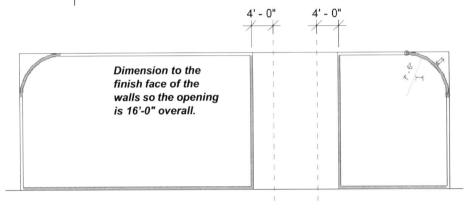

Dimension to the finish face of the walls so the opening is 16'-0" overall.

Figure 7–36

9. Double-click on the related floor and edit the boundary to fit the new outline.

10. Change the type to **Floor: Cobblestone**.

11. View the floors in 3D.

12. Save the project.

7.3 Creating Sloped Floors

Floors can have slopes applied to them. To make a floor slope in one direction, as shown in Figure 7–37, you can place a *slope arrow* in the sketch of the floor. Once the floor is created, you can add multiple drainage points and cause the floor to warp toward them.

Floors : Floor : Brick Path : R1

Figure 7–37

• These tools also work with roofs and structural slabs.

How To: Slope a Floor in One Direction

1. Select the floor that you want to slope. In the *Modify | Floors* tab>Mode panel, click (Edit Boundary).
2. In the *Modify | Floors>Edit Boundary* tab>Draw panel, click (Slope Arrow).

3. Select two points to define the arrow. The first point is the tail and the second is the head. The tail and head locations are points at which you can specify heights. The direction of the arrow determines the orientation of the slope, as shown in Figure 7–38.

The slope arrow only displays while Sketch mode is active.

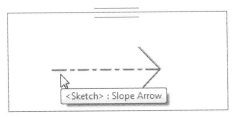

Figure 7–38

4. In Properties, specify the *Level* and *Offset* at the *Tail* and *Head*, as shown in Figure 7–39.

Constraints	⌃
Specify	Height at Tail
Level at Tail	Default
Height Offset at Tail	1' 0"
Level at Head	Default
Height Offset at Head	0' 0"

Figure 7–39

Creating Multiple Slopes for Drainage

When you need to have multiple slopes to show drainage patterns for hardscapes, you can warp a floor, as shown in Figure 7–40. Several tools provide ways of creating points for the drain locations, as well as creating lines to define how the slope is going to drain. You can also use these tools to create sloped floors that take the place of topography in more urban projects.

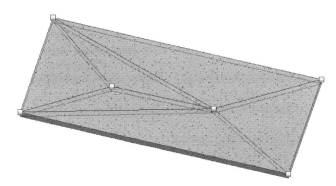

Figure 7–40

• These tools work with floors, roofs, and structural floors.

- Warping a floor also warps a floor pattern. Depending on the level of detail that you want to show, you might not want to actually model the points as outlined here but rather to annotate the plan view to show the location for drains.

How To: Create Multiple Slopes in a Floor

1. Select the required flat floor, roof, or slab.
2. In the *Modify | Floors* tab>Shape Editing panel (shown in Figure 7–41), select the tools to define the slopes.

Figure 7–41

	Add Point: Specify the location of the low or high points on the surface. In the Options Bar, set the *Elevation*. By default, the elevation is relative to the top of the surface. Clear the **Relative** option if you want to use the project elevation.  • displays when you place the point. Slope lines are automatically added from the corners of the surface to the point.
	Add Split Line: Define smaller areas on the surface when you place more than one drain. Depending on the size of the area you are working with, you might want to create these before adding drains. Select **Chain** if you want to add more than one connected segment.
	Pick Supports: Select structural beams that define the split lines.
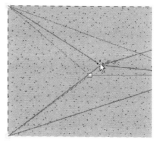	**Modify Sub-Elements:** Change the elevation of edges and points and change the location of points. You can also move points using shape handles without clicking (Modify Sub-Elements), as shown below. Press <Tab> to cycle through the options to reach the element that you want to modify.

- If you want to remove the slopes from a surface, click (Reset Shape).

- Floors, roofs, and slabs use styles set to a constant thickness (where the entire element slopes) or to a variable thickness (where only the top layer slopes), as shown in Figure 7–42.

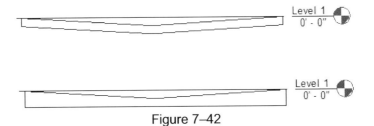

Figure 7–42

Practice 7c

Create Sloped Floors

Estimated time for completion: 10 minutes

Practice Objective

- Slope floors using shape editing tools.

In this practice, you will modify a floor, change it base height, and then add split lines and modify the points to create a "hill", as shown in Figure 7–43

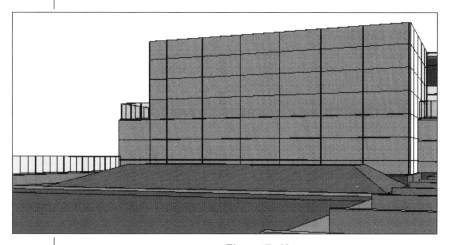

Figure 7–43

Task 1 - Create a sloped floor.

1. Open the project **Urban-Garden-Slope.rvt** from the practice files folder.

2. Open the **Floor Plans: 02 Roof Garden Materials and Layout Plan** view. (This view does not show the floor patterns, which could get in the way as you modify the slope of a floor.)

3. Type **ZF** to fit the view in the window.

4. Zoom in on the right side of the garden. This area will become a "hill".

5. Select the existing floor, as shown in Figure 7–44.

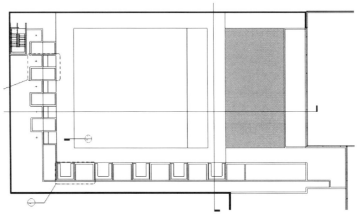

Figure 7–44

6. In Properties, set the *Height Offset from Level* to **4'-2"**.

7. In the *Architecture* tab>Work Plane panel, click

   (Reference Plane).

8. Add three reference planes, as shown in Figure 7–45.

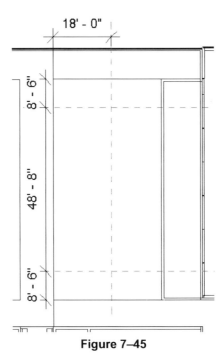

Figure 7–45

9. Select the floor again.

10. In the *Modify | Floors* tab>Shape Editing panel, click

    (Add Split Line) and use the reference planes to help you place the split lines, as shown in Figure 7–46.

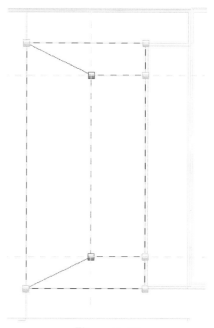

Figure 7–46

11. In the *Modify | Floors* tab>Shape Editing panel, click

    (Modify Sub Elements).

12. Select the four outer points. (Hold <Ctrl> to select more than one.)

13. In the Options Bar, set the *Elevation* to (negative) **-4'-2"**.

14. A Warning dialog box displays as shown in Figure 7–47. Read it and close it.

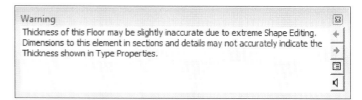

Warning
Thickness of this Floor may be slightly inaccurate due to extreme Shape Editing. Dimensions to this element in sections and details may not accurately indicate the Thickness shown in Type Properties.

Figure 7–47

15. Click **Modify** to finish the shape editing commands.

16. Save the project.

Task 2 - Create a 3D Camera view.

1. Zoom out to see the full roof garden.

2. In the Quick Access Toolbar, expand 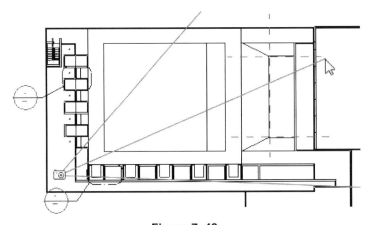 (Default 3D View) and click (Camera).

3. Select a point on the left of the roof and then a second point looking at the modified "hill", as shown in Figure 7–48.

Figure 7–48

4. When the camera view displays, set the *Visual Style* to **Shaded**.

5. In the Project Browser, in the 3D Views area, right-click on the new view and select **Rename**. Rename the view **Roof Garden Hill**.

6. Use the controls to modify the crop region, as required.

7. Save the project.

7.4 Working with Materials and Floor Types

When working with landscape designs, the **Floor** command is the primary way you create hardscapes. You can split a floor into several different areas and apply different materials, as shown in Figure 7–49. You can also create custom floors by duplicating an existing floor and modifying the type.

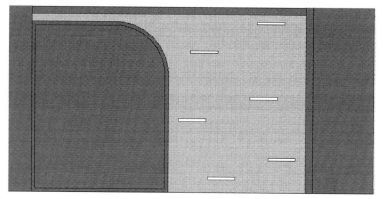

Figure 7–49

Splitting Faces

You can split a face into separate surfaces so you can apply different materials to each part. A sketch defines the split, which must be a closed shape completely inside the face, or an open shape that touches the face edges, as shown in Figure 7–50. Windows are cut out of faces automatically.

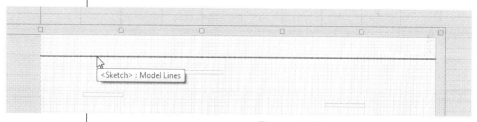

Figure 7–50

How To: Create a Split Face

1. Open a plan or 3D view.

2. In the *Modify* tab>Geometry panel, click (Split Face).

*If you have **Select elements by face** toggled on you can click directly on the face.*

3. Select the edge of the face that you want to modify. Use <Tab> as required, to toggle through the available faces.

4. In the *Modify | Split Face>Create Boundary* tab>Draw panel, use the sketch tools to create a sketch as required, to define the split.

5. Click ✅ (Finish Edit Mode).

• To save time, use a floor type that includes the primary material that you want to use on the split face. For example, if you are working with brick, set the floor to a type that has a brick face. This way, you can work with the brick courses when you are creating the split face.

• When using a material, such as brick, you can snap to the pattern and even lock the split lines to the pattern, as shown in Figure 7–51.

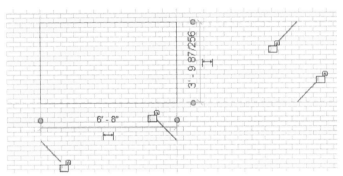

Figure 7–51

• You can double-click on the edge of the split face lines to switch to the Edit Boundary mode. If you double-click on the face (with **Select elements by face** toggled on), it switches to the Edit Profile mode, which impacts the entire wall, not just the split face boundary.

Applying Materials

Once you have a face split into sections, you can apply different materials to each part. For example, you might want to create a pattern of two different colored cobblestones. First, you would create the split face and then apply the new material using **Paint**, as shown in Figure 7–52.

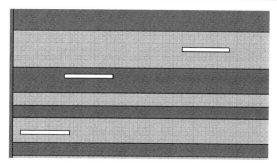

Figure 7–52

How To: Apply Material with Paint

1. In the *Modify* tab>Geometry panel, click 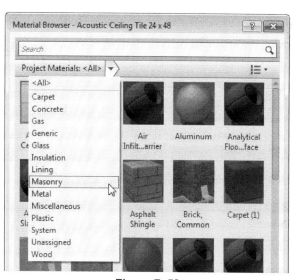 (Paint) or type **PT**.
2. In the Material Browser, select a material. You can run a search or filter the list using specific types of materials, as shown in Figure 7–53.

The browser remains open as you apply the paint.

Figure 7–53

3. Move the cursor over the face that you want to paint. It should highlight. Click on the face to apply the material.
4. Continue selecting materials and painting other faces, as required.
5. In the Material Browser, click **Done** to finish the command.

- Some material patterns display as shaded when you zoom out. Zoom in to display the pattern. Other material patterns only display when you are in the ⬜ (Realistic) Visual Style.

- To change the material applied to a face, in the *Modify* tab> Geometry panel, expand 🗔 (Paint) and click 🗔 (Remove Paint). Select the face(s) from which you want to remove the material.

Move and Rotate Patterns

When using floors with patterns, you can reposition the locations by aligning the pattern to other elements in the project, moving them (as shown in Figure 7–54), or rotating the lines, as shown in Figure 7–55.

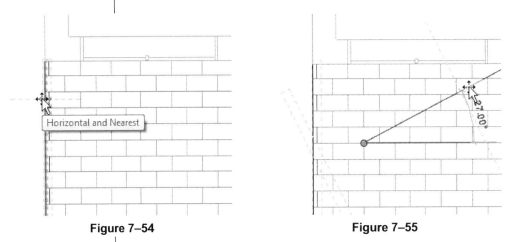

Figure 7–54   Figure 7–55

- To change a rectangular pattern from horizontal to vertical, select a line and rotate it 90 degrees.

How To: Align a Pattern

1. In the *Modify* tab>Modify panel, click 🗔 (Align).
2. Select a line on the building or any other feature to which you want to align the pattern of the floor.
3. Select the line in the floor pattern.

How To: Move a Pattern

1. Select a line in the pattern that you want to modify.

2. In the *Modify | Floors* tab>Modify panel, click ✛ (Move).
3. Move the cursor to one side and type a distance or select another element or alignment line.

How To: Rotate a Pattern

1. Select a line in the pattern that you want to modify.

2. In the *Modify | Floors* tab>Modify panel, click ⟳ (Rotate).

3. In the Options Bar, type an *Angle* value or use ↺ (Rotate) to visually select the angle.

Creating Floor Types

Another way to specify the correct top material for a floor and to assign the layers of materials that make up a floor (as shown in Figure 7–56) is to create floor types.

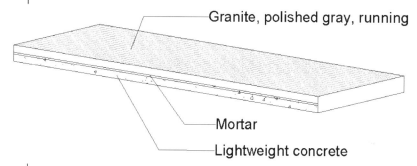

Granite, polished gray, running

Mortar

Lightweight concrete

Figure 7–56

- This method is also used to create and modify wall, ceiling, and roof types.

- You can create as many layers as required to define the structure.

- You can use floor types to create area plantings.

How To: Create a Compound Floor Type

1. Start the **Floor** command.
2. In Properties, select a type similar to the one you want to create and click ⊞ (Edit Type).
3. In the Type Properties dialog box, click **Duplicate....**
4. In the Name dialog box, enter a name for the new type and click **OK**.
5. Next to the **Structure** parameter, click **Edit....**
6. In the Edit Assembly dialog box, modify the layers of the assembly as required, and click **OK**.
7. Modify any Type Parameters in the Type Properties dialog box.
8. Click **OK** to close the dialog box.

Editing Floor Assemblies

In the Edit Assembly dialog box, you can define the layers that make up the compound structure, as shown in Figure 7–57.

*To better visualize the wall, click **<< Preview** to open a view of the layers in the structure. You can preview the structure in a plan or section view, and zoom or pan in the preview screen.*

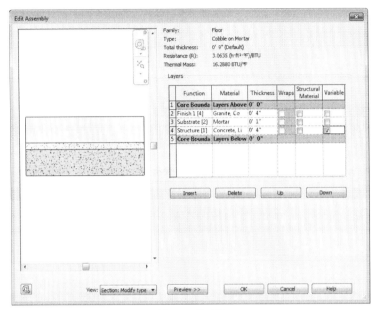

Figure 7–57

Assembly Information

The top of the dialog box lists the *Family* (such as **Basic Wall** or **Floor**), the *Type* that you gave to the new type, and the *Total thickness* (the sum of the layers), as shown in Figure 7–58. It also includes *Resistance (R)* and *Thermal Mass*, which are automatically calculated from the materials assigned to the layers. You can also set a *Sample Height* if you are creating a wall type.

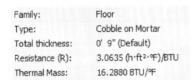

Figure 7–58

Layers

When you specify the layers for the compound element, you assign them a *Function*, *Material*, and *Thickness*, as shown in Figure 7–59.

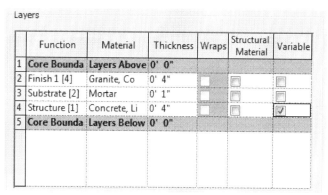

Figure 7–59

- Use the buttons to insert additional layers and to rearrange them in the layer list. You can also delete layers from the list.

- The *Core Boundary* function defines the layers above and below the wrapping; a heavier line is displayed when a plan or section view is cut.

- Editing a wall assembly works from the exterior side at the top of the list to the interior side at the bottom. For floors and roofs, you can work around the layers above and below the wrap of the *Core Boundary*.

Options

Function	Select from a set list of functions in the drop-down list with a priority of highest (1) to lowest (5). High priority layers connect before low priority layers.
Structure [1]	The structural support for the wall, floor, or roof.
Substrate [2]	A material that acts as a foundation for another material, such as plywood or gypsum board.
Thermal/ Air Layer [3]	An open layer for air space.
Finish 1 [4]	The exterior finish layer, such as brick for a wall.
Finish 2 [5]	The interior finish layer, such as drywall for a wall.
Membrane Layer	A vapor barrier. Typically, this is set to a zero thickness. Therefore, it does not have a priority code.

| Structural Deck (1) | (Floors only) A structural support based on a Deck Profile. You can also specify the Deck Usage with a Bound Layer Above or a Standalone Deck.

Structural Deck Properties
Deck Profile
Form Deck_Non-Composite : 2" x 6 ▼
Deck Usage
Bound Layer Above ▼
Bound Layer Above
Standalone Deck |
| --- | --- |
| Material | Select from a list of available materials. Layers clean up if they share the same material. If they do not, a line displays at the join. |
| Thickness | Set the thickness of the particular layer. |

Wall Only Options

Sample Height	Displays the height of a wall in section when you are creating it. It does not impact the height of the wall in the project.
Default Wrapping	Set up how the heavy line style wraps around openings in walls: at Inserts (**Do not wrap**, **Interior**, **Exterior**, or **Both**), and at Ends (**None**, **Exterior**, or **Interior**). Wrapping is only visible in plan view.
Wraps	Set up individual layers to wrap - select the **Wraps** option at the end of each layer.

- Roofs, floors, and structural slabs have an additional parameter that relates to sloping for drains. When *Variable* is not selected, the slab is set to a constant thickness and the entire element slopes, as shown on the top in Figure 7–60. When *Variable* is selected, only the top layer slopes, as shown on the bottom in Figure 7–60.

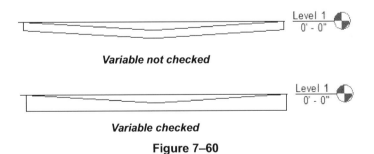

Variable not checked

Variable checked

Figure 7–60

- Retaining walls are a specific wall type whose *Function* is set to **Retaining** in the Type Properties, as shown in Figure 7–61.

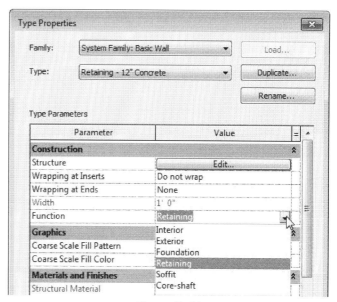

Figure 7–61

Practice 7d

Work with Materials and Floor Types

Practice Objectives

- Create a Floor Type
- Split faces of existing floors and paint the surfaces with materials.
- Modify the patterns of the materials to fit the location.

Estimated time for completion: 10 minutes

In this practice, you will create a new floor type and modify one of the floors to use this type. You will also use **Split Face** to separate parts of floors and then apply a new material to part of the floor. You will then use modify tools to align the patterns, as shown in Figure 7–62.

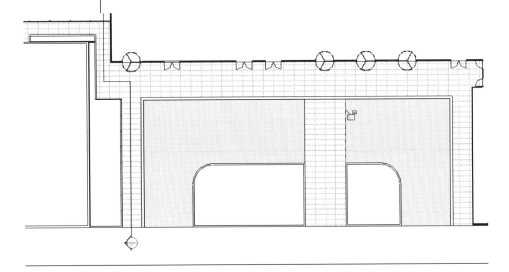

Figure 7–62

Task 1 - Create a Floor Type

1. Open the project **Urban-Garden-Materials.rvt** from the practice files folder.

2. Open the **Floor Plans: -01 Motor Court** view.

3. In the View Control Bar, set the *Visual Style* to **Shaded**.

4. Select the floor shown in Figure 7–63.

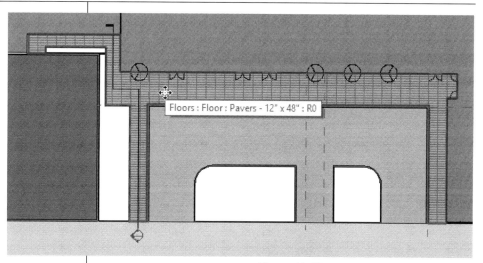

Figure 7–63

5. In Properties, click **Edit Type**.

6. In the Type Properties dialog box, click **Duplicate**.

7. In the Name dialog box, type the name shown in Figure 7–64, and click **OK**.

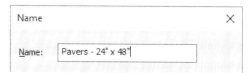

Figure 7–64

8. In the Type Parameters, beside *Structure*, click **Edit...**

9. In the Edit Assembly dialog box, click on the Browse button in the *Material* column, as shown in Figure 7–65.

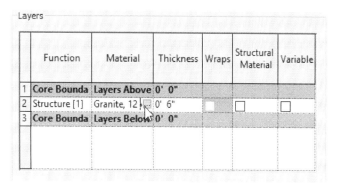

Figure 7–65

10. In the Material Browser, select **Granite, 24" x 48" Pavers** and click **OK**.

11. Click **OK** until the Type Properties dialog box closes. The floor uses the new type pattern, as shown in Figure 7–66.

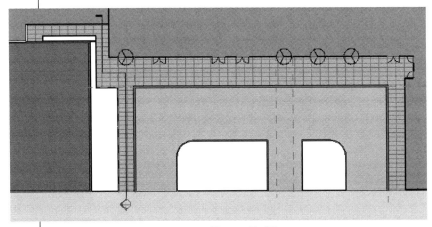

Figure 7–66

12. Save the project.

Task 2 - Split the faces of existing floors and apply new materials to parts of the floors.

---

1. In the *Modify* tab>Geometry panel, click (Split Face).

2. Select the edge of the cobblestone floor.

3. In the Options bar, clear the **Chain** option.

4. Draw lines to split the face into three, as shown in Figure 7–67.

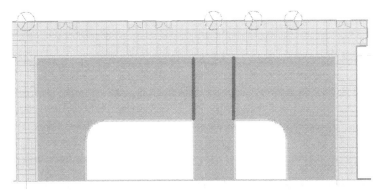

Figure 7–67

5. Click 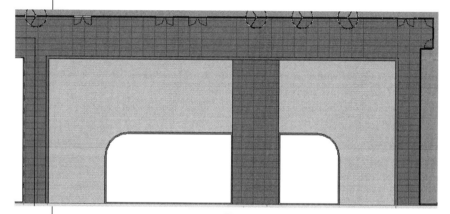 (Finish Edit Mode).

6. In the *Modify* tab>Geometry panel, expand **Paint** and click (Paint).

7. In the Material Browser, expand the *Project Materials* list and select **Stone**. Several different sized and colors pavers are available.

8. Select **Granite, 24" x 48" Pavers**.

9. Select the middle face you just created. The material is applied as shown in Figure 7–68.

Figure 7–68

10. Click **Modify**.

11. Save the project.

Task 3 - Align the material patterns.

1. Change the *Visual Style* to **Hidden Line.**

2. Select one of the reference planes and type **VH**. This hides all reference planes in this view.

3. Zoom in on the floor closest to the main entrance so that you can see the pattern clearly.

4. In the *Modify* tab>Modify panel, click (Align) or type **AL**.

5. Select the vertical edge of the split between the cobblestone and other pavers and then select one of the vertical patterns in the paving, as shown in Figure 7–69. Align the vertical lines of the floor above as well, as shown in Figure 7–70.

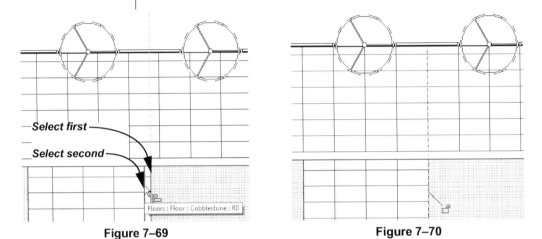

Figure 7–69   Figure 7–70

6. Align any other patterns nearby, as required.

7. Save the project.

8. If time permits, you can also split the face of the cobblestone floors and apply a different color, as shown in the example in Figure 7–71. The default material for the floor is **Granite, Cobblestone, gray** and there is an additional **Granite, Cobblestone, black** material you can use in contrast.

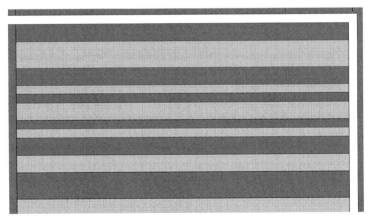

Figure 7–71

7.5 Modeling Stairs, Ramps and Railings

As with other Autodesk Revit elements, stairs are *smart* parametric elements. With just a few clicks, you can create stairs of varying heights and designs, complete with railings. Stairs can be created by assembling stair components (as shown in Figure 7–72), or by sketching a custom layout, as shown in Figure 7–73.

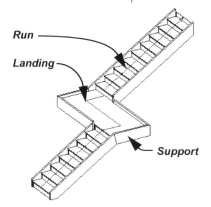

Figure 7–72

Figure 7–73

Creating Stairs

When creating stairs, there are three parts of a stair that can be assembled, as shown in Figure 7–72:

- **Runs:** The actual stair tread and riser elements. These include straight runs which can be combined for multi-landing stairs, spiral stairs and L-shaped and U-shaped Winders.

- **Landings:** The platform between runs. These are typically created automatically and then modified if required.

- **Supports:** The stringer or carriage that structurally holds the stair elements. These can be created automatically or you can pick the edges where you want the different types to go. These can be placed on either side of the stairs or in the center of the stairs.

- Railings are typically added in the **Stair** command. They display after you complete the stair.

- You can select and edit each of the components while you are in edit mode or after the stair has been created.

- Each component of the stair is independent but also has a relationship to the other components. For example, if steps are removed from one run, they are added to connected runs to maintain the overall height, as shown in Figure 7–74.

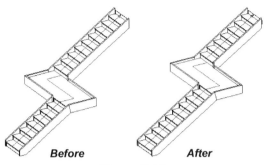

Before   **After**

Figure 7–74

Creating Runs

Stairs can include a mix of the different types of runs.

To create a stair, you must first place the run elements. There are six different options available in the Components panel, as shown in Figure 7–75. They are described as follows:

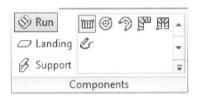

Figure 7–75

▥	**Straight**	Draws a straight run by selecting the start and end points of the run.
◎	**Full-Step Spiral**	Draws a spiral run based on a start point and radius.
◈	**Center-Ends Spiral**	Draws a spiral run based on a center point, start point, and end point.
▱	**L-Shape Winder**	Draws an L-shaped winder based on the lower end.
▦	**U-Shape Winder**	Draws a U-shaped winder based on the lower end.
✎	**Create Sketch**	Opens additional tools where you can sketch stair boundary and risers individually.

Hint: Stairs and Views

When creating stairs, you can work in either plan or 3D views. It can help to have the plan view and a 3D view open and tiled side by side. Only open the views in which you want to work and type **WT** to tile the views.

How To: Create a Component-based Stair with Straight Runs

The stair type can impact all of the other settings. Therefore, it is important to select it first.

1. In the *Architecture* tab>Circulation panel, click  (Stair).
2. In the Type Selector, select the stair type, as shown in Figure 7–76.

Figure 7–76

3. In Properties (shown in Figure 7–77), set the *Base Level* and *Top Level*, and any other required information.

Multistory Top Level enables you to create multiple runs of stairs based on Levels. The levels need to be the same height for this to work.

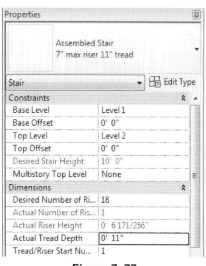

Figure 7–77

4. In the *Modify | Create Stairs* tab>Tools panel, click

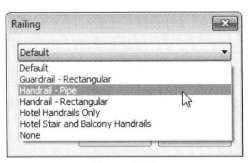 (Railing). In the Railings dialog box, select a railing type (as shown in Figure 7–78) and specify whether the *Position* is on the **Treads** or **Stringer**. Then, click **OK**.

Railings can also be added and modified after the stair has been placed.

Figure 7–78

5. In the *Modify | Create Stair* tab>Components panel, click

(Run) and then click (Straight).

6. In the Options Bar (shown in Figure 7–79), specify the following options:

- **Location Line:** Select **Exterior Support: Left**, **Run: Left**, **Run: Center**, **Run: Right**, or **Exterior Support: Right**.

- **Offset:** Specify a distance from the Location Line. This is typically used if you are following an existing wall but do not need to have the stairs directly against them.

- **Actual Run Width:** Specify the width of the stair run (not including the supports).

- **Automatic Landing:** Creates landings between stair runs (recommended).

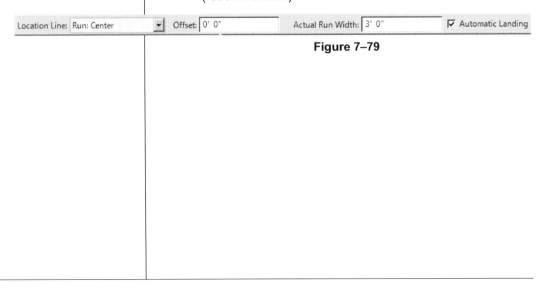

Figure 7–79

7. Click on the screen to select a start point for the run. A box displays, indicating the stair orientation and the number of risers created and remaining, as shown in Figure 7–80.

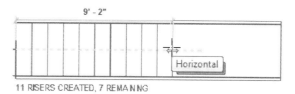

11 RISERS CREATED, 7 REMAINING

Figure 7–80

- For straight stairs of a single run, select a second point anywhere outside the box to create the run.
- For multi-landing or u-shaped stairs, select a second point inside the box for the length of the first run. Then, select a start point and an end point for the next run.

8. Click ✓ (Finish Edit Mode) to create the stairs, complete with railings.

How To: Sketch Custom Stairs

1. Open a plan or 3D view.

2. In the *Architecture* tab>Circulation panel, click 🗐 (Stair).
3. In the Type Selector, select the stair type.
4. In Properties, set the *Base Level* and *Top Level*. By default, a stair height is from level to level. In many cases, a custom stair is shorter and should be set using an offset from a level, as shown in Figure 7–81.

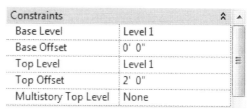

Figure 7–81

5. In the *Modify | Create Stair* tab>Components panel, click ✏ (Create Sketch).
6. In the *Modify | Create Stairs Sketch* tab>Draw panel, click ⌐ (Boundary) and sketch the outline of the stairs. Do not put boundaries at the top and bottom of the stairs.

*If you are creating a complex stair pattern, sketch reference planes in the **Stairs** command to help you select the start and end points of each run.*

If the stair is going in the wrong direction, click ⊞ (Flip) in the Modify | Create Stair tab>Tools panel.

7. In the Draw panel, click ⬚ (Riser) and sketch the risers. The risers must touch the boundary at each end. The number of risers still required displays below the sketch, as shown in Figure 7–82.

In this example, the boundaries are up against the wall. If it were a free standing stair, the boundaries would be along the sides of the stairs.

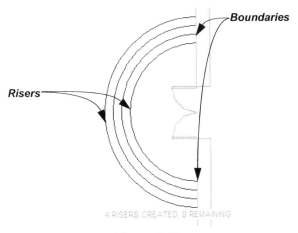

Figure 7–82

8. Click ✓ (Finish Edit Mode).

• In edit mode, riser lines are black and boundaries are green. The number of risers must be appropriate for the properties of the stair type.

• You can edit stair properties and modify the type when you select a custom stair, but you cannot select individual components. Using controls, you can move the *UP* text or flip the stair direction, as shown in Figure 7–83.

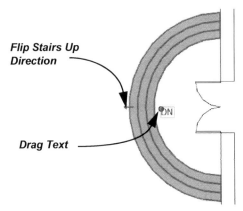

Figure 7–83

- To edit the boundary of the stairs, double-click on the stair or in the *Modify | Stairs* tab>Mode panel, click 🗒 (Edit Sketch).

- You can modify the Boundaries and Risers and also use standard editing commands, such as **Move** and **Trim** to edit the stair sketch.

Creating Ramps

The process of creating ramps is similar to that of creating stairs with runs and automatic landings. You can also sketch a boundary with risers at the start and end of each slope. Ramps are most often used for short vertical distances (as shown in Figure 7–84), as they require a lot of space for their runs. Check the local building codes to determine the maximum length of a run before a landing is required.

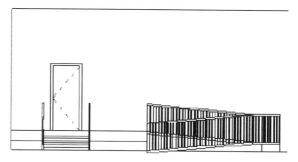

Figure 7–84

How To: Create a Ramp using Runs

1. In the *Architecture* tab>Circulation panel, click ⬭ (Ramp).
2. In the Type Selector, select the ramp type.
3. In the *Modify | Create Ramp Sketch* tab>Tools panel, click 🪜 (Railing) and select a railing type in the Railing Types dialog box. Click **OK**.
4. In Properties, specify the *Constraints,* especially **Base Level** and **Top Level** and their offsets (as shown in Figure 7–85), and other properties. The **Width** of the ramp is set in the *Dimensions* area.

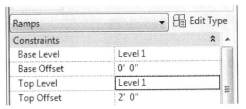

Figure 7–85

5. Draw reference planes to specify the locations of the run start and end points before creating the ramp. The run is based on the centerline of the ramp.

6. In the Draw panel, click ⊞ (Run) and select a start point for the run. A preview box displays the ramp's orientation and length. Click ⟋ (Line) or ⌒ (Center-ends Arc) to switch between linear and curved runs.

    •   Landings are automatically created between runs, as shown in Figure 7–86.

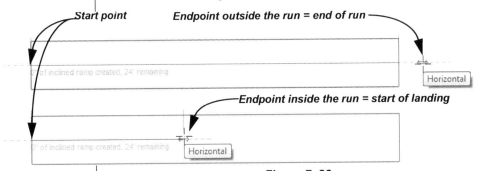

Figure 7–86

7. Click ✓ (Finish Edit Mode). The ramp (including railings) is created.

How To: Sketch a Ramp using Boundary and Riser

1. Click ⬭ (Ramp) and set up the ramp type and Properties.
2. In the *Modify | Create Ramp Sketch* tab>Draw panel, click

    ⌐ (Boundary).
3. Use the Draw tools to outline the sides (not the ends) of the ramp, as shown by the green lines in Figure 7–87.
4. In the *Modify | Create Ramp Sketch* tab>Draw panel, click

    ⌐ (Riser).

5. Use the Draw tools to specify the ends of the slope of each ramp, as shown by the black lines in Figure 7–87.

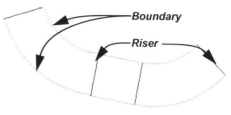

Figure 7–87

6. Click (Finish Edit Mode).

Working with Railings

Enhanced
in 2018

Hosts for sketched railings include floors, slabs, slab edges, the top of walls and roofs. You can also add railings to topographic surfaces.

Railings are automatically created with stairs, but you can modify or delete them independently of the stair element. You can also add railings separate from the stairs for other locations, as shown in Figure 7–88.

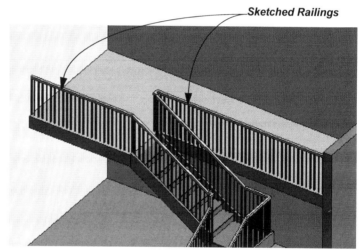

Figure 7–88

• You can add railings to existing stairs and ramps if they were not included when they were created.

How To: Add Railings by Sketching

1. Open a plan or 3D view.
2. In the *Architecture* tab>Circulation panel, expand

   (Railing) and click (Sketch Path).
3. In the Type Selector, specify the railing type.

4. In the *Modify | Create Railing Path* tab>Tools panel, click

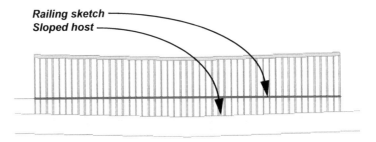 (Pick New Host) and select the element with which the railing is associated, such as a stair or floor.

- If you are working in a 3D or section view, you can select **Preview** in the *Modify | Create Railing Path* tab>Options panel so that the railing displays while you are still in edit mode. This only works if you have selected a host.
- If the host is sloped, the railing will follow the slope, as shown in Figure 7–89.

Railing sketch
Sloped host

Figure 7–89

5. Use the Draw tools to sketch the lines that define the railings.

6. Click 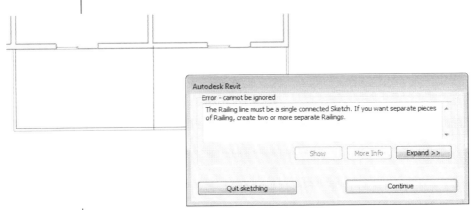 (Finish Edit Mode) to create the railing.

- The railing must be a single connected sketch. If it is not, you are prompted with a warning, as shown in Figure 7–90.

Autodesk Revit
Error - cannot be ignored
The Railing line must be a single connected Sketch. If you want separate pieces of Railing, create two or more separate Railings.

Show   More Info   Expand >>

Quit sketching   Continue

Figure 7–90

How To: Add Railings by Selecting a Host

1. In the *Architecture* tab>Circulation panel, expand

    ![icon] (Railing) and click ![icon] (Place on Host).
2. In the *Modify | Create Railing Place on Host* tab>Position

    panel, click ![icon] (Treads) or ![icon] (Stringer).
3. Select the stair or ramp where you want to add the railings.

- **Place on Host** only works if there are no railings on the stair. If you want to add an additional railing (e.g., down the middle of a wide stair), you need to sketch the railing.

Practice 7e

Model Stairs, Ramps, and Railings

Practice Objectives

- Create a ramp.
- Sketch custom stairs.
- Add railings.

Estimated time for completion: 15 minutes

In this practice, you will add a ramp on the Club Roof terrace. You will then add stairs by sketching the boundaries and riser lines. Finally, you will add railings to the stairs, as shown in Figure 7–91.

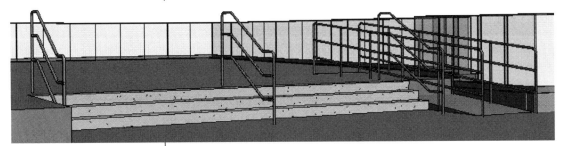

Figure 7–91

Task 1 - Add a ramp.

1. Open the project **Urban-Garden-Stairs.rvt** from the practice files folder.

2. Open the **Floor Plans: -03 Club Roof** view (the working model view).

3. Add a camera view looking from the building out to the edge of the roof, similar to that shown in Figure 7–92, so you can see the change of height between the two pools.

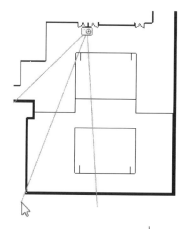
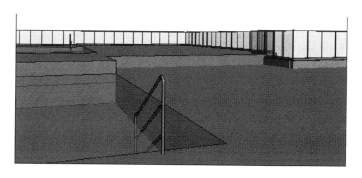

Figure 7–92

4. Return to the plan view.

5. In the *Architecture* tab>Work Plane panel, click 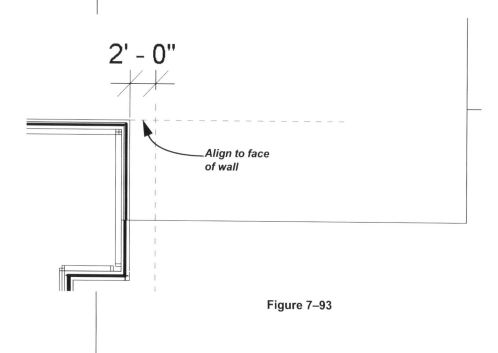 (Ref Plane).

6. Add two reference planes, as shown in Figure 7–93. These help you place the ramp. Ensure that you align it to the face of the walls.

2' - 0"

—*Align to face
of wall*

Figure 7–93

The roof deck is 1'-0 above the level.

7. In the *Architecture* tab>Circulation panel, click (Ramp).

8. In the Type Selector, select **Ramp: Pool Ramp**.

9. In Properties, set the following:
   - *Base Level:* **03 Club Roof**
   - *Base Offset:* **1'-0"**
   - *Top Level:* **03 Club Roof**
   - *Top Offset:* **2'-6"**
   - *Width:* **3'-0"**

10. In the *Modify | Create Ramp Sketch* tab>Tools panel, click (Railing).

11. In the Railing dialog box, select **Multi_Line-ATR-6M-3 Rail-Embedded** and click **OK**.

12. In the Draw panel, verify that (Run) is selected.

13. Draw the ramp sketch starting with the intersection of the reference planes, as shown in Figure 7–94. Pick a point past the end of the ramp to place it.

14. Click (Finish Edit Mode).

15. The ramp is not as wide as expected. In Properties, change the *Width* to **4'-0"**. The ramp now displays as shown in Figure 7–95.

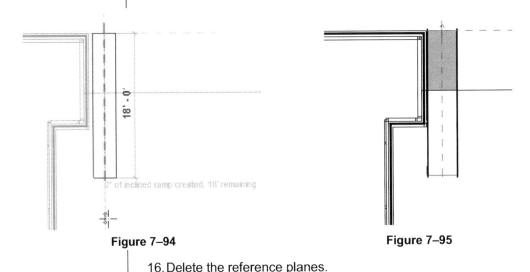

Figure 7–94   Figure 7–95

16. Delete the reference planes.

17. Open the 3D view. You can see the new ramp and railing but note that the roof needs to be modified. Since this in the architectural model, you would need to refer this back to the architect to change.

18. Save the project

Task 2 - Sketch Custom Stairs.

1. Return to the **Floor Plans: -03 Club Roof** view.

2. In the *Architecture* tab>Circulation panel, click ✎ (Stair).

3. In the Type Selector, select **Cast-In-Place Stair: Monolithic Stair**.

4. In the Options Bars, set the following:
   - *Location Line:* **Run: Right**,
   - *Offset:* **0'-0"**
   - *Actual Run Width:* **8'-0"**
   - *Automatic Landing:* **select**

5. In Properties, set the following:
   - *Base Level:* **03 Club Roof**
   - *Base Offset:* **1'-0"**
   - *Top Level:* **03 Club Roof**
   - *Top Offset:* **2'-6"**
   - *Desired Number of Risers:* **4**
   - *Actual Tread Depth*: **1'-0"**

6. In the *Modify | Create Ramp Sketch* tab>Tools panel, click ▨ (Railing).

7. In the Railing dialog box, select **None** and click **OK**. (The railings will be added separately.)

8. In the view, place the stairs by selecting the two points shown in Figure 7–96.

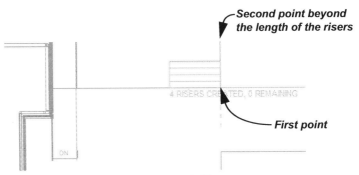

Figure 7–96

9. Select the riser component. Controls enable you to modify the size of the stairs, as shown in Figure 7–97.

10. Use the control on the left to change the width of the stairs, as shown in Figure 7–98.

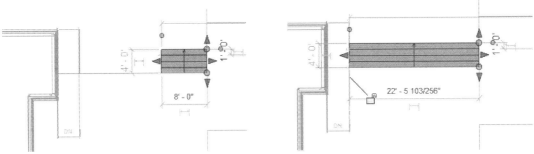

Figure 7–97　　　　　　　　　　**Figure 7–98**

11. Click ✔ (Finish Edit Mode).

12. The stairs may be running in the wrong direction. Select the finished stairs and click the **Flip Stairs Up Direction** control so the stairs are running correctly, as shown in Figure 7–99.

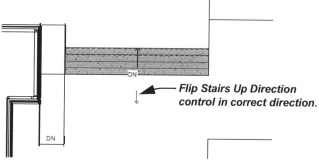

Figure 7–99

13. Use the same process to create a set of stairs on the other side of the pools.

14. View the stairs in 3D.

15. Save the project.

Task 3 - Add Railings.

1. Return to the **Floor Plans: -03 Club Roof** view.

2. In the *Architecture* tab>Circulation panel, expand (Railing) and click (Sketch Path).

3. In the Type Selector, select **Railing: Multi_Line - ATR - 3 Rail - Embedded**.

4. Sketch the railing path. Start by drawing a line from midpoint at the top of the stair up 4'-0". Then, add a 1'-0" line on each end, as shown in Figure 7–100.

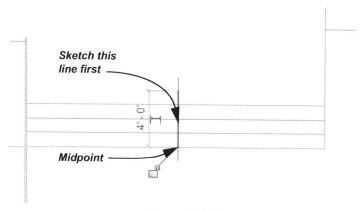

Figure 7–100

5. Click ✓ (Finish Edit Mode).

6. Open the 3D camera view. You can see that the railing is not working as expected, as shown in Figure 7–101.

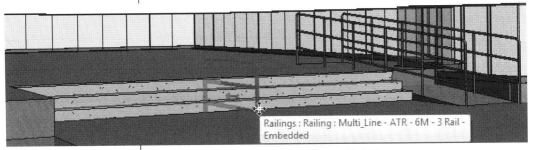

Railings : Railing : Multi_Line - ATR - 6M - 3 Rail - Embedded

Figure 7–101

7. With the railing selected, in the *Modify | Railings* tab>Tools panel, click 𝄃° (Pick New Host) and select the stairs. The railings take the correct configuration, as shown in Figure 7–102.

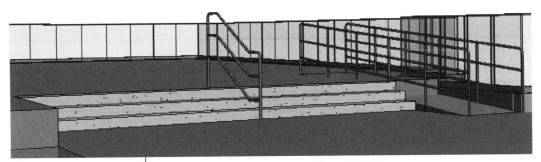

Figure 7–102

8. Return to the plan view and copy the railing to either end of the stairs. In the Options Bar, select **Constain** so you can only move horizontally or vertically.

9. Select all three railings and copy them to the other stair.

10. Create another camera view that is looking toward the other stair. The railings are not hosted by this stair.

11. Select each railing, click 𝄃° (Pick New Host), and select the stair.

12. Save the project.

Chapter Review Questions

1. What type of view do you need to be in to modify the profile of a wall so that it slopes or otherwise changes shape, as shown in Figure 7–103? (Select all that apply.)

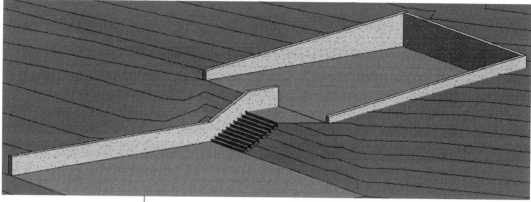

Figure 7–103

   a. Floor Plan

   b. Section

   c. Elevation

   d. 3D

2. When creating a floor, the boundary sketch must be...

   a. Open

   b. Closed

   c. It does not matter.

3. How do you change the thickness and material of a floor, such as those shown in Figure 7–104?

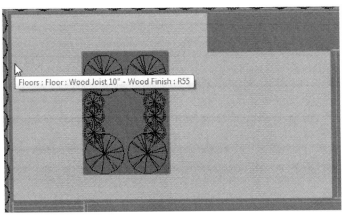

Floors : Floor : Wood Joist 10" - Wood Finish : R55

Figure 7–104

   a. In the Type Selector, change the *Floor Type*.

   b. In the Options Bar, change the *Floor Thickness*.

   c. In Properties, change the *Floor Thickness*.

   d. In the contextual ribbon, change the *Offset*.

4. How do you create a floor that has alternating materials, as shown in Figure 7–105?

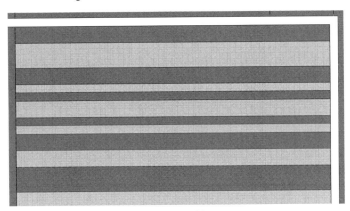

Figure 7–105

   a. Create a material that includes the pattern.

   b. Model multiple floors where the pattern repeats.

   c. Create filled regions over the floor face.

   d. Split the face of the floor and then paint the material on the new face.

5. When creating a sloped floor, △ (Add Point) places a point at...

   a. The end of the floor where you want the slope to end.

   b. The end of the floor where you want the slope to begin.

   c. A point where several slopes converge.

   d. A point where two slopes converge.

6. Which of the following elements is most helpful in specifying the start and end runs of ramps?

   a. Walls

   b. Stairs

   c. Sketch Lines

   d. Reference Planes

7. When do you need to use the ⧉ (Railing) command? (Select all that apply.)

   a. When you want an extra railing in the middle of very wide stairs.

   b. When you create a stair or ramp.

   c. When you create railings that are not attached to stairs or ramps.

   d. When you use the **Stair by Sketch** command.

Command Summary

Button	Command	Location
Walls		
	Wall	• **Ribbon:** *Architecture* tab>Build panel
	Wall Opening	• **Ribbon:** *Architecture* tab>Opening panel
Floors and Shape Editing Tools		
	Add Point	• **Ribbon:** *Modify	Floors* tab>Shape Editing panel
	Add Split Line	• **Ribbon:** *Modify	Floors* tab>Shape Editing panel
	Floor: Architectural	• **Ribbon:** *Architecture* tab>Build panel> expand Floor
	Floor: Structural	• **Ribbon:** *Architecture* tab>Build panel> expand Floor
	Modify Sub Elements	• **Ribbon:** *Modify	Floors* tab>Shape Editing panel
	Pick Supports	• **Ribbon:** *Modify	Floors* tab>Shape Editing panel
	Reset Shape	• **Ribbon:** *Modify	Floors* tab>Shape Editing panel
	Shaft	• **Ribbon:** *Architecture* tab>Opening panel
Stairs, Ramps, and Railings		
	Edit Stairs	• **Ribbon:** *Modify	Stairs* tab>Edit panel
	Stair	• **Ribbon:** *Architecture* tab>Circulation panel
	Ramp	• **Ribbon:** *Architecture* tab>Circulation panel
	Edit Path (Railings)	• **Ribbon:** *Modify	Railings* tab>Mode panel
	Pick New Host	• **Ribbon:** *Modify	Create Railing Path (Railings)* tab>Tools Panel
	Railing	• **Ribbon:** *Modify	Create Stair (Create Stairs Sketch) (Create Ramp)* tab> Tools panel

	Railing>Place on Host	• **Ribbon:** *Architecture* tab>Circulation panel>expand Railing
	Railing>Sketch Path	• **Ribbon:** *Architecture* tab>Circulation panel>expand Railing

8

Adding Planting and Other Landscape Components

When constructing a landscape model, you will likely add component families such as trees, shrubs, bollards, and lighting fixtures. These components can be included in your company's template or loaded from the Autodesk® Revit® library or a custom library. For area plantings, you can customize floor types to create planting beds of many sizes and shapes.

Learning Objectives in this Chapter

- Place components in a project to further develop the design.
- Load components from the Autodesk Revit library and a custom library.
- Purge unused component elements to increase the processing speed of the model.
- Use custom floor types for planting areas.
- Use groups to place and update sets of elements.

8.1 Adding Landscape Components

Many types of elements are added to a project using component families. These can include freestanding components, such as the plants, bollards, and benches. They can also include wall, ceiling, floor, roof, face and line-hosted components. These hosted components must be placed on the referenced element, such as the wall-hosted lighting fixtures shown in Figure 8–1.

Figure 8–1

- Several components are included in the default template, making them automatically available in new projects. You can load more components into a project or create your own, as required.

- Components are located in family files with the extension RFA. For example, a component family named **RCP Tree.rfa** can contain several types and sizes.

How To: Place a Component

1. In the *Architecture* tab>Build panel, click ⬛ (Place a Component), or type **CM**.
2. In the Type Selector, select the component that you want to add to the project.

RCP stands for Rich Photorealistic Content. These components help make renderings more lifelike.

3. Proceed as follows, based on the type of component used:

If the component is...	Then...
Not hosted	Set the *Level* and *Offset* in Properties, as shown in Figure 8–2.
Wall hosted	Set the *Elevation* in Properties, as shown in Figure 8–3.
Face hosted	Select the appropriate method in the contextual tab> Placement panel, as shown in Figure 8–4. • Vertical Faces include walls and columns. • Faces include ceilings, beams, and roofs. • Work Planes can be set to levels, faces, and named reference planes.

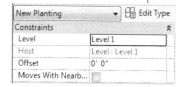

Figure 8–2

Figure 8–3

Figure 8–4

4. Place the component in the model.

• A fast way to add components that match those already in your project is to select one, right-click on it, and select **Create Similar**. This starts the **Component** command with the same type selected.

• In the *Massing & Site* tab>Model Site panel, there are two component commands specific to site components: ⬠ (Site Component) and ▥ (Parking Component).

Create Similar works with all elements.

Working with Host Elements

When you place a component on an element, such as a floor or toposurface, it recognizes this as a host, as shown in Figure 8–5. When the host is moved, the component moves with it. If you place components where there is no host, they are typically associated with a level.

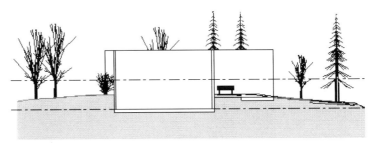

Figure 8–5

If you need to move a component from another host or the level on which it was inserted, you can change its host. For example, one of the shrubs shown in Figure 8–6 is floating above the floor. It was placed on the level when it was inserted, but needs to be located on the surface that is below the level.

Figure 8–6

How To: Pick a New Host Element

1. Select a component.
2. In the *<component type>* contextual tab>Host panel, click

    (Pick New Host).
3. Select the new host (e.g., the floor or toposurface).

- You can select a floor, toposurface, or level to be the new host for the components depending on the requirements of the component.

Loading Components

If the components you are looking for are not available, you can look in the Autodesk Revit Library, which contains many options. You can also check which components your company has. As you start building a custom library, you can find vendor-specific components on BIMobject Cloud Solutions.

How To: Load a Family

You can also load a family from the Modify | Place Component tab> Mode panel when placing a component.

1. In the *Insert* tab>Load from Library panel, click

   (Load Family).
2. In the Load Family dialog box, locate the folder that contains the family or families you want to load and select them, as shown in Figure 8–7. To load more than one family at a time, hold <Ctrl> while selecting.

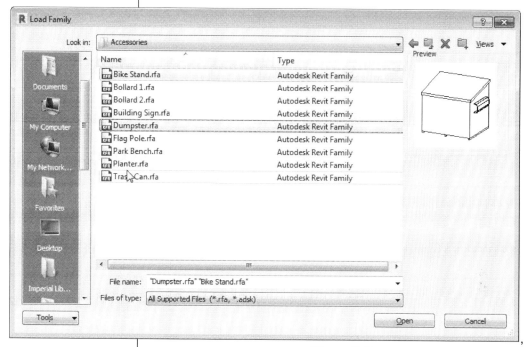

Figure 8–7

3. Click **Open**.

4. Once the family (or families) is loaded, click 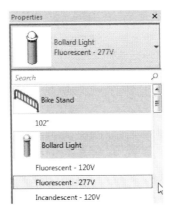 (Component) and select the type you want to use from the Type Selector, as shown in Figure 8–8.

Figure 8–8

- The Autodesk Revit family library includes the *Site* folder, with sub-folders for *Accessories*, *Logistics*, *Parking*, and *Utilities*.

    - *Accessories*: Items such as bike stands and trash cans.

    - *Logistics*: Trucks, cranes, and other construction equipment.

    - *Parking*: Parking spaces, islands, direction arrows, and an ADA-compliant curb cut, parking space, and symbol.

    - *Utilities:* Catch basins, fire hydrants, manhole covers, and more.

- Additional trees and shrubs can be loaded from the *Planting* folder in the Library. Each family (Shrub, Conifer, and Deciduous) contains a variety of types and heights of trees.

- Many components (not just site specific components) are face-based. If the components are added in a view in which the toposurface is visible, they can use a toposurface as a host.

Purging Unused Elements

You can remove unused elements from a project, including individual component types, as shown in Figure 8–9.

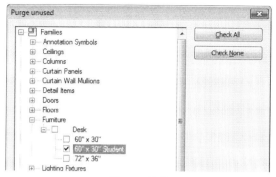

Figure 8–9

- Some elements are nested in other elements and it might require several rounds of purging the project to remove them.

How To: Purge Unused Elements

1. In the *Manage* tab>Settings panel, click ⌷ (Purge Unused).
2. In the Purge unused dialog box, click **Check None** and select the elements that you want to purge.
3. Click **OK**.

- Purging unused components not only helps simplify the component list, but also reduces the project file size.

Practice 8a

Add Landscape Components

Practice Objectives

- Load and add components.

Estimated time for completion: 10 minutes

In this practice, you will add tree and shrub components and copy and array them into place. You will also add floor-based light fixtures in the motor court and add bollard lights along the edge of the walkway near the building. Finally, you will add a linear trellis fence, as shown in Figure 8–10.

Figure 8–10

- The planting components used in this practice have been customized to work well with landscape-specific schedules.

Task 1 - Add trees and shrubs.

1. Open the project **Urban-Garden-Components.rvt** from the practice files folder.

2. Open the **Floor Plans: 01 Motor Court - Planting Plan** view.

3. Type **ZF** to fit the view in the window, if required.

4. In the View Control Bar, change the *Visual Style* to **Shaded**. You can see that some floors are made with an Earth material and other features have been added to the planting beds on the left side of the motor court, as shown in Figure 8–11.

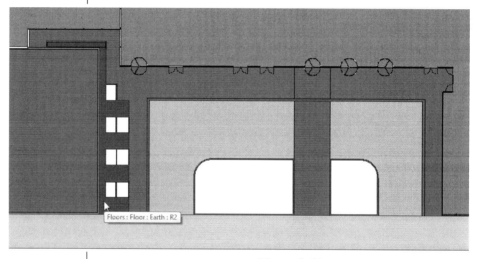

Figure 8–11

5. Select the one of the earth floors and note that the *Height Offset from Level* is **3'-6"**.

6. Return the *Visual Style* to **Hidden Line**.

7. In the *Architecture* tab>Build panel, click (Component).

8. In the Type Selector, select **RPC Tree - Deciduous: American Hornbeam**.

9. Place four trees in the planting beds to the left of the driveway, as shown in Figure 8–12.

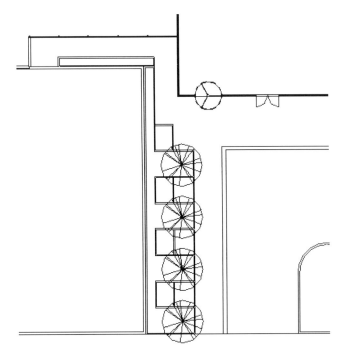

Figure 8–12

10. Select the four trees. You can see in Properties that the *Host* for the trees is automatically set to **Floor: Earth**.

11. Start the **Component** command again. In the Type Selector, select **RPC Tree-Shrub: Common Boxwood**. (**Hint:** In the search box, start typing **boxwood** and the options display as shown in Figure 8–13.)

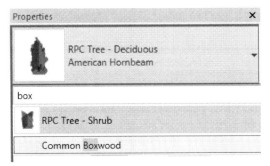

Figure 8–13

12. Place one boxwood at the lower left of the planter, as shown in Figure 8–14.

13. Click **Modify** and select the new shrub.

When the boxwood is rendered in a 3D view, it looks like it is floating. Setting the Offset below the host makes it look better.

14. In Properties, set the *Offset* to (negative) **-6"**.

15. Type **AR** to start the **Array** command.

16. In the Options Bar, set the following:

   - Click 🔲 (Linear).
   - Select **Group and Associate**.
   - *Number:* **20**
   - *Move to:* **Last**

17. Pick two points to define the first and last points of the array, as shown in Figure 8–14. Copies of the element are placed at equal distance between the selected points, as shown in Figure 8–15.

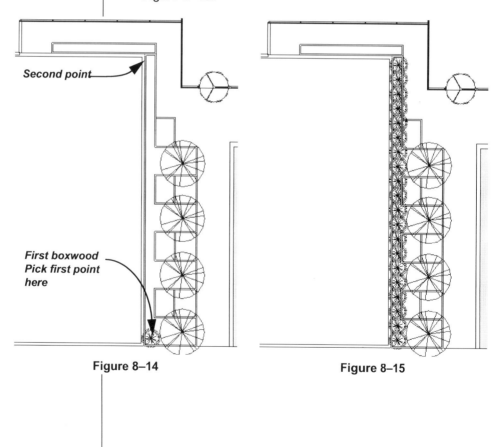

Second point

First boxwood
Pick first point
here

Figure 8–14   Figure 8–15

18. When **Group and Associate** is on, you can modify the number of elements in the array, if required. Click **Modify**.

19. Add copies of the component **Bamboo-2D** at **2'-0" O.C.** (on center) to the planter, as shown in Figure 8–16.

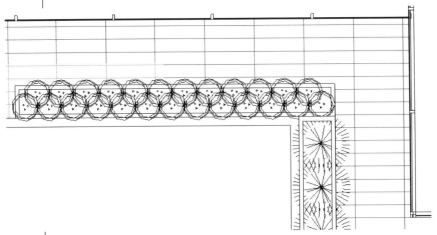

Figure 8–16

• Use the **Copy** or **Array** commands.

20. Save the project.

Task 2 - Add Lighting Components.

1. Open the **-01 Motor Court Plan** view.

2. Start the **Component** command and in the Type Selector, select **Flush In-ground Light-floor based**.

3. Hover the cursor over the planting area and you will see that you cannot place the component because there is no floor for it to be placed on, as shown on the right in Figure 8–17.

4. Hover the cursor over the cobblestone driveway and you can place the light, as shown on the left in Figure 8–17.

Figure 8–17

5. Zoom in so you can see the newly placed light, as shown in Figure 8–18.

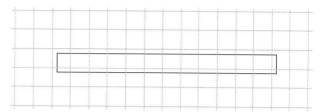

Figure 8–18

6. Use **Align** to line it up with the cobblestone pattern, as shown in Figure 8–19.

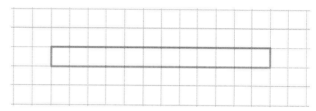

Figure 8–19

7. Copy the aligned light fixture to various places around the cobblestone driveway, similar to that shown in Figure 8–20.

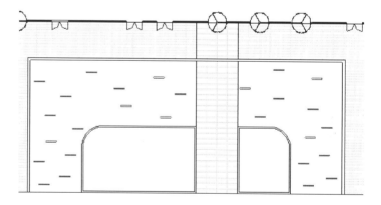

Figure 8–20

8. Add Square Bollard components along the curb of the driveway, as shown in Figure 8–21. They should be **8'-0" O.C.**. You will need to move some of them over so they line up with the pattern change at the main entrance.

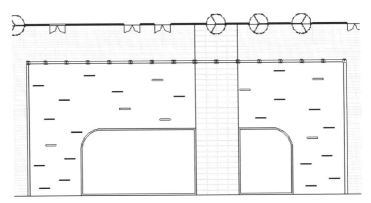

Figure 8–21

9. Open the **3D Views: 01 Motor Court Planting** view.

10. Set the *Visual Style* to **Realistic** so you can see the new components.

11. Save the project.

Task 3 - Add a linear component.

---

1. Open the **-01 Motor Court Plan** view.

2. In the *Insert* tab>Load from Library panel, click (Load Family).

Note: This is a manufacturer supplied component.

3. In the Load Family dialog box, navigate to the practice files> *Trellis-Freestanding-Green_Screen-Fence* folder, select **Trellis-Freestanding-Green_Screen-Fence.rfa**, and click Open.

4. In the Specify Types dialog box, select **Panel Size - 10'x4'**, as shown in Figure 8–22, and click **OK**. This family file needs to be updated.

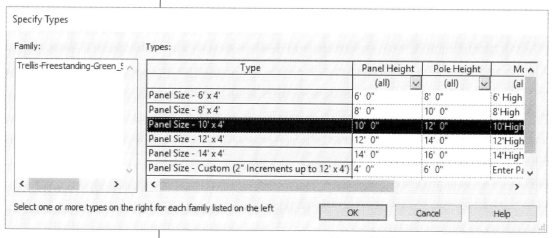

Figure 8–22

5. Start the **Component** command.

6. In the Type Selector, select **Trellis-Freestanding-Green_ Screen-Fence: Panel Size - 10'x4'**.

7. Press <Spacebar> to rotate the component so it is vertical. Then, place the component over to the left in an open area, as shown in Figure 8–23.

8. Use the controls to lengthen the component, as shown in Figure 8–23. It expands in 4'-0" increments.

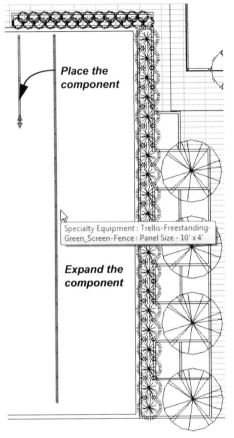

Place the component

Specialty Equipment : Trellis-Freestanding-Green_Screen-Fence : Panel Size - 10' x 4'

Expand the component

Figure 8–23

9. Move the expanded trellis over to the planter behind the boxwood.

10. Open the **3D Views: 01 Motor Court Planting** view.

11. Set the *Visual Style* to **Realistic** to see the new planting components.

12. Save the project.

13. If time permits, you can add components to the other levels and the park topography as well.

8.2 Creating Planting Areas and Groups

Individual plants, such as trees and shrubs, can be placed in a design using component families. You can group components and place the groups to fill areas, but there are no families designed specifically for planting areas. A work-around for this is to create floor types that define areas planted with smaller plants, as shown in Figure 8–24.

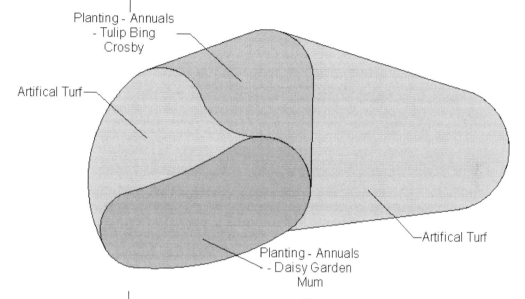

Planting - Annuals
- Tulip Bing
Crosby

Artifical Turf

Artifical Turf

Planting - Annuals
- Daisy Garden
Mum

Figure 8–24

- The process of adding planting areas using floors is the same as adding paving.

- Check with your BIM Manager to verify which floor types you should use.

Hint: Temporary Hide/Isolate

You might want to temporarily remove elements from a view, modify the project, and then restore the elements. Instead of completely toggling the elements off, you can temporarily hide them.

Select the elements that you want to hide (make invisible) or isolate (keep displayed while all other elements are hidden) and click 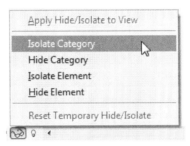 (Temporary Hide/Isolate). Select the method that you want to use, as shown in Figure 8–25.

Apply Hide/Isolate to View

Isolate Category

Hide Category

Isolate Element

Hide Element

Reset Temporary Hide/Isolate

Figure 8–25

Either elements or categories can be hidden or isolated. A cyan border displays around the view with a note in the upper left corner, as shown in Figure 8–26. It indicates that the view contains temporarily hidden or isolated elements.

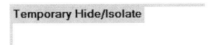

Temporary Hide/Isolate

Figure 8–26

- Click 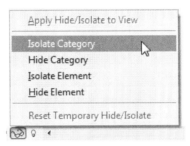 (Temporary Hide/Isolate) again and select **Reset Temporary Hide/Isolate** to restore the elements to the view.

- If you want to permanently hide the elements in the view, select **Apply Hide/Isolate to View**.

- Elements that are temporarily hidden in a view are not hidden when the view is printed.

Grouping Model Elements

Groups enable you to gather elements together to work as one unit. They can be used multiple times in a project. For example, if you are creating a planting bed with multiple plants and planting areas, you can create a group (as shown in Figure 8–27) and then copy the group rather than place the individual planting components.

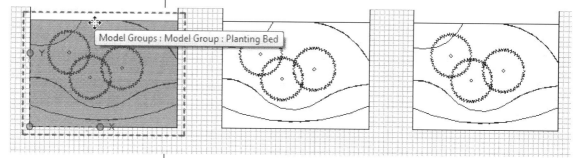

Figure 8–27

- Model Groups consist of model elements only. You can also create groups made up of detail elements or a mix of model and detail elements.

How To: Create a Model Group

1. Select the model elements that you want to include in the group.
2. In the *Modify contextual* tab>Create panel, click ▣ (Create Group) or type **GP**.
3. Enter a name in the Create Model Group dialog box, as shown in Figure 8–28. If you want to modify the group before creating it, select **Open in Group Editor**.

Figure 8–28

4. Click **OK** to create the group.

5. By default, the group origin is at the center of the group, as shown in Figure 8–29. Click and drag the origin to a new location, as shown in Figure 8–30. The new origin is used by any new instances of the group.

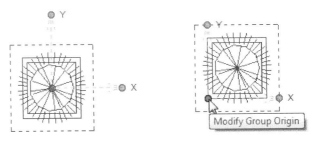

Figure 8–29   Figure 8–30

How To: Create a Group and Add Elements

1. In the *Architecture* or *Structure* tab>Model panel, expand (Model Group) and click (Create Group).
2. In the Create Group dialog box, name the group and select **Model**, as shown in Figure 8–31.

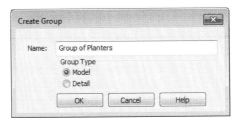

Figure 8–31

3. Click **OK**.
4. The Group Editor opens with the Edit Group panel, as shown in Figure 8–32.

Elements that are not part of the group are grayed out.

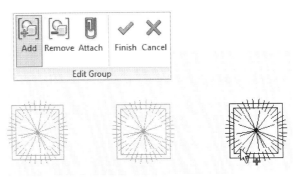

Figure 8–32

5. Add elements to the group.

- Click 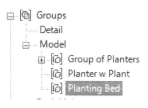 (Add) or type **AP** and select any existing elements that you want to include in the group.
- Anything you draw or insert while in the Group Editor is added to the group.
- You can copy elements, which become part of the group.
- Click (Remove) or type **RG** to remove existing elements from the group. The elements are not removed from the project unless you delete them.
- To add or remove multiple elements from the group, hold <Ctrl> when selecting the elements.

*The type of elements that you can select or insert depends on the Group Type (**Model** or **Detail**).*

Using Groups in a Project

You can add groups to a project by selecting them in the Project Browser, in the *Groups* node, and dragging them into the view, as shown in Figure 8–33. You can also use the Place Group commands.

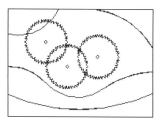

Figure 8–33

- If a model group has a detail group, you need to attach it separately.

How To: Add Model Groups from the Ribbon

1. In the *Architecture* or *Structure* tab>Model panel, expand (Model Group) and click (Place Model Group).
2. In Properties, in the Type Selector, select the group that you want to add.
3. Click in the drawing screen to place the group. You can add multiple copies.

- If you selected a model group with a hosted element (such as a door or window) that does not include the host (wall), you can only place one group at a time.

Modifying Groups

Groups can be copied, moved, mirrored, and rotated like most elements in the program. You can also cut, copy, and paste them to the clipboard. Individual instances of groups can be changed, but you can also change a group definition that impacts all instances of that group.

- If you no longer want an instance of a group to act as a group (as shown in Figure 8–34), select it and click

  (Ungroup) in the Group panel or type **UG**.

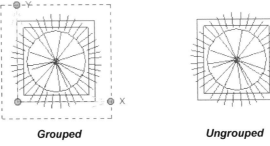

Grouped   *Ungrouped*

Figure 8–34

- To delete a group definition from the project, you must first delete all instances of the group in the project. You can then select the group name in the Project Browser, right-click, and select **Delete**.

- To modify individual instances of a group, use <Tab> to select one element in a group. Then, click on the *Group Member* icon (as shown in Figure 8–35) to remove the element from that instance of the group

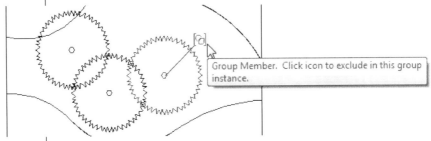

Group Member. Click icon to exclude in this group instance.

Figure 8–35

- To replace one group with a different one, select the required group. In Properties, select another group's name, as shown in Figure 8–36. The selected groups are replaced.

If you are replacing groups, it helps to match the groups' origin and rotation.

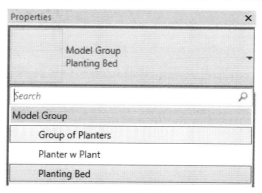

Figure 8–36

- To modify all instances of a group definition, in the *Modify |*

  Model Groups tab>Group panel, click 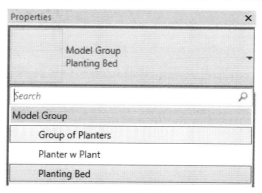 (Edit Group) or type **EG**. In the Group Editor, make changes to the group, as required. Use the floating Edit Group toolbar to add, remove, and attach elements.

- To change the name of a group, right-click on the group in the Project Browser and select **Rename**.

Practice 8b | Create Planting Areas and Groups

Practice Objectives

- Add floors using custom floor types set up for planting.
- Create and modify groups.

Estimated time for completion: 15 minutes

In this practice, you will create planting areas in the Motor Court using custom floor types designed for planting, as shown in Figure 8–37. You will also create planting areas on the Roof Garden, create a group, and then copy the group to other planting beds. You will modify one of the groups and see how the rest of the groups update.

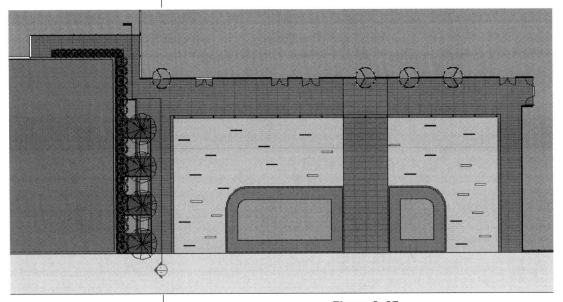

Figure 8–37

- The floor types used in this practice have been customized to work well with landscape-specific schedules.

Task 1 - Add planting areas using floor types.

1. Open the project **Urban-Garden-Areas.rvt** from the practice files folder.

2. Open the **Floor Plans: -01 Motor Court** view.

3. Zoom in on the planting beds in the middle of the driveway.

4. In the *Architecture* tab>Build panel, click 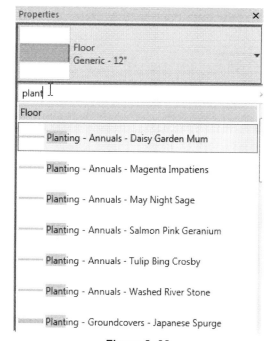 (Floor).

5. Expand the Type Selector and in the search field start typing **planting**. A number of floor types that start with the word **Planting** are provided in this project, as shown in Figure 8–38.

The floor types designed as planting areas are also divided by Annuals, Groundcovers, and Shrubs.

Properties ✕

Floor
Generic - 12"

plant

Floor

Planting - Annuals - Daisy Garden Mum

Planting - Annuals - Magenta Impatiens

Planting - Annuals - May Night Sage

Planting - Annuals - Salmon Pink Geranium

Planting - Annuals - Tulip Bing Crosby

Planting - Annuals - Washed River Stone

Planting - Groundcovers - Japanese Spurge

Figure 8–38

6. Scroll down or type **shrub** in the search box and select **Floor : Planting - Shrubs - Dwarf Boxwood**.

7. In the *Modify | Create Floor Boundary* tab>Draw panel, click (Pick Lines).

8. In the Options Bar, select **Lock**.

9. Select the interior lines of the curbs around both planting beds, as shown in Figure 8–39.

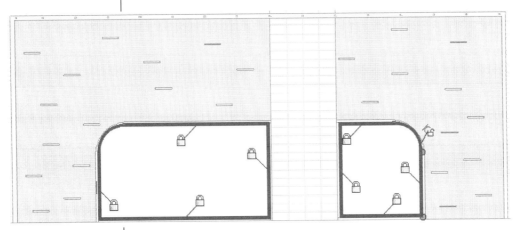

Figure 8–39

- By locking the sketch to the curbs the floor will automatically update if the curb locations are changed.
- In this case, these planting beds will include the same mix of plants. If there were two separate types of plants, you would need to create each one independently.

10. In the Options Bar, set the *Offset* to **4'-0"**. Hover the cursor over one set of the new lines and press <Tab> until they are all highlighted and click to select them when you see the dashed lines on the inside of the area, as shown in Figure 8–40.

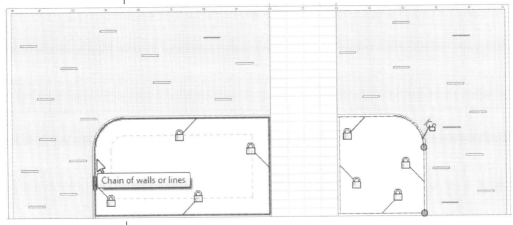

Chain of walls or lines

Figure 8–40

11. Click ✓ (Finish Edit Mode).

12. The planting beds are created as shown in Figure 8–41

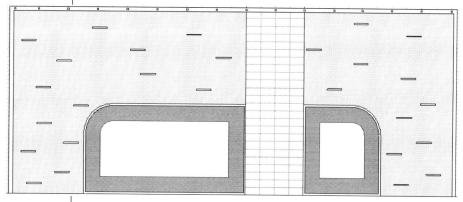

Figure 8–41

13. Create separate floors inside the boxwood planting areas using one of the annual planting types.

14. Set the *Visual Style* to **Shaded** to see the different colors connected with the new elements.

15. Pan over to the planting beds to the left of the driveway.

16. Select one of the trees and one of the boxwood elements.

17. In the View Control Bar, click 🎨 (Temporary Hide/Isolate) and select **Hide Category**. All of the trees and other plants are temporarily hidden.

18. Create three floors using the floor types shown in Figure 8–42. The dwarf boxwood is a 1'-0" edging around the roses.

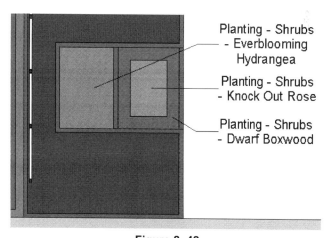

Planting - Shrubs - Everblooming Hydrangea

Planting - Shrubs - Knock Out Rose

Planting - Shrubs - Dwarf Boxwood

Figure 8–42

19. Select the three new planting beds and copy them to the other two openings. Then, copy just the hydrangea planting bed to the additional opening at the top of the group.

20. In the View Control Bar, click ⌇ (Temporary Hide/Isolate) and select **Reset Temporary Hide/Isolate**. The final layout is shown in Figure 8–43.

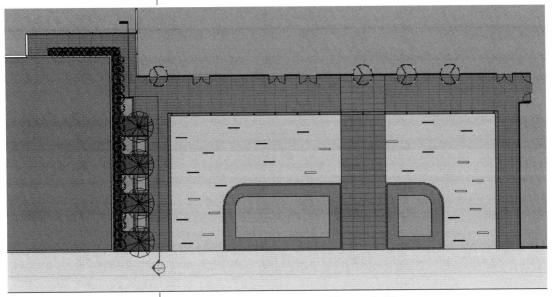

Figure 8–43

21. Save the project.

Task 2 - Create and Modify Groups.

1. Open the **Floor Plans: 02 Roof Garden- Planting Plan** view. Zoom to fit if required.

2. Select one of the trees and temporarily hide the category.

3. Zoom in on the top planting bed on the top left of the building and add the planting floor types shown in Figure 8–44. Do not lock the sketch lines to the boundary walls.

A warning about highlighted floors overlapping displays. Ignore it for this step.

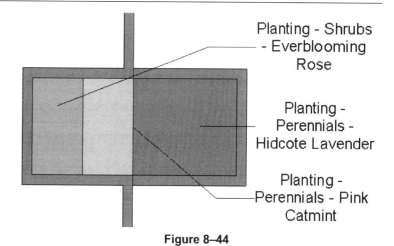

Planting - Shrubs - Everblooming Rose

Planting - Perennials - Hidcote Lavender

Planting - Perennials - Pink Catmint

Figure 8–44

4. Set the *Visual Style* to **Shaded**. You cannot see the colors because the floors are overlapping the roof.

5. Select the three planting elements and in Properties, change the *Height Offset from Level* to **6"**. The floors no longer overlap and the colors now display.

6. With the three planting elements still selected, in the *Modify | Multi-Select* tab>Create panel, click [icon] (Create Group) or type **GP**.

7. In the Create Model Group dialog box, type in the *Name:* **Planting Bed - Roof** and click **OK**.

8. Drag the group origin to the upper left corner of the wall, as shown in Figure 8–45.

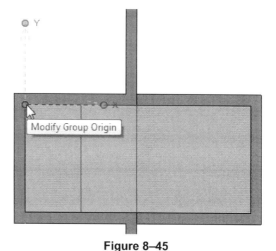

Figure 8–45

9. Pan down so you can see the rest of the planting beds on the same side.

10. Copy the entire group to each of the other planting beds, as shown in Figure 8–46.

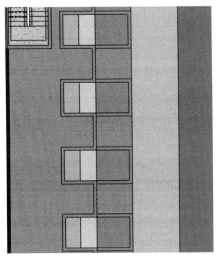

Figure 8–46

11. Select one of the groups.

12. In the *Modify | Model Groups* tab>Group panel, click (Edit Group).

13. The Edit Group toolbar displays with the edited group in full color with everything else in the view grayed out.

14. Double-click on the floor with the lavender planting type to edit the boundary.

15. Add a **2'-0"** circle in the center of the space. This creates a hole in the floor. Click (Finish Edit Mode).

16. Add a new floor using a different type in the opening. Select the new floor and change the *Height Offset from Level* to **6"**. The modifications display as shown in Figure 8–47.

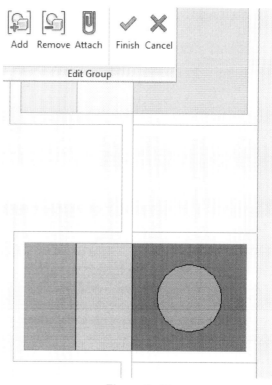

Figure 8–47

17. Click ✔ (Finish). All of the groups update to match the change.

18. In the View Control Bar, expand 🕶 (Temporary Hide/Isolate) and select **Reset Temporary Hide/Isolate**.

19. Save the project.

Chapter Review Questions

1. When inserting a component, you select the family that you want to use in the...

   a. Quick Access Toolbar

   b. Type Selector

   c. Options Bar

   d. Properties Palette

2. If the component that you want to use is not available in the current project, where can you get it from? (Select all that apply.)

   a. Copy the component to the clipboard from another project and paste it into the current one.

   b. In the current project, use  (Insert from File) and select the family from the list in the dialog box.

   c. In the current project, use (Load Family) and select the family from the list in the dialog box.

3. Which of the following commands would you use if you want to move a planting component to a floor that is lower than the level where it was original placed, as shown in Figure 8–48?

Figure 8–48

   a. Use (Level) and add a Level at the height of the lower floor.

   b. Use (Ref Plane) and draw a plane aligned with the lower floor.

   c. Use (Pick New Host) and select the lower floor.

   d. Use (Edit Family) and change the work plane in the family so that it matches the height of the lower floor.

4. Which of the following types of elements can be used to add planting areas to a project?

a. Areas

b. Floors

c. Planting Areas

d. Components

5. If you made a change to the model group shown in Figure 8–49, what would happen to the other two groups?

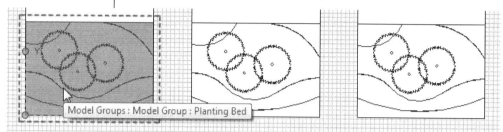

Model Groups : Model Group : Planting Bed

Figure 8–49

a. Only the one model group changes.

b. You have to select and update the other groups using the Type Selector.

c. All of the model groups change.

d. You have to select **Update Group** for the other groups to change.

Command Summary

Button	Command	Location
	Load Family	• **Ribbon:** *Modify	Place Component* tab> Load panel or *Insert* tab>Load from Library panel
	Pick New Host	• **Ribbon:** *Modify	Multi-Select* or *component type* contextual tab>Host panel
	Place Component	• **Ribbon:** *Architecture* tab>Build panel> expand Component • **Shortcut:** CM
	Place on Face	• **Ribbon:** *Modify	Place Component* tab> Placement panel
	Place on Vertical Face	• **Ribbon:** *Modify	Place Component* tab> Placement panel
	Place on Work Plane	• **Ribbon:** *Modify	Place Component* tab> Placement panel
	Purge Unused	• **Ribbon:** *Manage* tab>Settings panel

Groups

Button	Command	Location
	Add to Group	• **Floating Panel:** Edit Group • **Shortcut:** AP (when a group is in edit mode)
	Create Group (elements selected)	• **Ribbon:** *Modify* contextual tab>Create panel • **Shortcut:** GP
	Create Group (Model)	• **Ribbon:** *Architecture* or *Structure* tab> Model panel>expand Model Group • **Shortcut:** GP
	Edit Group	• **Ribbon:** *Modify	Model (or Detail) Groups* tab>Group panel • **Shortcut:** EG (when a group is selected)
	Remove from Group	• **Floating Panel:** Edit Group • **Shortcut:** RG (when a group is in edit mode)
	Ungroup	• **Ribbon:** *Modify	Model* (or *Detail*) *Groups* tab>Group panel • **Shortcut:** UG (when a group is selected)

Chapter 9

Creating Construction Documents

The accurate creation of construction documents in the Autodesk® Revit®
software ensures that the design is correctly communicated to downstream users.
Construction documents are created primarily in special views called sheets.
Knowing how to select titleblocks, assign titleblock information, place views, and
print the sheets are essential steps in the construction documentation process.

Learning Objectives in this Chapter

- Add Sheets with titleblocks and views of a project.
- Enter the titleblock information for individual sheets and for an entire project.
- Place and organize views on sheets.
- Print sheets using the default Print dialog box.

9.1 Setting Up Sheets

While you are modeling a project, the foundations of the working drawings are already in progress. Any view (such as a floor plan, section, callout, or schedule) can be placed on a sheet, as shown in Figure 9–1.

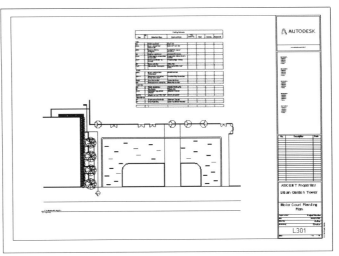

Figure 9–1

- Company templates can be created with standard sheets using the company (or project) titleblock and related views already placed on the sheet.

- The sheet size is based on the selected title block family.

- Sheets are listed in the *Sheets* area in the Project Browser.

- Most information on sheets is included in the views. You can add general notes and other non-model elements directly to the sheet.

How To: Set Up Sheets

1. In the Project Browser, right-click on the *Sheets* area header and select **New Sheet...**, or in the *View* tab>Sheet Composition panel, click 🗋 (Sheet).

2. In the New Sheet dialog box, select a titleblock from the list as shown in Figure 9–2. Alternatively, if there is a list of placeholder sheets, select one or more from the list.

*Click **Load...** to load a sheet from the Library.*

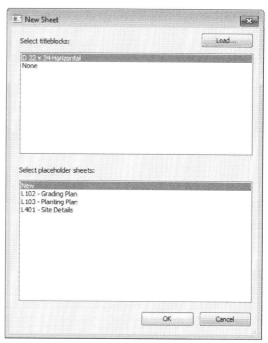

Hold <Ctrl> to select multiple placeholder sheets.

Figure 9–2

3. Click **OK**. A new sheet is created using the preferred title block.
4. Fill out the information in the title block, as required.
5. Add views to the sheet.

• When you create sheets, the next sheet is incremented numerically.

• When you change the *Sheet Name* and/or *Number* in the title block, it automatically changes the name and number of the sheet in the Project Browser.

• The plot stamp on the side of the sheet automatically updates according to the current date and time. The format of the display uses the regional settings of your computer.

• The Scale is automatically entered when a view is inserted onto a sheet. If a sheet has multiple views with different scales, the scale displays **As Indicated.**

Sheet (Title Block) Properties

Each new sheet includes a title block. You can change the title block information in Properties, as shown in Figure 9–3, or by selecting any blue label you want to edit (Sheet Name, Sheet Number, Drawn by, etc.), as shown in Figure 9–4.

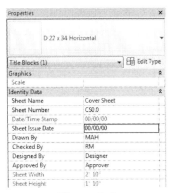

Figure 9–3

Figure 9–4

Properties that apply to all sheets can be entered in the Project Properties dialog box, as shown in Figure 9–5. In the *Manage* tab>Settings panel, click (Project Information).

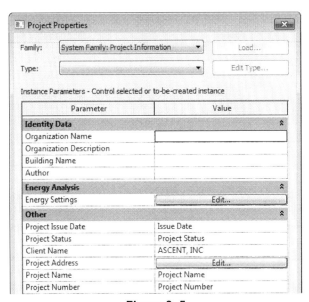

Figure 9–5

9.2 Placing and Modifying Views on Sheets

You can easily add views to a sheet by dragging and dropping a view from the Project Browser onto the required sheet. The new view on the sheet displays at the scale specified in the original view. The view title displays the name, number, and scale of the view, as shown in Figure 9–6.

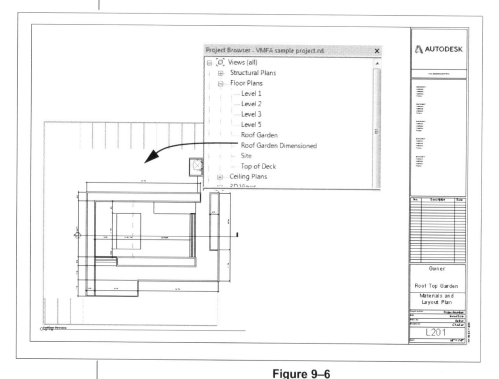

Figure 9–6

How To: Place Views on Sheets

Alignment lines from existing views display to help you place additional views.

1. Set up the view as you want it to display on the sheet, including the scale and visibility of elements.
2. Create or open the sheet where you want to place the view.
3. Select the view in the Project Browser and drag and drop it onto the sheet.
4. The center of the view is attached to the cursor. Click to place it on the sheet.

Placing Views on Sheets

- Views can only be placed on a sheet once. However, you can duplicate the view and place that copy on a sheet.

- Views on a sheet are associative. They automatically update to reflect changes to the project.

- Each view on a sheet is listed under the sheet name in the Project Browser, as shown in Figure 9–7.

Figure 9–7

- You can also use two other methods to place views on sheets:
    - In the Project Browser, right-click on the sheet name and select **Add View...**
    - In the *View* tab>Sheet Composition panel, click

     (Place View).

    Then, in the Views dialog box (shown in Figure 9–8), select the view you want to use and click **Add View to Sheet**.

This method lists only those views which have not yet been placed on a sheet.

Figure 9–8

- To remove a view from a sheet, select it and press <Delete>. Alternatively, in the Project Browser, expand the individual sheet information to show the views, right-click on the view name, and select **Remove From Sheet**.

Hint: Setting up the Project Browser

To view and change the Project Browser's types, select the top level node of the Project Browser (which is set to *Views (all)* by default) and select the type that you want to use from the Type Selector. For example, you can set the Browser to only display views that are not on sheets, as shown in Figure 9–9.

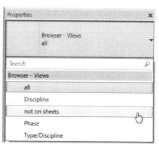

Figure 9–9

Moving Views and View Titles

*You can also use the **Move** command or the arrow keys to move a view.*

- To move a view on a sheet, select the edge of the view and drag it to a new location. The view title moves with the view.

- To move only the view title, select the title and drag it to the new location.

- To modify the length of the line under the title name, select the edge of the view and drag the controls, as shown in Figure 9–10.

1. North-South Entry
   1/8" = 1'-0"

Figure 9–10

- To change the title of a view on a sheet without changing its name in the Project Browser, in Properties, in the *Identity Data* area, type a new title for the *Title on Sheet* parameter, as shown in Figure 9–11.

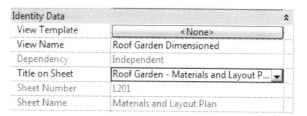

Identity Data	
View Template	<None>
View Name	Roof Garden Dimensioned
Dependency	Independent
Title on Sheet	Roof Garden - Materials and Layout P...
Sheet Number	L201
Sheet Name	Materials and Layout Plan

Figure 9–11

Rotating Views

- When creating a vertical sheet, you can rotate the view on the sheet by 90 degrees. Select the view and set the direction of rotation in the Rotation on Sheet drop-down list in the Options Bar, as shown in Figure 9–12.

Figure 9–12

- To rotate a view to an angle other than 90 degrees, open the view, toggle on the crop region and select it. Use the **Rotate** command to change the angle.

Working Inside Views

To make small changes to a view while working on a sheet:

- Double-click *inside* the view to activate it.
- Double-click *outside* the view to deactivate it.

Only elements in the viewport are available for modification. The rest of the sheet is grayed out, as shown in Figure 9–13.

Only use this method for small changes. Significant changes should be made directly in the view.

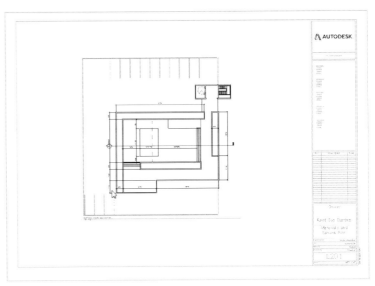

Figure 9–13

- You can activate and deactivate views by right-clicking on the edge of the view or by using the tools found on the *Modify | Viewports* and *Views* tab>Sheet Composition panel.

- Changes you make to elements when a view is activated also display in the original view.

- If you are unsure which sheet a view is on, right-click on the view in the Project Browser and select **Open Sheet**. This item is grayed out if the view has not been placed on a sheet and is not available for schedules and legends which can be placed on more than one sheet.

Resizing Views on Sheets

Each view displays the extents of the model or the elements contained in the crop region. If the view does not fit on a sheet (as shown in Figure 9–14), you might need to crop the view or move the elevation markers closer to the building.

If the extents of the view change dramatically based on a scale change or a crop region, it is easier to delete the view on the sheet and drag it over again.

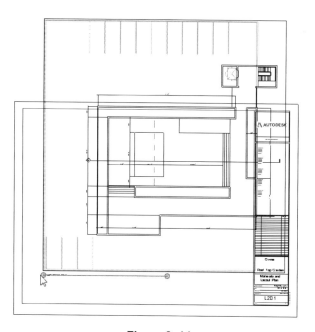

Figure 9–14

Hint: Add an Image to a Sheet

Company logos and renderings saved to image files (such as .JPG and .PNG) can be added directly on a sheet or in a view.

1. In the *Insert* tab>Import panel, click  (Image).
2. In the Import Image dialog box, select and open the image file. The extents of the image display as shown in Figure 9–15.

Figure 9–15

3. Place the image where you want it.
4. The image displays. Pick one of the grips and extend it to modify the size of the image.

- In Properties, you can adjust the height and width and also set the *Draw Layer* to either **Background** or **Foreground**, as shown in Figure 9–16.

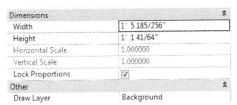

Dimensions	☆
Width	1' 5 185/256"
Height	1' 1 41/64"
Horizontal Scale	1.000000
Vertical Scale	1.000000
Lock Proportions	☑
Other	☆
Draw Layer	Background

Figure 9–16

- You can select more than one image at a time and move them as a group to the background or foreground.

Practice 9a

Create Construction Documents

Practice Objectives

- Set up project properties.
- Create sheets individually.
- Modify views to prepare them to be placed on sheets.
- Place views on sheets.

Estimated time for completion: 20 minutes

In this practice, you will complete the project information, add new sheets and use existing sheets. You will fill in title block information and then add views to sheets, such as the Materials and Layout Plan sheet shown in Figure 9–17. Complete as many sheets as you are able to during the given time.

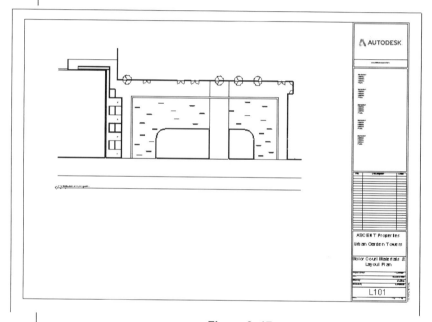

Figure 9–17

Task 1 - Complete the project information.

1. Open the project **Urban-Garden-Sheets.rvt** from the practice files folder.

2. In the *Manage* tab>Settings panel, click (Project Information).

These properties are used across the entire sheet set and do not need to be entered on each sheet.

3. In the Project Properties dialog box, in the *Other* area, set the following parameters:
   - *Project Issue Date:* **Issue Date**
   - *Project Status:* **Design Development**
   - *Client Name:* **Ascent Properties**
   - *Project Address:* Click **Edit...** and enter your address
   - *Project Name:* **Urban Garden Towers**
   - *Project Number:* **1234-567**

4. Click **OK**.

5. Save the project.

Task 2 - Create a Cover Sheet and Floor Plan Sheets.

1. In the *View* tab>Sheet Composition panel, click  (Sheet).

2. In the New Sheet dialog box, select the **E1 30 x42 Horizontal** titleblock.

3. Click **OK**.

4. Zoom in on the lower right corner of the title block. The Project Properties filled out earlier are automatically added to the sheet.

5. Continue filling out the title block, as shown in Figure 9–18.

ASCENT Properties

Urban Garden Towers

Cover Sheet

Project Number	1234-567
Date	Issue Date
Drawn By	Author
Checked By	Checker

CS000

| Scale | |

Figure 9–18

6. Zoom out to see the entire sheet.

7. In the Project Browser, expand the **3D Views** node. Drag and drop the **01 Motor Court Planting** view on to the sheet, as shown in Figure 9–19. The view is rather small and there are two items that are not required on the cover sheet, the viewport title and crop region.

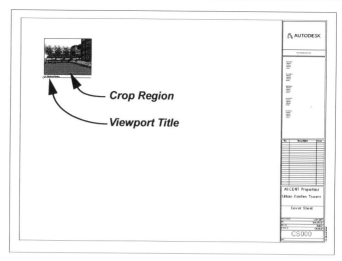

Crop Region

Viewport Title

Figure 9–19

8. Select the edge of the viewport. In the Type Selector, select **Viewport: No Title**.

9. Double-click inside the viewport. The title block grays out and you can modify the actual view.

10. Select the edge of the crop region.

11. In the *Modify | Cameras* tab>Crop panel, click (Size Crop).

12. In the Crop Region Size dialog box, in the *Change* area, select **Scale (locked proportions)** and set the *Width* to **18**, as shown in Figure 9–20. Click **OK**.

Figure 9–20

13. In Properties, in the *Extents* area, clear the checkmark from **Crop Region Visible**. (This could also be done in the View Control Bar.)

14. Double-click outside the viewport to return to the sheet and move the view as required, to fit on the sheet.

15. In the Sheet Composition panel, click 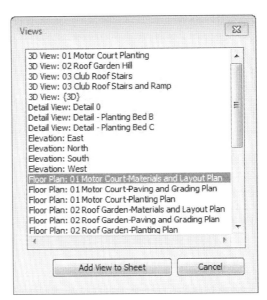 (Sheet). Using the same sized title block, create the following new sheets:
    - **L101 - Motor Court Materials & Layout Plan**
    - **L201 - Motor Court Paving & Grading Plan**
    - **L301 - Motor Court Planting Plan**
    - **L400 - Site Details**

16. Save the project.

Task 3 - Add views to sheets.

1. Open the sheet **L101 - Motor Court Materials & Layout Plan**.

2. In the Project Browser, right click on the sheet and select **Add View...**.

3. In the Views dialog box, scroll down and select **Floor Plan: 01 Motor Court Material and Layout Plan**, as shown in Figure 9–21. Click **Add View to Sheet** and place the view on the sheet.

Views

3D View: 01 Motor Court Planting
3D View: 02 Roof Garden Hill
3D View: 03 Club Roof Stairs
3D View: 03 Club Roof Stairs and Ramp
3D View: {3D}
Detail View: Detail 0
Detail View: Detail - Planting Bed B
Detail View: Detail - Planting Bed C
Elevation: East
Elevation: North
Elevation: South
Elevation: West
Floor Plan: 01 Motor Court-Materials and Layout Plan
Floor Plan: 01 Motor Court-Paving and Grading Plan
Floor Plan: 01 Motor Court-Planting Plan
Floor Plan: 02 Roof Garden-Materials and Layout Plan
Floor Plan: 02 Roof Garden-Paving and Grading Plan
Floor Plan: 02 Roof Garden-Planting Plan

Add View to Sheet   Cancel

Figure 9–21

4. Open the **L201 - Motor Court Paving and Grading Plan** sheet and add the related floor plan view to the sheet.

   • The **01 Motor Court Material and Layout Plan** view is no longer available because it has already been added to a sheet.

5. Repeat the process with the **L301- Motor Court Planting Plan** sheet and view.

6. Open the **L400 - Site Details** sheet.

7. From the *Detail Views (Detail)* node in the Project Browser, drag and drop the three detail views on to the sheet using alignment lines to help you place them as shown in Figure 9–22.

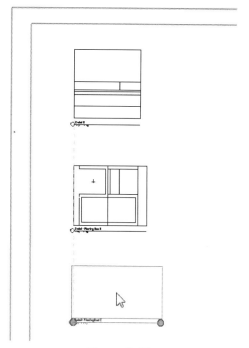

Figure 9–22

8. In the Project Browser, right-click on one of the planting bed detail views and select **Find Referring Views...**.

9. In the Go To View dialog box, select the view and click **Open View**.

10. Zoom in on one of the markers. Note that it has now been automatically assigned a detail and a sheet number, as shown in Figure 9–23.

Your numbers might not exactly match the numbers in the example.

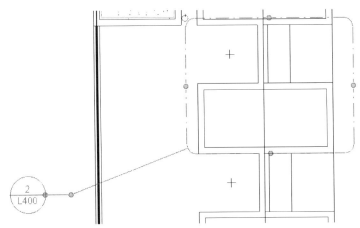

Figure 9–23

11. If time permits, create sheets for the other levels.

- Modify crop regions and hide unnecessary elements in the views. Toggle off crop regions after you have modified them.

- Verify the scale of a view in Properties before placing it on a sheet.

- Change the view title, if required, to more accurately describe what is on the sheet.

- To make minor changes to a view once it is on a sheet, double-click inside the viewport to activate the view. To return to the sheet, double-click outside the viewport to deactivate the view.

12. Save the project.

9.3 Printing Sheets

Using the **Print** command, you can print individual sheets or a list of selected sheets. You can also print an individual view or a portion of a view for check prints or presentations. To open the Print dialog box (shown in Figure 9–24), in the *File* tab, click

 (Print).

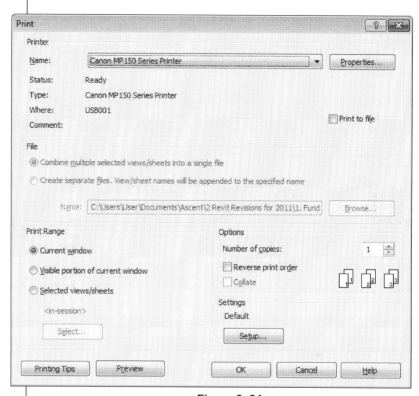

Figure 9–24

Printing Options

The Print dialog box is divided into the following areas: *Printer*, *File*, *Print Range, Options*, and *Settings*. Modify them as required, to produce the plot you want.

*   **Printing Tips:** Opens Autodesk WikiHelp online, in which you can find help with troubleshooting printing issues.

*   **Preview:** Opens a preview of the print output so that you can see what is going to be printed.

Printer

Select from the list of available printers, as shown in Figure 9–25. Click **Properties...** to adjust the properties of the selected printer. The options vary according to the printer. Select **Print to file** to print to a file rather than directly to a printer. You can create .PLT or .PRN files.

You must have a .PDF print driver installed on your system to print to PDF.

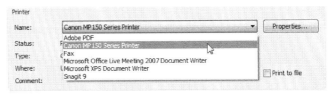

Figure 9–25

File

The *File* area is only available if the **Print to file** option has been selected in the *Printer* area or if you are printing to an electronic-only type of printer. You can create one file or multiple files depending on the type of printer you are using, as shown in Figure 9–26. Click **Browse...** to select the file location and name.

Figure 9–26

Print Range

The *Print Range* area enables you to print individual views/sheets or sets of views/sheets, as shown in Figure 9–27.

Figure 9–27

- **Current window:** Prints the entire current sheet or view you have open.

- **Visible portion of current window:** Prints only what displays in the current sheet or view.

- **Selected views/sheets:** Prints multiple views or sheets. Click **Select...** to open the View/Sheet Set dialog box to choose what to include in the print set. You can save these sets by name so that you can more easily print the same group again.

Options

If your printer supports multiple copies, you can specify the number in the *Options* area, as shown in Figure 9–28. You can also reverse the print order or collate your prints. These options are also available in the printer properties.

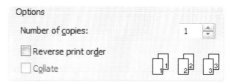

Figure 9–28

Settings

Click **Setup**... to open the Print Setup dialog box, as shown in Figure 9–29. Here, you can specify the *Orientation* and *Zoom* settings, among others. You can also save these settings by name.

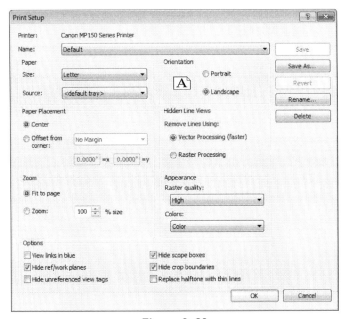

Figure 9–29

- In the *Options* area, specify the types of elements that you want to print or not print. Unless specified, all of the elements in a view or sheet are set to print.

Chapter Review Questions

1. How do you specify the size of a sheet?

   a. In the Sheet Properties, specify the **Sheet Size**.

   b. In the Options Bar, specify the **Sheet Size**.

   c. In the New Sheet dialog box, select a title block to control the Sheet Size.

   d. In the Sheet view, right-click and select **Sheet Size**.

2. How is the title block information filled in as shown in Figure 9–30? (Select all that apply.)

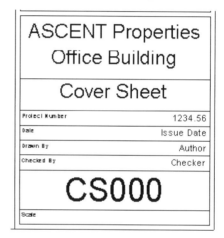

Figure 9–30

   a. Select the title block and select the label that you want to change.

   b. Select the title block and modify it in Properties.

   c. Right-click on the Sheet in the Project Browser and select **Information**.

   d. Some of the information is filled in automatically.

3. On how many sheets can a view be placed?

   a. 1

   b. 2-5

   c. 6+

   d. As many as you want.

4. Which of the following is the best method to use if the size of a view is too large for a sheet, as shown in Figure 9–31?

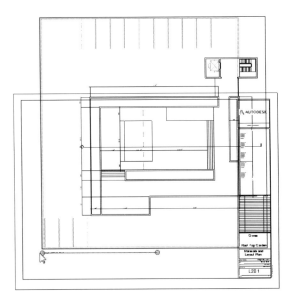

Figure 9–31

a. Delete the view, change the scale and place the view back on the sheet.

b. Activate the view and change the View Scale.

5. How do you set up a view on a sheet that only displays part of a floor plan, as shown in Figure 9–32?

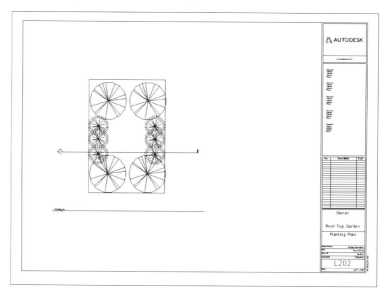

Figure 9–32

a. Drag and drop the view to the sheet and use the crop region to modify it.

b. Activate the view and rescale it.

c. Create a callout view displaying the part that you want to use and place the callout view on the sheet.

d. Open the view in the Project Browser and change the View Scale.

Command Summary

Button	Command	Location
	Activate View	• **Ribbon:** (*select the view*) *Modify | Viewports* tab>Viewport panel
		• **Double-click:** *(in viewport)*
		• **Right-click:** (*on view*) Activate View
	Deactivate View	• **Ribbon:** *View* tab>Sheet Composition panel>expand Viewports
		• **Double-click:** *(on sheet)*
		• **Right-click:** (*on view*) Deactivate View
	Place View	• **Ribbon:** *View* tab>Sheet Composition panel
	Print	• **Ribbon:** *File* tab
	Sheet	• **Ribbon:** *View* tab>Sheet Composition panel

Annotating Construction Documents

When creating construction documents, annotations such as dimensions, detail lines, text, tags, and symbols are required to show the design intent. Annotations can be added to views at any time during the creation of a project. They are also view-specific and only display in the view in which they are added.

Learning Objectives in this Chapter

- Add dimensions to the model as a part of the working drawings.
- Add text to a view and use leaders to create notes pointing to a specific part of the model.
- Draw detail lines to further enhance the documentation view.
- Tag elements in views using different tag types.
- Add view-specific annotation symbols for added clarity.

10.1 Working with Dimensions

You can create permanent dimensions using aligned, linear, angular, radial, diameter, and arc length dimensions. These can be individual or a string of dimensions, as shown in Figure 10–1. With aligned dimensions, you can also dimension entire walls with openings, grid lines, and/or intersecting walls.

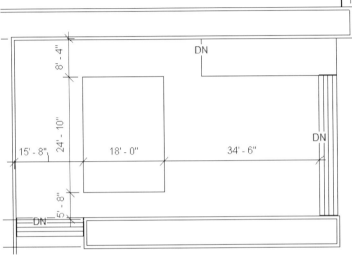

Figure 10–1

- Dimensions referencing model elements must be added to the model in a view. You can dimension on sheets, but only to items added directly on the sheets.

- Dimensions are available in the *Annotate* tab>Dimension panel and the *Modify* tab>Measure panel, as shown in Figure 10–2.

(Aligned) is also located in the Quick Access Toolbar.

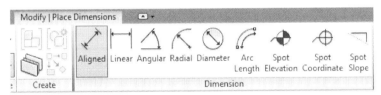

Figure 10–2

How To: Add Aligned Dimensions

1. Start the ✎ (Aligned) command or type **DI.**
2. In the Type Selector, select a dimension style.
3. In the Options Bar, select the location line of the wall to dimension from, as shown in Figure 10–3.

    • This option can be changed as you add dimensions.

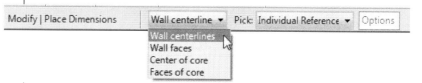

Figure 10–3

4. In the Options Bar, select your preference from the Pick drop-down list:

    • **Individual References:** Select the elements in order (as shown in Figure 10–4) and then click in an empty space to position the dimension string.

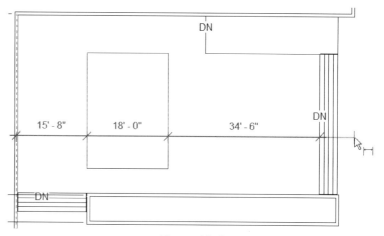

Figure 10–4

*The **Entire Walls** option is most often used in architectural documents.*

    • **Entire Walls:** Select the wall that you want to dimension and then click the cursor to position the dimension string. The openings, intersecting walls, and/or intersecting grids are automatically dimensioned according to the method you set up in the options.

How To: Add Other Types of Dimensions

*When the **Dimension** command is active, the dimension methods are also accessible in the Modify | Place Dimensions tab> Dimension panel.*

1. In the *Annotate* tab>Dimension panel, select a dimension method.

⟋	**Aligned**	Most commonly used dimension type. Select individual elements or entire walls to dimension.
⊢⊣	**Linear**	Used when you need to specify certain points on elements.
△	**Angular**	Used to dimension the angle between two elements.
⟨	**Radial**	Used to dimension the radius of circular elements.
⟨	**Diameter**	Used to dimension the diameter of circular elements.
⟋	**Arc Length**	Used to dimension the length of the arc of circular elements.

2. In the Type Selector, select the dimension type.
3. Follow the prompts for the selected method.

Modifying Dimensions

When you move elements that are dimensioned, the dimensions automatically update. You can also modify dimensions by selecting a dimension or dimension string and making changes, as shown in Figure 10–5.

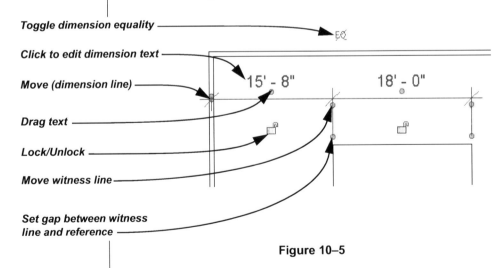

Toggle dimension equality

Click to edit dimension text

Move (dimension line)

Drag text

Lock/Unlock

Move witness line

Set gap between witness line and reference

Figure 10–5

- To move the dimension text, select the **Drag text** control under the text and drag it to a new location. It automatically creates a leader from the dimension line if you drag it away. The style of the leader (arc or line) depends on the dimension style.

- To move the dimension line (the line parallel to the element being dimensioned), simply drag the line to a new location or select the dimension and drag the ✛ (Move) control.

- To change the gap between the witness line and the element being dimensioned, drag the control at the end of the witness line.

- To move the witness line (the line perpendicular to the element being dimensioned) to a different element or face of a wall, use the **Move Witness Line** control in the middle of the witness line. Click repeatedly to cycle through the various options. You can also drag this control to move the witness line to a different element, or right-click on the control and select **Move Witness Line**.

Adding and Deleting Dimensions in a String

- To add a witness line to a string of dimensions, select the dimension and in the *Modify | Dimensions* tab>Witness Lines panel, click (Edit Witness Lines). Select the element(s) that you want to add to the dimension. Click in an empty space to finish.

- To delete a witness line, drag the **Move Witness Line** control to a nearby element. Alternatively, you can hover the cursor over the control, right-click, and select **Delete Witness Line**.

- To delete one dimension in a string and break the string into two separate dimensions, select the string, hover the cursor over the dimension that you want to delete, and press <Tab>. When it highlights (as shown on top in Figure 10–6), select it and press <Delete>. The selected dimension is deleted and the dimension string is separated into two elements, as shown on the bottom in Figure 10–6.

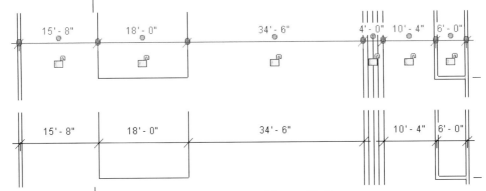

Figure 10–6

Modifying the Dimension Text

Because the Autodesk® Revit® software is parametric, changing the dimension text without changing the elements dimensioned would cause problems throughout the project. These issues could cause problems beyond the model if you use the project model to estimate materials or work with other disciplines.

You can append the text with prefixes and suffixes (as shown in Figure 10–7), which can help you in renovation projects.

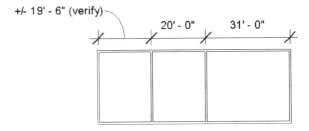

Figure 10–7

Double-click on the dimension text to open the Dimension Text dialog box (shown in Figure 10–8) and make modifications, as required.

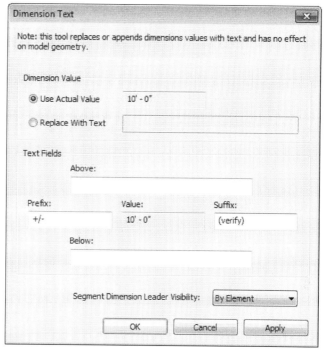

Figure 10–8

Setting Constraints

The three types of constraints that work with dimensions are locks and equal settings (as shown in Figure 10–9), as well as labels.

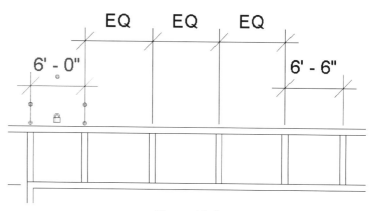

Figure 10–9

Locking Dimensions

When you lock a dimension, the value is set and you cannot make a change between it and the referenced elements. If it is unlocked, you can move it and change its value.

- Note that when you use this and move an element, any elements that are locked to the dimension also move.

Setting Dimensions Equal

For a string of dimensions, select the **EQ** symbol to constrain the elements to be at an equal distance apart. This actually moves the elements that are dimensioned.

- The equality text display can be changed in Properties, as shown in Figure 10–10. The style for each of the display types is set in the dimension type.

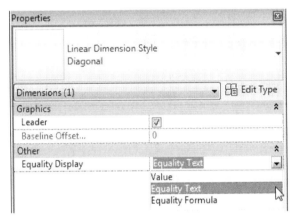

Figure 10–10

Labeling Dimensions

If you have a distance that needs to be repeated multiple times, such as the *Wall to Window* label shown in Figure 10–11, or one where you want to use a formula based on another dimension, you can create and apply a global parameter, also called a label, to the dimension.

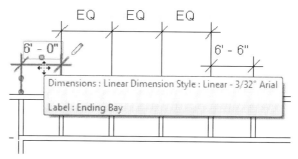

Figure 10–11

- To apply an existing label to a dimension, select the dimension and in the *Modify | Dimension* tab>Label Dimension panel, select the label from the drop-down list, as shown in Figure 10–12.

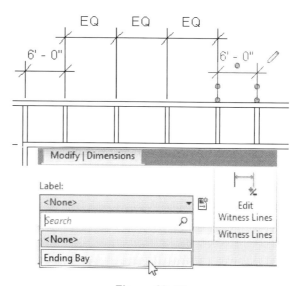

Figure 10–12

How To: Create a Label

1. Select a dimension.
2. In the *Modify | Dimension* tab>Label Dimension panel, click
   🗒 (Create Parameter).
3. In the Global Parameter Properties dialog box, type in a
   Name, as shown in Figure 10–13. Click **OK**.

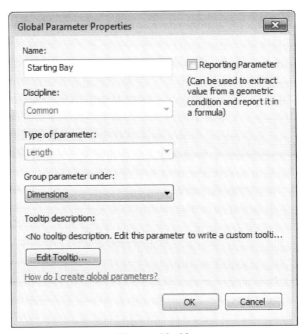

Figure 10–13

4. The label is applied to the dimension.

How To: Edit the Label Information

1. Select a labeled dimension.
2. Click **Global Parameters**, as shown in Figure 10–14.

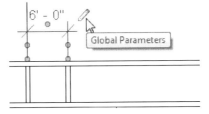

Figure 10–14

3. In the Global Parameters dialog box, in the *Value* column, type the new distance, as shown in Figure 10–15.

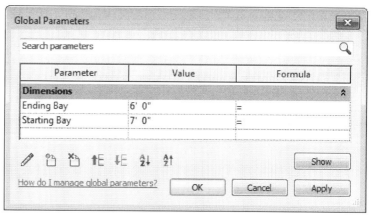

Figure 10–15

4. Click **OK**. The selected dimension and any other dimensions using the same label are updated.

- You can also edit, create, and delete Global Parameters in this dialog box.

Working with Constraints

To find out which elements have constraints applied to them, in the View Control Bar, click ⊡ (Reveal Constraints). Constraints display as shown in Figure 10–16.

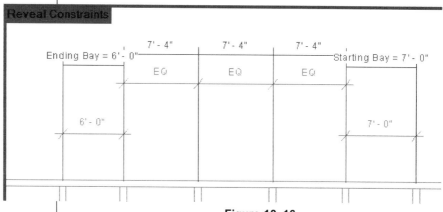

Figure 10–16

- If you try to move the element beyond the appropriate constrains, a warning dialog box displays, as shown in Figure 10–17.

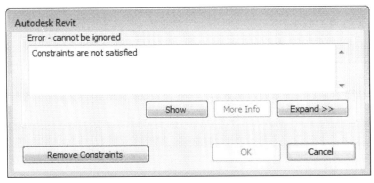

Figure 10–17

- If you delete dimensions that are constrained, a warning dialog box displays, as shown in Figure 10–18. Click **OK** to retain the constraint or **Unconstrain** to remove the constraint.

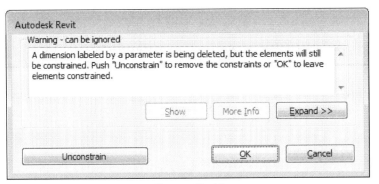

Figure 10–18

Practice 10a | Work with Dimensions

Practice Objectives

- Add detail lines.
- Add dimensions.
- Modify dimensions.

Estimated time for completion: 10 minutes

In this practice, you will draw detail lines used to point out alignments to the building. You will add dimensions based on the alignment lines and other model elements. You will modify dimension text to add a suffix (TYP.) and change a dimension to V.I.F. You will then add a string of dimension set to equal and finally, add dimensions and update the model elements so the correct dimension displays. The final view is shown in Figure 10–19.

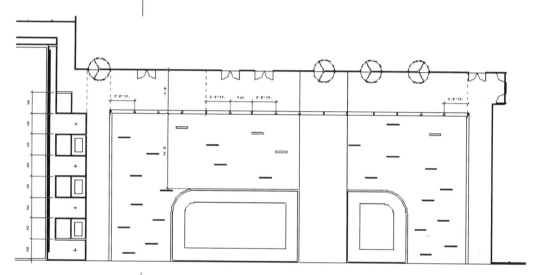

Figure 10–19

Task 1 - Add detail lines to show alignments.

1. Open the project **Urban-Garden-Dimensions.rvt** from the practice files folder.

2. Open the **01 Motor Court-Materials and Layout Plan** view.

3. In the *Annotate* tab>Detail panel, click 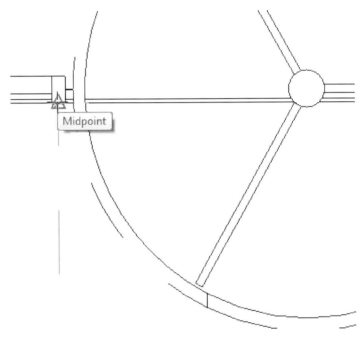 (Detail Line).

4. In the *Modify | Place Detail Lines* tab>Line Style panel, expand the drop-down list and select **Hidden Lines**.

5. In the Draw panel, verify that ⟋ (Line) is selected.

6. Zoom in close on the left revolving door and draw a line from the midpont of the curtain wall mullion, as shown in Figure 10–20.

*Type **SM** to override the default snap so it snaps to the midpoint.*

Figure 10–20

7. Draw another line from the midpoint of the mullion on the other side of the door.

8. Click **Modify**.

9. Zoom out slightly and drag the endline of each line down to the curbs, as shown in Figure 10–21.

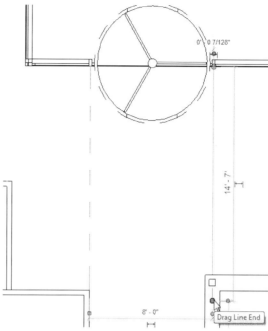

Figure 10–21

10. Select the detail line on the right and copy it 32'-0" to the right. (This lines up with one of the other 8'-0" O.C. mullions in the curtain wall.)

11. Copy it again to the far right where it aligns with mullion next to the double doors, as shown in Figure 10–22.

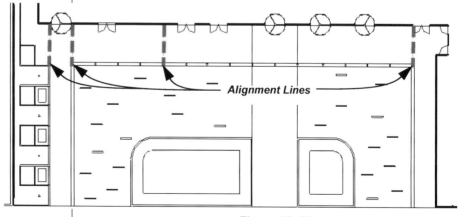

Figure 10–22

12. Save the project.

Task 2 - Add and modify dimensions.

1. In the Quick Access Toolbar, click ⚲ (Aligned).

2. Select the alignment line and then the bollard light (use the internal alignment line that displays at the center line of the bollard) and place the dimension above the light, as shown in Figure 10–23.

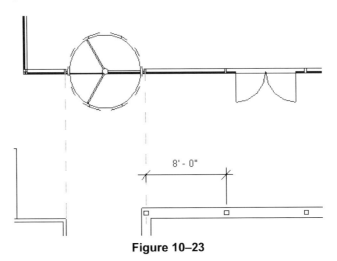

Figure 10–23

3. Add dimensions to the bollards based off of the other alignment lines as shown in Figure 10–24.

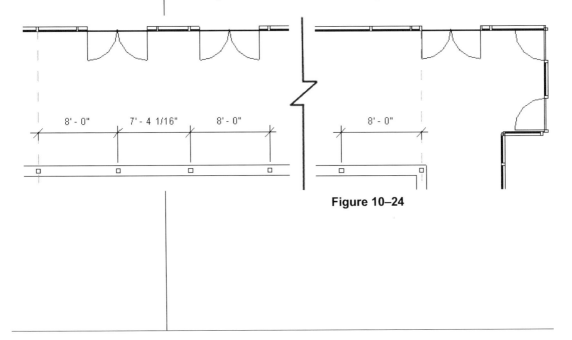

Figure 10–24

4. Select one of the 8'-0" dimensions and then double-click on the dimension text.

5. In the Dimension Text dialog box, type in the *Suffix* **TYP.** as shown in Figure 10–25. Click **OK**.

Remember that you want the model elements to control the actual value. If one is not correct then you need to change the element, not the dimension.

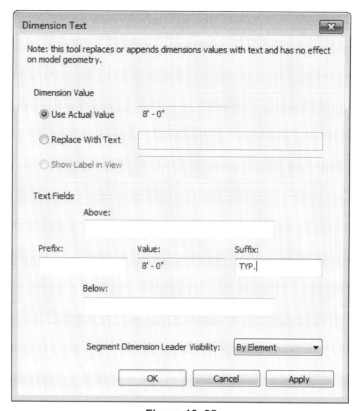

Figure 10–25

6. Repeat the process with the other three 8'-0" dimensions.

In most cases, you will not totally replace dimension text. This is one instance where doing so is OK.

7. Select the 7'-4 1/16" dimension text. In the Dimension Text dialog box, select **Replace with Text** and type in **V.I.F.** (verify in field).

8. Start the **Aligned Dimension** command again.

9. In the Options Bar, in the drop-down list, select **Wall centerline**.

10. Select the center line of each wall of the planting beds and click to place the dimension to the left, as shown in Figure 10–26. Select the EQ control and the dimensions change to EQ, as shown in Figure 10–27.

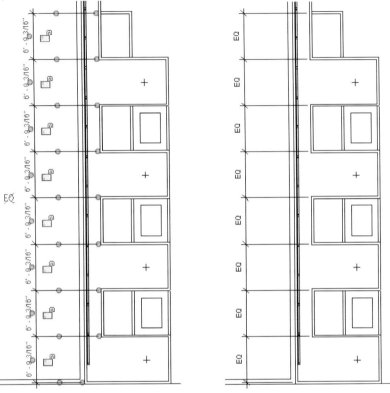

Figure 10–26   **Figure 10–27**

- The planting beds were already created equal distance from each other but if they had not been selecting the EQ control would have moved them equal distance apart.

11. Start the **Aligned Dimension** command again.

12. In the Options Bar, select **Wall faces** and add the dimensions shown in Figure 10–28. The lower dimension was expected to be 24'-0" rather than 24' -1 1/4" which is what displays. Do not modify the dimension.

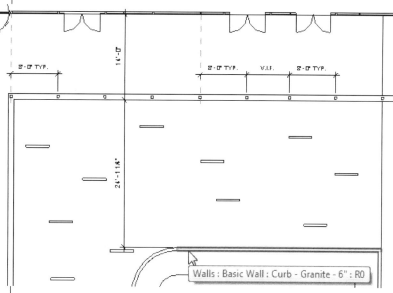

Figure 10–28

13. Select the curb wall shown in Figure 10–28. The dimension text turns blue. Click the text and change it to **24'-0"**. The wall moves and the dimension is updated.

14. The curb wall on the other side also needs to be updated. Start the **Align** command and align the walls as shown in Figure 10–29.

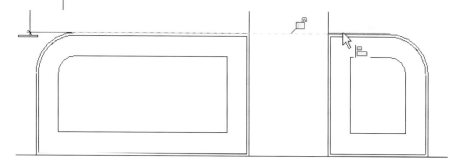

Figure 10–29

15. Save the project.

10.2 Working With Text

The **Text** command enables you to add notes to views or sheets, such as the detail shown in Figure 10–30. The same command is used to create text with or without leaders.

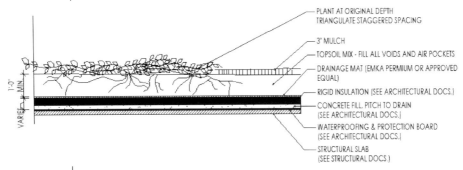

Figure 10–30

The text height is automatically set by the text type in conjunction with the scale of the view (as shown in Figure 10–31, using the same size text type at two different scales as well as tags and a section view marker). Text types display at the specified height, both in the views and on the sheet.

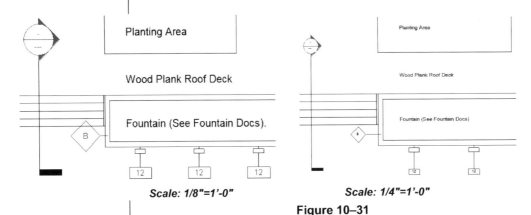

Figure 10–31

How To: Add Text

1. In the Quick Access Toolbar or in the *Annotate* tab>Text panel, click **A** (Text).
2. In the Type Selector, set the text type.

The text type sets the font and height of the text.

3. In the *Modify | Place Text* tab>Leader panel, select the method that you want to use: A (No Leader), ←A (One Segment), ⟋A (Two Segments), or ⟋A (Curved).

4. In the Paragraph panel, set the overall justification for the text and leader, as shown in Figure 10–32.

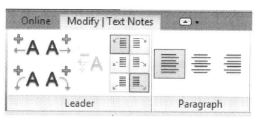

Figure 10–32

Use alignment lines to help you align the text with other text elements.

5. Select the location for the leader and text.

- If **No leader** is selected, select the start point for the text and begin typing.

- If using a leader, the first point places the arrow and you can then select points for the leader. The text starts at the last leader point.

- To set a word wrapping distance, click and drag to set the start and end points of the text.

6. Type the required text. In the *Edit Text* tab, specify additional options for the font and paragraph, as shown in Figure 10–33.

Figure 10–33

7. In the *Edit Text* tab>Edit Text panel, click ☒ (Close) or click outside the text box to complete the text element.

- Pressing <Enter> after a line of text starts a new line of text in the same text window.

How To: Add Text Symbols

New
in 2018

1. Start the **Text** command and click to place the text.
2. As you are typing text and need to insert a symbol, right-click and select **Symbols** from the shortcut menu. Select from the list of commonly used symbols, as shown in Figure 10–34.

Figure 10–34

3. If the symbol you need is not listed, click **Other**.
4. In the Character Map dialog box, click on a symbol and click **Select**, as shown in Figure 10–35.

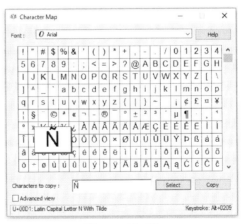

Figure 10–35

5. Click **Copy** to copy the character to the clipboard and paste it into the text box.

- The Font in the Character Map must match the font used by the text type. You cannot use a different font for symbols.

Editing Text

Editing text notes takes place at two levels:

- Modifying the text note, which includes the **Leader** and **Paragraph** styles.

- Editing the text, which includes changes to individual letters, word, and paragraphs in the text note.

Modifying the Text Note

Click once on the text note to modify the text box and leaders using controls (as shown in Figure 10–36) or using the tools in the *Modify | Text Notes* tab.

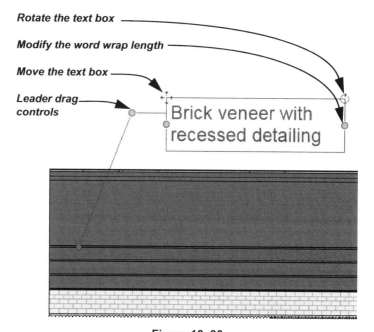

Figure 10–36

How To: Add a Leader to Text Notes

1. Select the text note.
2. In the *Modify | Text Notes* tab>Leader panel, select the direction and justification for the new leader, as shown in Figure 10–37.
3. The leader is applied, as shown in Figure 10–38. Use the drag controls to place the arrow, as required.

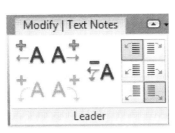

Modify | Text Notes
Leader

Figure 10–37

Brick veneer with
recessed detailing
Drag

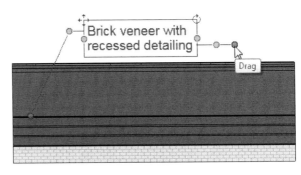

Figure 10–38

- You can remove leaders by clicking (Remove Last Leader).

Editing the Text

The *Edit Text* tab enables you to make various customizations. These include modifying the font of selected words as well as creating bulleted and numbered lists, as shown in Figure 10–39.

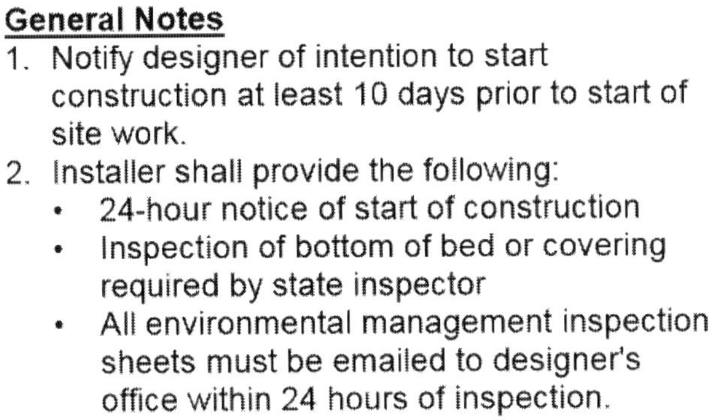

General Notes
1. Notify designer of intention to start construction at least 10 days prior to start of site work.
2. Installer shall provide the following:
• 24-hour notice of start of construction
• Inspection of bottom of bed or covering required by state inspector
• All environmental management inspection sheets must be emailed to designer's office within 24 hours of inspection.

Figure 10–39

- You can **Cut**, **Copy**, and **Paste** text using the clipboard. For example, you can copy text from a document and then paste it into the text editor in Revit.

- To help you see the text better as you are modifying it, in the *Edit Text* tab, expand the Edit Text panel and select one or both of the options, as shown in Figure 10–40.

Figure 10–40

How To: Modify the Font

1. Select Individual letters or words.
2. Click on the font modification that you want to include:

B (Bold)	X$_2$ (Subscript)
I (Italic)	X^2 (Superscript)
U̲ (Underline)	ᵃA (All Caps)

- When pasting text from a document outside of Autodesk Revit the font modifications such as **Bold** and *Italic* are retained.

How To: Create Lists

1. In Edit Text mode, place the cursor in the line where you want to add to a list.
2. In the *Edit Text* tab>Paragraph panel, click the type of list that you want to create:

(Bullets)	(Uppercase Letters)
(Numbers)	(Lowercase Letters)

The indent distance is setup by the Text Type Tab Size.

3. As you type, press <Enter> and the next line in the list is incremented.

4. To include sub-lists, at the beginning of the next line, click

    (Increase Indent). This indents the line and applies the next level of lists, as shown in Figure 10–41.

4. The applicant shall be responsible:
   A. First Indent
      a. Second Indent
         • Third Indent

Figure 10–41

- You can change the type of list after you have applied the first increment. For example, you might want to use a list of bullets instead of letters, as shown in Figure 10–42.

5. Click (Decrease Indent) to return to the previous list style.

- Press <Shift>+<Enter> to create a blank line in a numbered list.

- To create columns or other separate text boxes that build on a numbering system (as shown in Figure 10–42), create the second text box and list. Then, place the cursor on one of the lines and in the Paragraph panel, click (Increment List Value) until the list matches the next number in the sequence.

General Notes
1. Notify designer of intention to start construction at least 10 days prior to start of site work.
2. Installer shall provide the following:
   - 24-hour notice of start of construction
   - Inspection of bottom of bed or covering required by state inspector
   - All environmental management inspection sheets must be emailed to designer's office within 24 hours of inspection.
3. Site layout and required inspections to be made by designer:
   - Foundations and OWTS location and elevation
   - Inspection of OWTS bottom of trench
4. The applicant shall be responsible for:
   - New Application for redesign.
   - As-built location plans

General Notes (cont.)
5. The installer/applicant shall provide the designer with materials sheets for all construction materiasl prior to designer issuing certificate of construction.
6. The applicant shall furnish the original application to the installer prior to start of constuction

— *List Incremented*

Figure 10–42

- Click (Decrement List Value) to move back a number.

Hint: Model Text

Model text is different from annotation text. It is designed to create full-size text on the model itself. For example, you would use model text to create a sign on a door, as shown in Figure 10–43. One model text type is included with the default template. You can create other types, as required.

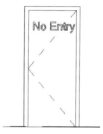

Figure 10–43

- Model text is added from the *Architecture* tab>Model panel, by clicking (Model Text).

Spell Checking

The Spelling dialog box displays any misspelled words in context and provides several options for changing them, as shown in Figure 10–44.

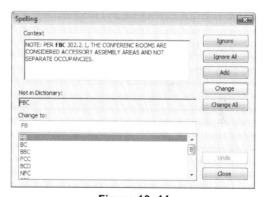

Figure 10–44

- To spell check all text in a view, in the *Annotate* tab>Text panel, click (Spelling) or press <F7>. As with other spell checkers, you can **Ignore**, **Add**, or **Change** the word.

- You can also check the spelling in selected text. With text selected, in the *Modify | Text Notes* tab>Tools panel, click (Check Spelling).

Practice 10b | Work with Text

Practice Objectives

- Add text notes.
- Add leaders to text notes.
- Copy and paste text from a document.
- Modify the numbering of a list.

Estimated time for completion: 15 minutes

In this practice, you will add text notes, some with leaders and some without, as shown in Figure 10–45. You will rotate the text and add leaders. You will add planting notes to a sheet by copying and pasting text from a document and then modifying the numbering of the list.

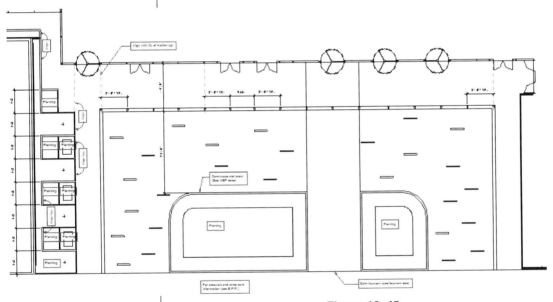

Figure 10–45

Task 1 - Add text notes with leaders to a view.

1. Open the project **Urban-Garden-Text.rvt** from the practice files folder.

2. Open the **01 Motor Court-Materials and Layout Plan** view.

3. In the Quick Access Toolbar, click **A** (Text).

4. In the Type Selector, select **Text: 3/32" Arial**.

5. In the planting area, pick two points to locate the text, as shown in Figure 10–46.

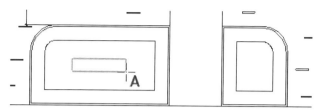

Figure 10–46

6. Type the word **Planting**. (It will be very small.)

7. Move the cursor over to the other planting bed and ensure that the text is aligned with the first text. Click to place the text and type **Planting** again.

8. In the *Modify | Place Text* tab>Edit Text panel, click ☒ (Close).

9. Note that you are still in the **Place Text** command, but you now have access to the leader options. In the Leader panel, click ⦫A (Two Segments).

10. Point to the alignment line near the revolving door to place the arrow location. Then click two points to place the horizontal segment. Type **Align with CL of mullion typ**., as shown in Figure 10–47.

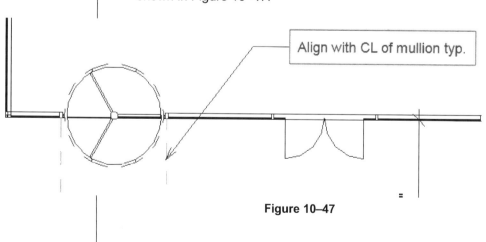

Align with CL of mullion typ.

Figure 10–47

11. Add the additional text shown in Figure 10–48. (The scale of this view has been modified so the text is easier to read.)

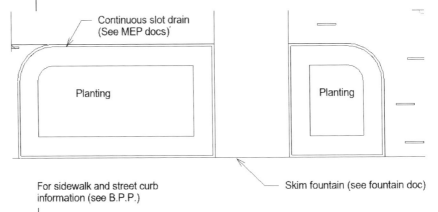

Figure 10–48

12. Copy the text "Planting" to the other planting areas.

Task 2 - Rotate text and add leaders.

1. Add text and use the **Rotate** control to orient it, as shown in Figure 10–49.

2. With the text still selected, in the *Modify | Text Notes* tab> Leader panel, click ⁺A (Add Left Side Arc Leader) and A⁺ (Add Right Side Arc Leader) to add leaders, as shown in Figure 10–50.

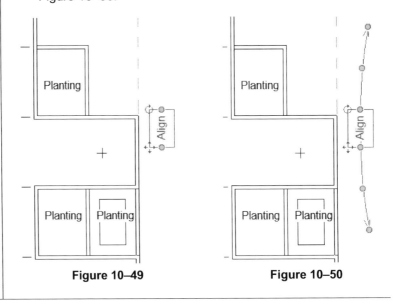

Figure 10–49   **Figure 10–50**

3. Modify the arc leaders so that they point to the alignment line and the curb.

4. Copy the text and leaders to other places where it is required, similar to that shown in Figure 10–51.

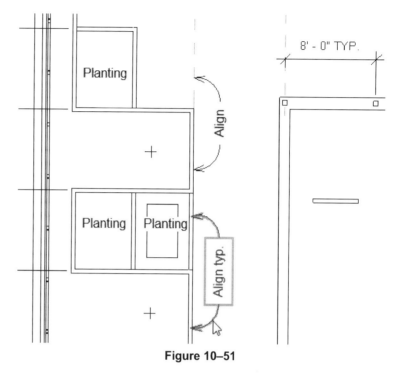

Figure 10–51

5. Save the project.

Task 3 - Create Text with a List.

---

1. In a text editor (such as NotePad or Microsoft Word), navigate to the practice files folder and open either **Planting Notes.docx** or **Planting Notes.txt**.

2. Copy the entire contents of the file to the clipboard.

3. In the Autodesk Revit software, open the Sheet **L301 - Motor Court Planting Plan**.

4. Start the **Text** command.

5. Verify that no leader is selected, set the text type to **3/32"
   Arial** and draw a text box similar to the one shown in
   Figure 10–52.

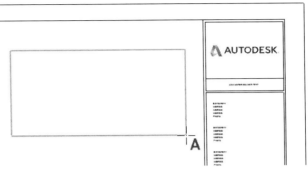

Figure 10–52

6. In the Edit Text dialog box> Clipboard panel, click
   (Paste).

7. Remain in **Edit Text** mode and zoom in on the text box.Note
   that there are numbered lists in the text but they are not
   entirely correct.

8. Select all of the text and in the *Edit Text* tab>Paragraph
   panel, click (List: Numbers).

9. The paragraphs are recognized and numbered but the
   existing numbers are still there.

10. Zoom in and remove the additional numbers, as shown in
    Figure 10–53.

1. Any plant substitutions must be approved by landscape architect prior to purchase.
2. Contractor shall implement the planting plan as shown. Plants shall be located as close as possible to layout provided or as directed in the field by the landscape architect.
3. Planting beds shall receive a layer of bark chip mulch, as indicated on the planting details.
4. Material will be inspected and approved at place of growth by the landscape architect. However, plant material which has become damaged or diseased or which is unacceptable to the landscape architect may be rejected upon delivery to the site
5. Should there be any discrepancies between the quantities and/or sized called for on the plant list and those indicated on the plan, the greater quantity shall govern.
6. At all times, the site shall be kept neat and free of debris left from the planting operation.
7. All plants in the same planting area shall be placed and planted at the same time. If because of delivery schedule, any plants remain on the site for more than 24 hours, shall be heeled-in on site to maintain their health and vitality. Plants shall be otherwise protected and maintained, including but not limited to water and shade. Any plants deemed not in satisfactory health or condition at the time of planting shall be replaced at the contractor's expense.
8. All plant material to be vigorous, and free of injury or defects. All plant material to be true representatives of their species.
9. All plant tags must remain on the plant material until the landscape architect reviews the layout and approves quantities.
10. Discrepancies in plant size, quantity, or selection must be brought to the attention of the landscape architect by the contractor prior to bid.

Figure 10–53

11. At the beginning of the list, add the text **Planting Notes**. Make it bold and underlined, as shown in Figure 10–54.

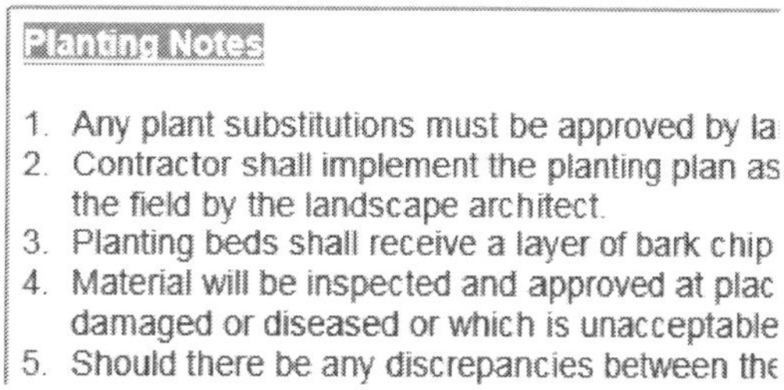

Planting Notes

1. Any plant substitutions must be approved by la
2. Contractor shall implement the planting plan as the field by the landscape architect.
3. Planting beds shall receive a layer of bark chip
4. Material will be inspected and approved at plac damaged or diseased or which is unacceptable
5. Should there be any discrepancies between the

Figure 10–54

12. Click outside the text box and use the controls if required, to relocate or resize the text note.

13. Zoom out to see the full sheet.

14. Save the project.

10.3 Adding Tags and Symbols

Tags identify elements that are listed in schedules. Tags can be added at any time to specific views, as required. Many types of tags are available in the Autodesk Revit software, such as wall tag, plant tags and floor tags, as shown in Figure 10–55. Symbols are view-specific annotation elements that are not connected with model elements and are used for items such as the centerline symbol and north arrows.

Additional tags are stored in the Library in the Annotations folder.

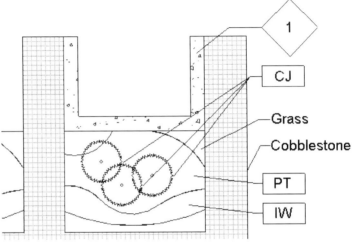

Figure 10–55

*   The **Tag by Category** command works for most elements, except for a few that have separate commands.

*   Tags can be letters, numbers, or a combination of the two.

You can place three types of tags:

*   (Tag by Category): Tags according to the category of the element. It places door tags on doors and wall tags on walls.

*   (Multi-Category): Tags elements belonging to multiple categories. The tags display information from parameters that they have in common.

*   (Material): Tags that display the type of material. They are typically used in detailing.

How To: Add Tags

1. In the *Annotate* tab>Tag panel, click  (Tag by Category), (Multi-Category), or (Material Tag), depending on the type of tag you want to place.
2. In the Options Bar, set the options as required, as shown in Figure 10–56.

| Modify | Tag | Horizontal ▼ | Tags... | ☑ Leader | Attached End ▼ | ↦ 1/2" |

Figure 10–56

3. Select the element that you want to tag. If a tag for the selected element is not loaded, you are prompted to load it from the Library.

Tag Options

*   You can set tag options for leaders and tag rotation, as shown in Figure 10–57. You can also press <Spacebar> to toggle the orientation while placing or modifying the tag.

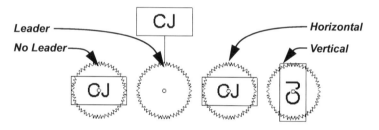

Figure 10–57

*   Leaders can have an **Attached End** or a **Free End**, as shown in Figure 10–58. The attached end must be connected to the element being tagged. A free end has an additional drag control where the leader touches the element.

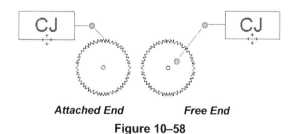

Figure 10–58

- If you change between **Attached End** and **Free End**, the tag does not move and the leader does not change location.

- The **Length** option specifies the length of the leader in plotting units. It is grayed out if **Leader** is not selected or if a **Free End** leader is defined.

- If a tag is not loaded, a warning box opens as shown in Figure 10–59. Click **Yes** to open the Load Family dialog box in which you can select the appropriate tag.

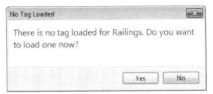

Figure 10–59

- Tags can be pinned. If you move the element, the tag stays in place. This is primarily used when tags have leaders, as shown in Figure 10–60.

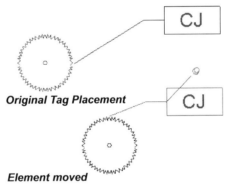

Figure 10–60

- Most landscape related tags are type tags. To modify a type tag, you can either double-click directly on the number in the tag and modify it (as shown in Figure 10–61), or select the element and in Properties, click ⊞ (Edit Type). In the Type Properties dialog box, in the *Identity Data* area, modify the *Type Mark*, as shown in Figure 10–62. All instances of this element then update.

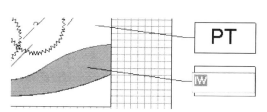

Figure 10–61

Parameter	Value	=
Identity Data		≫
Type Image		
Keynote		
Model		
Manufacturer		
Type Comments		
URL		
Description		
Assembly Description	Floor Construction	
Assembly Code	B1010	
Type Mark	TW	
Cost		

Figure 10–62

- When you change a type tag, an alert box opens to warn you that changing a type parameter affects other elements. If you want this tag to modify all other elements of this type, click **Yes**.

- If a type tag displays with a question mark, it means that no Type Mark has been assigned yet.

Using Symbols

Symbols are 2D elements that only display in one view, while components can be in 3D and display in many views.

Many of the annotations used in working drawings are frequently repeated. Several of them have been saved as symbols in the Autodesk Revit software, such as the North Arrow, Center Line, and Graphic Scale annotations, as shown in Figure 10–63.

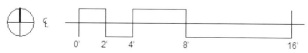

Figure 10–63

- You can also create or load custom annotation symbols.

How To: Place a Symbol

1. In the *Annotate* tab>Symbol panel, click ⬚ (Symbol).
2. In the Type Selector, select the symbol that you want to use.
3. In the *Modify | Place Symbol* tab>Mode panel, click ⬚ (Load Family) if you want to load other symbols.
4. In the Options Bar (shown in Figure 10–64), set the *Number of Leaders* and select **Rotate after placement** if you want to rotate the symbol as you insert it.

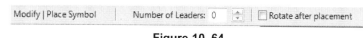

Figure 10–64

5. Place the symbol in the view. Rotate it if you selected the **Rotate after placement** option. If you specified leaders, use the controls to move them into place.

- In the *Annotate* tab>Symbol panel, click 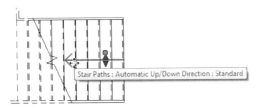 (Stair Path) to label the slope direction and walk line of a stair, as shown in Figure 10–65.

Figure 10–65

How To: Add Multiple Tags

Enhanced in 2018

*To tag only some elements, select them before starting this command. In the Tag All Not Tagged dialog box, select **Only selected objects in current view**.*

1. In the *Annotate* tab>Tag panel, click (Tag All).
2. In the Tag All Not Tagged dialog box (shown in Figure 10–66), select the checkbox beside one or more categories to tag. Selecting the checkbox beside the *Category* column heading selects all of the tags.

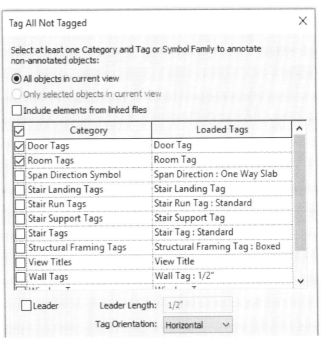

Figure 10–66

3. Set the *Leader* and *Tag Orientation*, as required.
4. Click **Apply** to apply the tags and stay in the dialog box. Click **OK** to apply the tags and close the dialog box.

- When you select a tag, the properties of that tag display. To display the properties of the tagged element, in the

  Modify | <contextual> tab>Host panel click  (Select Host).

- To have one tag with multiple leaders place all the tags and then move the tag on top of each other so they all overlap.

How To: Load Tags and Symbols

1. In the *Annotate* tab, expand the Tag panel and click

   (Loaded Tags And Symbols) or, when a Tag command is active, in the Options Bar, click **Tags...**.
2. In the Loaded Tags And Symbols dialog box (shown in Figure 10–67), click **Load Family...**.

Category	Loaded Tags	Loaded Symbols
Floors	Floor Tag : Standard	Span Direction : One
Furniture		
Furniture Syste...		
Generic Models		
Lighting Fixtures		
Mass		
Mass Floor		
Mechanical Eq...		
Parking		
Parts		
Planting	Planting Tag : Boxed	
Plumbing Fixt...		

Loaded Tags And Symbols

Select an available Tag or Symbol Family for each Family Category listed
Note: Multi-Category Tag Families are not shown below.

Filter list: Architecture ▼   Load Family...

OK   Cancel   Help

Figure 10–67

3. In the Load Family dialog box, navigate to the appropriate *Annotations* folder, select the tag(s) required and click **Open**.
4. The tag is added to the category in the dialog box. Click **OK**.

Tagging in 3D Views

You can add tags (and some dimensions) to 3D views (as shown in Figure 10–68), as long as the views are locked first. Note that you can only add tags in isometric views.

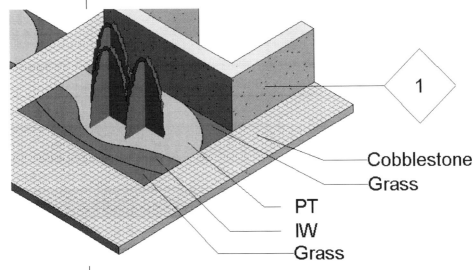

Figure 10–68

- Locked views can be used with perspective views. This enables you to create the view as required and then save it so the view direction cannot be modified.

How To: Lock a 3D View

1. Open a 3D view and set it up as required to display.

2. In the View Control Bar, expand 🏠 (Unlocked 3D View) and click 🏠 (Save Orientation and Lock View).

- If you are using the default 3D view and it has not been saved, you are prompted to name and save the view first.

- To modify the orientation of the view, expand 🏠 (Locked 3D View) and click 🏠 (Unlock View). This also removes any tags applied.

- To return to the previous locked view, expand 🏠 (Unlocked 3D View) and click 🏠 (Restore Orientation and Lock View).

Practice 10c | Add Tags and Symbols

Practice Objectives

- Add tags to a model.
- Set the Type Mark parameter for tags.
- Add symbols
- Place Spot Coordinates
- Load tags.

Estimated time for completion: 15 minutes

In this practice you will add tags to plans, updating the Type Mark through the tag and in Type Properties so the correct value displays. You will add centerline symbols and spot coordinates, as shown in Figure 10–69. You will tag plant components and load planting area tags.

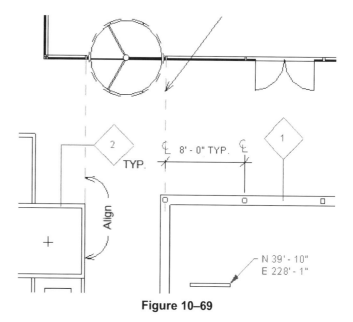

Figure 10–69

Task 1 - Add tags and update Type Properties.

1. Open the project **Urban Garden-Tags.rvt** from the practice files folder.

2. Open the **Floor Plans: 01 Motor Court - Materials and Layout Plan** view.

3. Select one of the floors. In the View Control Bar, click

   (Temporary Hide/Isolate) and select **Hide Category**. This makes it easier to tag the wall elements without accidentally tagging the floors.

4. In the *Annotate* tab>Tag panel, click (Tag by Category). In the Options Bar, select **Leader** and verify that the **Attached End** option is selected.

5. Select one of the curb walls.

6. The tag comes in with a question mark (as shown in Figure 10–70) because the wall does not have a *Type Mark* set yet. Click on the **?** in the tag and change the tag number to **1** and press <Enter>.

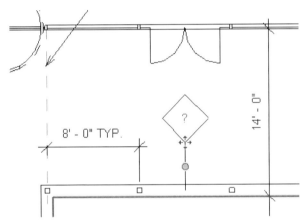

Figure 10–70

7. When alerted that you are changing a type parameter, click **Yes** to continue.

8. While still in the **Tag** command, tag one of the other curb walls. This time, the tag number **1** comes in automatically as it is the same wall type as the first one.

9. Tag one of the planter walls. This wall also comes in with a question mark.

10. Click (Modify).

11. Select one of the planter walls (**Basic Wall: Curb - Granite - 4"**).

12. In Properties, click (Edit Type).

13. In the Type Properties dialog box, in *Identity Data* area, set *Type Mark* to **2**, as shown in Figure 10–71. Click **OK**.

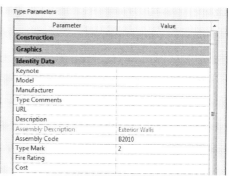

Figure 10–71

14. Select one of the curb walls around the large planting area and set the *Type Mark* to **3**.

15. Use 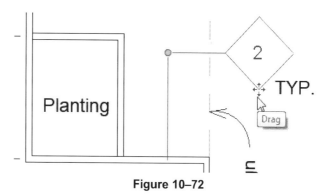 (Tag By Category) to tag one of each of the curb wall but not all of the planter walls. The Type Mark displays as set in the Type Properties.

16. Click **Modify** and select any tags that need to be moved. Then, use the drag controls to reposition them as required, as shown in Figure 10–72.

17. For the tag labeled **2**, add text beside it, as shown on the right in Figure 10–72.

Figure 10–72

18. Zoom out to display the entire floor plan.

19. In the View Control Bar, click (Temporary Hide/Isolate) and select **Reset Temporary Hide/Isolate**.

20. Save the project.

Task 2 - Add Symbols and Spot Coordinates.

1. In the *Annotate* tab>Symbol panel, click ⊞ (Symbol).

2. In the Type Selector, select **Centerline**.

3. Add the symbol over the end of the dimension, as shown in Figure 10–73.

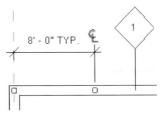

Figure 10–73

4. Copy or add other Centerline symbols to the related dimensions.

5. In the *Annotate* tab>Dimension panel, click ⊕ (Spot Coordinate).

6. In the Type Selector, select **Spot Coordinates: No Symbol**.

7. Select the upper right corner of one of the in-ground light fixtures and then place the leader and text as shown in Figure 10–74.

Figure 10–74

8. Continue placing spot coordinates at the same point on the rest of the lighting fixtures.

9. Open the sheet **L101- Motor Court Materials & Layout Plan**. All of the annotation added to this view displays on the sheet as shown in Figure 10–75.

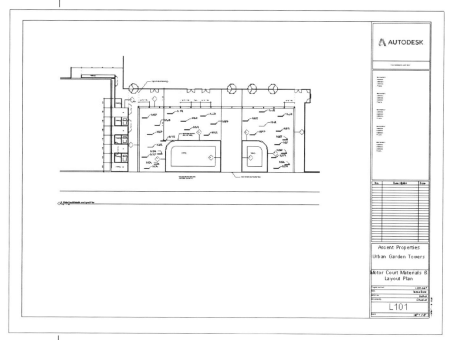

Figure 10–75

10. Open the sheet **L301 - Motor Court Planting Plan**. The annotation does not show in this view.

11. Save the project.

Task 3 - Add and modify Planting Tags.

1. Open the **Floor Plans: 01 Motor Court - Planting Plan** view.

2. In the *Annotate* tab>Tag panel, click (Tag by Category). In the Options Bar, select **Leader** and verify that the **Attached End** option is selected.

3. Select one of the trees. A warning displays saying that no planting tag is available in the project. Click **Yes** to load one.

4. In the Load Family dialog box, navigate to the *Annotation> Civil* folder, select **Planting Tag.rfa**, and click **Open**.

5. Select the tree again to place the tag. You can see that it is not fitting near the tree, as shown in Figure 10–76.

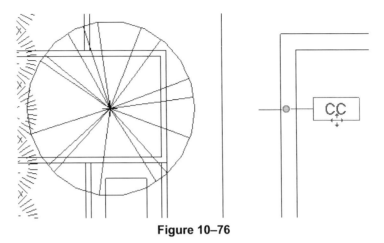

Figure 10–76

6. Click **Modify** and select the tag.

7. In the Options Bar, change *Attached End* to **Free End**.

8. Use the drag controls to place the end of the tag at the trunk of the tree.

9. Add text behind the tag, as shown in Figure 10–77

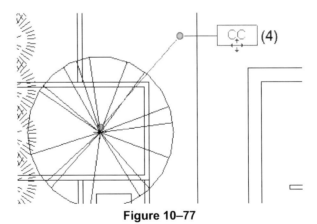

Figure 10–77

- Adding the number of plantings to a tag at this time requires advanced customization to Autodesk Revit.

10. Start the **Tag by Category** command again and in the Options Bar, change *Attached End* to **Free End**.

11. Tag the boxwood on the edge of the sidewalk and add text behind it for the number of boxwoods, as shown in Figure 10–78

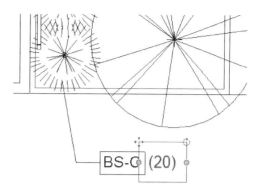

Figure 10–78

12. Tag one of the Bamboo plantings. This component does not have a type mark applied to it. Click on the **?** and change it to **Bamboo**. (It will not fit in the box but this will be updated later to the correct key when the exact type of bamboo is selected.)

13. Save the project.

Task 4 - Tag Planting Areas.

1. It is not necessary for the floor-based lighting fixtures to be showing in this view, but the floor element category does need to show so you can tag the planting areas. Select the cobblestone floor with lights, then right-click and select **Hide in View>Elements**. Only the selected floor is hidden.

2. Start the **Tag by Component** command again and place a tag on one of the planting areas (floors). A different type of tag that with the name of the type displays by default, as shown in Figure 10–79.

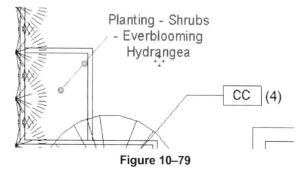

Figure 10–79

3. In the *Annotate* tab>Tag panel, expand the title and select
 (Loaded Tags and Symbols).

4. In the Loaded Tags and Symbols dialog box, note that the *Loaded Tag for Floors* is set to **Floor Tag: Standard**.

5. Click **Load Family...**.

6. In the Load Family dialog box, navigate to the practice files folder, select **Planting Area Tag.rfa**, and click **OK**. (This is a floor tag that has been optimized to work with the planting areas in this project.)

7. Select the existing **Planting- Shrubs** tag and in the Type Selector, select **Planting Area Tag: Boxed**. The tag updates to show the Type Mark of the tag (as shown in Figure 10–80), which is based on the Botanical Name of the plant type.

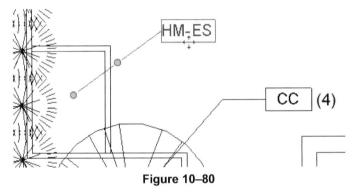

Figure 10–80

8. Tag the other planting areas. The information about how many plants are in each planting area will be supplied in the schedules.

9. Zoom out to see the full view.

10. Return to the sheet **L301 - Motor Court Planting Plan**. The planting tags now show in this view.

11. Save the project.

Chapter Review Questions

1. How do you update a dimension when a wall is moved, as shown in Figure 10–81?

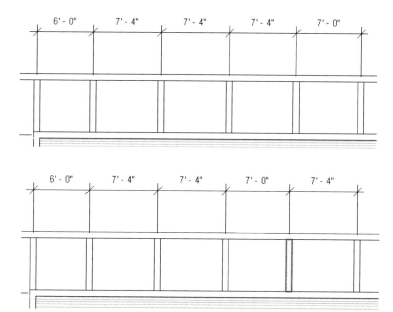

Figure 10–81

a. Edit the dimension and move it over.

b. Select the dimension and click **Update** in the Options Bar.

c. The dimension automatically updates.

d. Delete the existing dimension and add a new one.

2. When you edit text, how many leaders can be added using the leader tools shown in Figure 10–82?

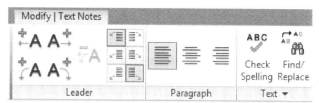

Figure 10–82

a. One

b. One on each end of the text.

c. As many as you want at each end of the text.

3. Detail Lines created in one view also display in the related view.

   a. True

   b. False

4. Which of the following describes the difference between a symbol and a component?

   a. Symbols are 3D and only display in one view. Components are 2D and display in many views.

   b. Symbols are 2D and only display in one view. Components are 3D and display in many views.

   c. Symbols are 2D and display in many views. Components are 3D and only display in one view.

   d. Symbols are 3D and display in many views. Components are 2D and only display in one view.

Command Summary

Button	Command	Location
Dimensions		
	Aligned (Dimension)	• **Ribbon:** *Annotate* tab>Dimension panel or *Modify* tab>Measure panel, expanded drop-down list • **Quick Access Toolbar** • **Shortcut:** DI
	Angular (Dimension)	• **Ribbon:** *Annotate* tab>Dimension panel or *Modify* tab>Measure panel, expanded drop-down list
	Arc Length (Dimension)	• **Ribbon:** *Annotate* tab>Dimension panel or *Modify* tab>Measure panel, expanded drop-down list
	Diameter (Dimension)	• **Ribbon:** *Annotate* tab>Dimension panel or *Modify* tab>Measure panel, expanded drop-down list
	Linear (Dimension)	• **Ribbon:** *Annotate* tab>Dimension panel or *Modify* tab>Measure panel, expanded drop-down list
	Radial (Dimension)	• **Ribbon:** *Annotate* tab>Dimension panel or *Modify* tab>Measure panel, expanded drop-down list
Other Annotations		
	Detail Line	• **Ribbon:** *Annotate* tab>Detail panel • **Shortcut:** DL
	Material Tag	• **Ribbon:** *Annotate* tab>Tag panel
	Multi-Category	• **Ribbon:** *Annotate* tab>Tag panel
	Stair Path	• **Ribbon:** *Annotate* tab>Symbol panel
	Symbol	• **Ribbon:** *Annotate* tab>Symbol panel
	Tag All Not Tagged	• **Ribbon:** *Annotate* tab>Tag panel
	Tag by Category	• **Ribbon:** *Annotate* tab>Tag panel • **Shortcut:** TG
	Text	• **Ribbon:** *Annotate* tab>Text panel • **Shortcut:** TX

Working with Schedules and Legends

Schedules are a critical component of construction documents and a great way to analyze the design model. Information stored in model elements is automatically extracted to schedules and updates when the elements are changed. Schedules can include data from both instance and type properties. Legends are annotation views that provide a place to document any symbols that are used in a project as well as create content required on multiple sheets, such as key plans.

Learning Objectives in this Chapter

- Modify schedule content including the instance and type properties of related elements.
- Add schedules to sheets as part of the construction documents.
- Create legend views and populate them with symbols of elements in the project.

11.1 Working with Schedules

Schedules extract information from a project and display it in table form. Each schedule is stored as a separate view and can be placed on sheets, as shown in Figure 11–1. Any changes you make to the project elements that affect the schedules are automatically updated in both views and sheets.

Schedules are typically created in template files. Check your company standards for more information.

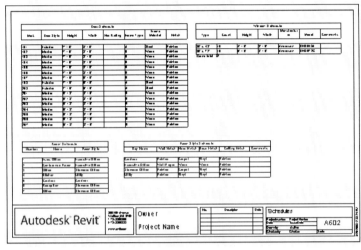

Figure 11–1

- The examples used in this learning guide include custom parameters for planting area floor types (as shown in Figure 11–2) and planting components. These parameters are then used to create custom schedules that show the information required by landscape designers.

Creating parameters, schedules, floor types, families, and templates is covered in the Autodesk Revit BIM Management: Template and Family Creation learning guide, by ASCENT - Center for Technical Knowledge.

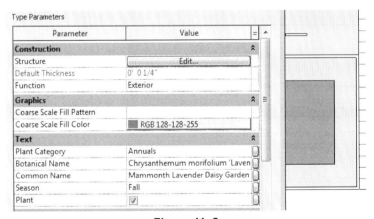

Figure 11–2

How To: Work with Schedules

1. In the Project Browser, expand the *Schedules/Quantities* area (as shown in Figure 11–3) and double-click on the schedule that you want to open.

Figure 11–3

2. Schedules are automatically filled out with the information stored in the instance and type parameters of related elements that are added to the model.
3. Fill out additional information in either the schedule or Properties.
4. Drag and drop the schedule onto a sheet.

Modifying Schedules

Information in schedules is bi-directional:

- If you make changes to elements, the schedule automatically updates.

- If you change information in the cells of the schedule, it automatically updates the elements in the project.

Hint: Key Schedules

A *key schedule* lists type information that is not automatically included in an element. The practice files included in this learning guide contain a key schedule, as shown in Figure 11–4. This enables you to assign a *Spacing ID* that can be used to calculate the number of plants in a planting area element.

			<_PLANT MATERIAL SPACING>			
A	B	C	D	E	F	G
SPACING ID	SPACING (IN)	SQ.FT./PLANT	PLANTS/SQ.FT.	SPACING (CM)	SQ.M/PLANT	PLANTS/SQ.M
6	6"	0.217 SF	4.608 SF	15.0	0.0201 m²	49.7164 m²
6 Bulb/SF		0.155 SF	0.000 SF			
9	9"	0.487 SF	2.053 SF	22.0	0.0453 m²	22.0962 m²
12	12"	0.866 SF	1.155 SF	30.0	0.0805 m²	12.4291 m²
18	18"	1.949 SF	0.513 SF	45.0	0.1810 m²	5.5248 m²
24	24"	3.464 SF	0.289 SF	60.0	0.3218 m²	3.1073 m²
30	30"	5.413 SF	0.185 SF	75.0	0.5029 m²	1.9886 m²
36	36"	7.794 SF	0.125 SF	90.0	0.7241 m²	1.3810 m²
42	42"	10.609 SF	0.094 SF	100.0	0.9856 m²	1.0146 m²

Figure 11–4

- Fields in key styles are typically controlled by instance parameters rather than by type parameters.

- Typically, you modify the elements, so in this case, you do not need to touch the key schedule at all.

How To: Modify Schedule Cells

1. Open the schedule view.
2. Select the cell that you want to change. Some cells have drop-down lists, as shown in Figure 11–5. Others have edit fields.

If you change a type parameter in the schedule, it applies to all elements of that type. If you change an instance parameter, it only applies to that one element.

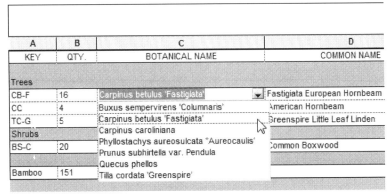

Figure 11–5

3. Add the new information. The change is reflected in the schedule, on the sheet, and in the elements of the project.

- If you change a type parameter, an alert box opens as shown in Figure 11–6.

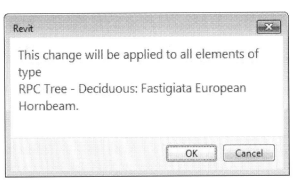

Figure 11–6

- When you select an element in a schedule, in the *Modify Schedule/Quantities* tab>Element panel, you can click

   (Highlight in Model). This opens a close-up view of the element with the Show Element(s) in View dialog box, as shown in Figure 11–7. Click **Show** to display more views of the element. Click **Close** to finish the command.

Figure 11-7

Hint: Basic Schedule Modification

Most schedules are established in template files so the general user does not need to know all the ends and outs of creating schedules. However, it helps to know some basics. Schedule Properties include access to each tab in the Schedule Properties dialog box, as shown in Figure 11-8.

Figure 11-8

One example is the *Filter* tab, where you can set up filters so that only elements meeting specific criteria are included in the schedule. For example, you might only want to show information for one level, as shown in Figure 11-9. You can create filters for up to eight values. All values must be satisfied for the elements to display.

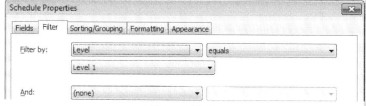

Figure 11-9

• The parameter that you want to use as a filter must be included in the schedule. You can hide the parameter once you have completed the schedule, if required.

Modifying a Schedule on a Sheet

Once you have placed a schedule on a sheet, you can manipulate it to fit the information into the available space. Select the schedule to display the controls that enable you to modify it, as shown in Figure 11–10.

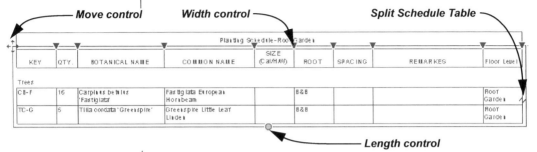

Figure 11–10

- The blue triangles modify the width of each column.

- The break mark splits the schedule into two parts.

- In a split schedule, you can use the arrows in the upper left corner to move that portion of the schedule table. The control at the bottom of the first table changes the length of the table and impacts any connected splits.

- To unsplit a schedule, drag the Move control from the side of the schedule that you want to unsplit back to the original column.

Practice 11a | Work with Schedules

Practice Objectives

- Update schedule information in schedules and through the elements.
- Modify schedule filters.
- Add schedules to a sheet.

Estimated time for completion: 20 minutes

In this practice, you will add information to a plant schedule and to elements that are connected to the schedule. You will also modify information in a planting area schedule. You will create duplicates of the schedules and filter them so that only specific levels display. You will also place the schedules on a sheet, as shown in Figure 11–11. If time permits, you can create additional floors and assign them to annual planting area types that display in an Annual Rotation Table.

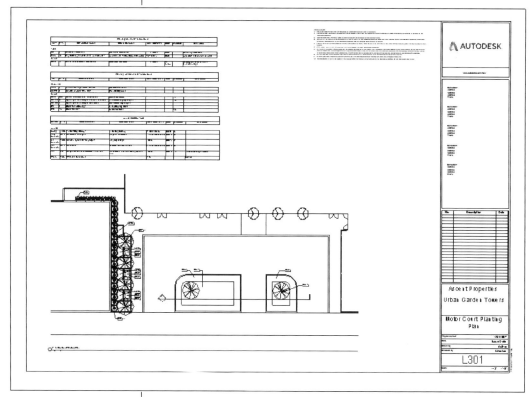

Figure 11–11

- This practice includes customized schedules and parameters. Many of the steps used in this practice may be different from how your templates are setup.

Task 1 - Fill in planting component schedules.

1. Open the project **Urban-Garden-Schedules.rvt** from the practice files folder.

2. Open the **Floor Plans: -01 Motor Court** and **-02 Roof Garden** views.

3. Close the **CS000 - Cover Sheet** view.

4. In the Project Browser, expand *Schedules/Quantities (all)*. Several schedules have been added to this project.

5. Double-click on **Planting Schedule** to open it. The existing plant components in the project are already populated with some of the basic information, as shown in Figure 11–12.

A	B	C	D	E	F	G	H	I
KEY	QTY.	BOTANICAL NAME	COMMON NAME	SIZE (Cal/H/W)	ROOT	SPACING	REMARKS	Floor Level
Trees								
CB-F	16	Carpinus betulus 'Fastigiata'	Fastigiata European Hornbeam					Roof Garden
CC	4	Carpinus caroliniana	American Hornbeam					
TC-G	5	Tilia cordata 'Greenspire'	Greenspire Little Leaf Linden					Roof Garden
Shrubs								
BS-C	20	Buxus sempervirens 'Columnaris'	Common Boxwood					
Bamboo	151							

Figure 11–12

- Planting Areas are in a separate schedule.

6. Switch back to one of the floor plan views and type **WT** to tile the three views. Move the views around so that the Planting Schedule is across the top and the two floor plan views are on the bottom, similar to Figure 11–13.

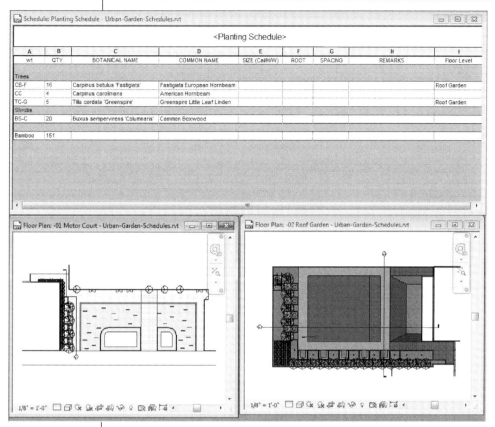

Figure 11–13

7. In the Planting Schedule view, select the Key **Bamboo**.

8. In the *Modify Schedules/Quantities* tab>Element panel, click (Highlight in Model). The related bamboo components are highlighted in both of the plan views.

9. In the Show Element(s) In View dialog box, click **Close**.

10. All of the bamboo elements are still selected. In Properties, click (Edit Type).

11. Use the drop-down lists in the value fields and set the following:

- *Plant Category:* **Trees**
- *Botanical Name:* **Phyllostachs aureosulcata "Aureocaulis"**
- *Common Name:* **Aureocaulis Yellow Groove Bamboo**
- *Type Mark:* **PA-A**

12. Click **OK** to finish. A warning about duplicate type mark values displays. Click **OK**. (There is a 3D component for the bamboo as well).

13. The information updates in the Planting schedule, as shown in Figure 11–14.

	A	B	C	D
	KEY	QTY.	BOTANICAL NAME	COMMON NAME
Trees				
	CB-F	16	Carpinus betulus 'Fastigiata'	Fastigiata European Hornbeam
	CC	4	Carpinus caroliniana	American Hornbeam
	PA-A	151	Phyllostachys aureosulcata "Aure	Aureocaulis Yellow Groove Ba
	TC-G	5	Tilla cordata 'Greenspire'	Greenspire Little Leaf Linden
Shrubs				
	BS-C	20	Buxus sempervirens 'Columnaris'	Common Boxwood

<Plantin

Figure 11–14

14. In the Motor Court view, zoom in to see the bamboo.

15. Window around the bamboo components. You will end up selecting other elements as well.

16. In the *Modify | Multi-Select* tab>Selection panel, click (Filter).

17. In the Filter dialog box, click **Check None** and then check **Planting**.

This is an example of a way to customize schedules with custom parameters.

18. In Properties, beside *Floor Level,* type **Motor Court** and click **Apply**. In a later step, you will separate out the schedules by the Floor Level so it is important to know which components are on each level.

19. In the Planting Schedule view, set the *Floor Level* to **Motor Court** for the American Hornbeam and Common Boxwoods. There are no instances of these trees and shrubs on the other levels at this time.

20. Continue working in the Planting Schedule view and add information about the *Size, Root,* and *Remarks*, as shown in Figure 11–15.

<Planting Schedule>

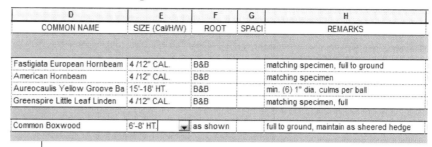

D	E	F	G	H
COMMON NAME	SIZE (Cal/H/W)	ROOT	SPACI	REMARKS
Fastigiata European Hornbeam	4 /12" CAL.	B&B		matching specimen, full to ground
American Hornbeam	4 /12" CAL.	B&B		matching specimen
Aureocaulis Yellow Groove Ba	15'-18' HT.	B&B		min. (6) 1" dia. culms per ball
Greenspire Little Leaf Linden	4 /12" CAL.	B&B		matching specimen, full
Common Boxwood	6'-8' HT.	as shown		full to ground, maintain as sheered hedge

Figure 11–15

21. Save the project.

Task 2 - Create Individual schedules for each level.

1. In the Project Browser, right-click on the Planting Schedule and select **Duplicate View> Duplicate**.

2. In the new schedule view, change the name to **Planting Schedule - Motor Court**, as shown in Figure 11–16.

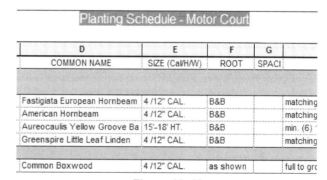

Planting Schedule - Motor Court

D	E	F	G	
COMMON NAME	SIZE (Cal/H/W)	ROOT	SPACI	
Fastigiata European Hornbeam	4 /12" CAL.	B&B		matching
American Hornbeam	4 /12" CAL.	B&B		matching
Aureocaulis Yellow Groove Ba	15'-18' HT.	B&B		min. (6)
Greenspire Little Leaf Linden	4 /12" CAL.	B&B		matching
Common Boxwood	4 /12" CAL.	as shown		full to gr

Figure 11–16

3. In Properties, beside *Filter* click **Edit...**.

4. In the Schedule Properties dialog box, in the *Filter* tab, set *Filter by* to **Floor Level equals Motor Court**, as shown in Figure 11–17.

Figure 11–17

5. Click **OK**. Only the plants listed on the Floor Level Motor court display in the schedule.

6. Right-click on the *Floor Level* column and select **Hide Columns**.

7. Duplicate the new **Planting Schedule - Motor Court** and rename it to **Planting Schedule - Roof Garden.**

8. In Properties, beside *Filter* click **Edit....**

9. In the Schedule Properties dialog box, in the *Filter* tab, change the *Filter by* to **Floor Level equals Roof Garden.**

10. Duplicate the newest schedule, rename it **Planting Schedule - Club Roof**, and change the *Filter by* to **Floor Level equals Club Roof**. (This schedule will be empty as there are no plants on this level at this point in the process.)

11. Save the project.

Task 3 - Add schedules to a sheet.

---

1. In the Project Browser, open the sheet **L301 - Motor Court Planting Plan**.

2. Drag and drop the **Planting Schedule - Motor Court** view onto the sheet, as shown in Figure 11–18.

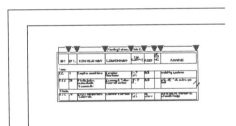

Figure 11–18

• Note that your schedule might look different than the one shown in Figure 11–18.

3. Zoom in and use the arrows at the top to modify the width of the columns so that the titles display correctly.

4. Click in empty space on the sheet to finish placing the schedule.

5. Move the plan view out of the way, as required.

6. Double-click inside the floor plan view on the sheet to activate it.

7. Copy one of the trees from the side planting bed to the center planting beds, as shown in Figure 11–19.

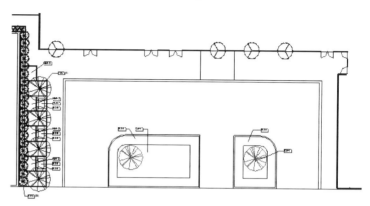

Figure 11–19

8. Double-click outside of the view and zoom in on the schedule. You can see the quantity updated from *4* to **6**, as shown in Figure 11–20.

			Planting Schedule - Motor Court	
KEY	QTY.	BOTANICAL NAME	COMMON NAME	SI
Trees				
CC	6	Carpinus caroliniana	American Hornbeam	4 /1
PA-A	25	Phyllostachys aureosulcata "Aureocaulis'	Aureocaulis Yellow Groove Bamboo	15'-
Shrubs				
BS-C	20	Buxus sempervirens 'Columnaris'	Common Boxwood	4 /1

Figure 11–20

9. Save the project.

Task 4 - Modify Planting Area Schedules.

1. Open the **Planting Area Schedule** view. No Quantities are available at this time.

2. Open the **Floor Plans: 01 Motor Court-Planting Plan** view and zoom in on the planting beds to the left of the driveway.

3. Select one of the Knock Out Rose planting areas, as shown in Figure 11–21.

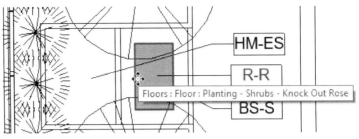

Figure 11–21

4. In Properties, collapse the sections you don't need by clicking near the double small arrows on the right of the title. Ensure that *Identity Data* and *Analysis Results* are expanded, as shown in Figure 11–22.

5. Expand the drop-down list beside *Spacing (o.c.)* and select **18**, as shown in Figure 11–23. (This is the key name for 18" on center.) The Analysis Results are populated.

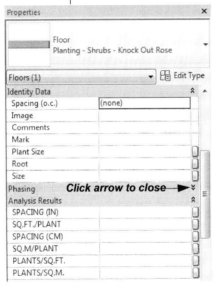

Figure 11–22

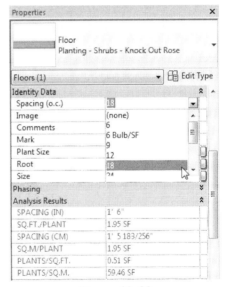

Figure 11–23

6. Press <Ctrl> + <Tab> to cycle back to the **Planting Area Schedule** view. The number of roses required for that planting area is updated as shown in Figure 11–24.

A	B	C	D
KEY	QTY.	Botanical Name	Common Name
Perennials			
LA-H	0	Lavandula angustifolia 'Hidcote'	Hidcote Lavender
NN-PC	0	Nepeta nervoca 'Pink Cat'	Pink Cat Catmint
Shrubs			
BS-S	0	Buxus sempervirens 'Suffruiticosa'	Dwarf Boxwood
HM-ES	0	Hydrangea macrophyla 'Endless Summer'	Everblooming Hydrangea
HM-NB	0	Hydrangea macrophyla 'Nikko Blue'	Nikko Blue Hydrangea
R-E	0	Rosa 'Everblooming'	Everblooming Rose
R-R	6	Rosa 'Radraz'	Knockout Rose

Figure 11–24

7. Return to the plan view, select the other two Knock Out Rose planting areas, and set the *Spacing (o.c.)* to **18**.

8. Select one of the HM-ES (Everblooming Hydrangea) planting areas. Right-click and select **Select All Instances>Visible in View**.

9. In Properties, set the *Spacing (o.c.)* to **18**.

10. Repeat the process with the BS-S (Dwarf Boxwood) and set the *Spacing (o.c.)* to **12**.

11. Return to the **Planting Area Schedule** view. All of the Motor Court based plantings are updated as shown in Figure 11–25

<Planting Area Schedule>

A	B	C	D	E	F	G
KEY	QTY.	Botanical Name	Common Name	SIZE (CAL/H/W)	ROOT	SPACING
Perennials						
LA-H	0	Lavandula angustifolia 'Hidcote'	Hidcote Lavender			
NN-PC	0	Nepeta nervoca 'Pink Cat'	Pink Cat Catmint			
Shrubs						
BS-S	880	Buxus sempervirens 'Suffruiticosa'	Dwarf Boxwood			12"
HM-ES	64	Hydrangea macrophyla 'Endless Summer'	Everblooming Hydrangea			18"
HM-NB	0	Hydrangea macrophyla 'Nikko Blue'	Nikko Blue Hydrangea			
R-E	0	Rosa 'Everblooming'	Everblooming Rose			
R-R	18	Rosa 'Radraz'	Knockout Rose			18"

Figure 11–25

- The *Spacing* column automatically displays the distance gathered from the key schedule.

12. Duplicate the Planting Area Schedule and name it **Planting Area Schedule - Motor Court**.

13. In Properties beside *Filter* click **Edit...**.

14. In the Schedule Properties dialog box, in the *Filter* tab, set the *Filter by* to **Level equals Motor Court** and click **OK**.

15. Open the sheet **L301 - Motor Court Planting Plan**.

16. Drag and drop the **Planting Area Schedule - Motor Court** view onto the sheet. Locate it under the Planting Schedule - Motor Court and modify the columns so they match.

17. Save the project.

Floor elements automatically know what level they are related to so you do not need to fill in this information.

Task 5 - (Optional) Work with Annual Rotation Tables.

---

1. The Annual Rotation Table includes an additional *Season* parameter, as shown in Figure 11–26. These plantings all need to be in the same location but include different plants for different seasons.

A	B	C
Season	QTY.	Botanical Name
Annuals		
Fall	0	Chrysanthemum morifolium 'Lavender'

Figure 11–26

2. Open the **Floor Plans: 01 Motor Court-Planting Plan** view.

3. In the Quick Access Toolbar, click ⌖ (Section) and draw a horizontal section through the annual planting beds, as shown in Figure 11–27. Use the controls to limit the depth.

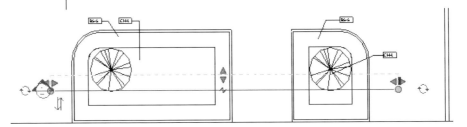

Figure 11–27

4. Click **Modify** and double-click on the section head to open the section view.

- Note that there is one thin floor in the view, as shown in Figure 11–28.

Floors : Floor : Planting - Annuals - Daisy Garden Mum

Figure 11–28

You may need to modify the section view in order to see all of the copied floors.

5. Create five copies of the floor below the level.

6. Zoom in so you can see the floors.

7. Select each floor. In the Type Selector, assign the floor to a different annual planting, as shown in Figure 11–29. The exact order does not matter.

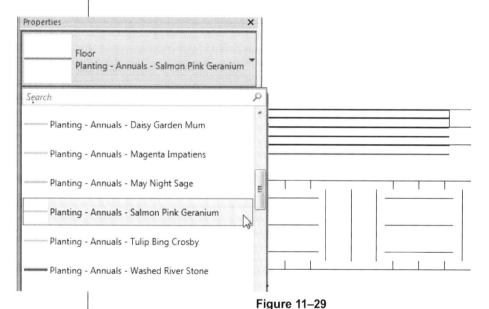

Figure 11–29

The Spacing (o.c.) values need to be assigned directly to the elements as this information does not show in the schedule.

8. Select each floor and in Properties, add the appropriate *Spacing (o.c.)* as follows:
- *Tulip 'Bing Crosby':* **6 Bulb/SF**
- *Magenta Impatiens:* **6**
- *May Night Sage:* **9**
- *Salmon Pink Geranium:* **6**
- *Daisy Garden Mum:* **12**
- *Washed River Stone:* **none**

9. Return to the Annual Rotation Table and fill out the rest of the information, as shown in Figure 11–30.

<Annual Rotation Table>

	D	E	F	G	H
	Common Name	SIZE (CAL/H/W)	ROOT	SPACING	REMARKS
	Tulip Bing Crosby	#1 Grade Bulb	BULB	6"	
	Magenta Impatiens	4" Peat Pot, 3–6" ht.	CONT.	6"	
	May Night Sage	2 Gal.	CONT.	9"	
	Salmon Pink Geraniuma	3" Peat Pot, 3–6" ht.	CONT.	6"	
	Mammonth Lavender Daisy Garden Mum	2 Gal.	CONT.	12"	Full Plant, Large Flower

Figure 11–30

10. Open the **Annual Rotation Table - Stone**, shown in Figure 11–31. This table automatically gathers information from the depth of the floor type (3") and applies it to the Quantity. This has to be separate because the calculations are different from the other area plantings.

A	B	C	D	E
Winter	165	Washed River Stone		3"

Figure 11–31

11. Open the sheet **L301 - Motor Court Planting Plan**.

12. Drag and drop both the **Annual Rotation Tables** views onto the sheet. Locate them under the other schedules and modify the columns so they match as much as possible. The Stone table does not include any titles so it fits up directly under the other table, as shown in Figure 11–32.

		Annual Rotation Table					
Season	QTY.	Botanical Name	Common Name	SIZE (CAL/H/W)	ROOT	SPACING	REMARKS
Annuals							
Spring	4266	Tulipa 'Bing Crosby'	Tulip Bing Crosby	#1 Grade Bulb	BULB	6"	
Early Summer	3047	Impatiens walleriana	Magenta Impatiens	4" Peat Pot, 3–6" ht.	CONT.	6"	
Mid Summer	1368	Salvia x sylvestris 'May Night'	May Night Sage	2 Gal.	CONT.	9"	
Late Summer	3047	Geranium	Salmon Pink Geraniuma	3" Peat Pot, 3–6" ht.	CONT.	6"	
Fall	764	Chrysanthemum morifolium 'Lavender'	Mammonth Lavender Daisy Garden Mum	2 Gal.	CONT.	12"	Full Plant, Large Flower
Winter	165	Washed River Stone		0 · 3"		661 SF	

Figure 11–32

13. Zoom out to fit the view.

14. Save the project.

11.2 Creating Legends

A legend is a separate view in which you can list the symbols used in your project and provide explanatory notes next to them, such as the Planting Legend shown in Figure 11–33. Legends can include a list of all annotation symbols used in working drawings, a list of materials, or elevations of wall types used in the project. Legends are also frequently used to create key plans that show the location of the part of the project covered on a sheet.

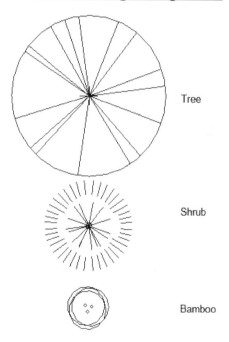

Planting Legend

Tree

Shrub

Bamboo

Figure 11–33

- You can use ◰ (Detail Lines) and **A** (Text) to create the table and explanatory notes. Once you have a legend view, you can use commands, such as ⬚ (Legend Component), ▧ (Detail Component) and ⬚ (Symbol), to place elements in the view.

- Unlike other views, legend views can be attached to more than one sheet.

- You can set a legend's scale in the View Status Bar.

- Elements in legends can be dimensioned.

How To: Create a Legend

1. In the *View* tab>Create panel, expand ▦ (Legends) and

   click ▦ (Legend) or in the Project Browser, right-click on the *Legends* area title and select **New Legend**.
2. In the New Legend View dialog box, enter a name and select a scale for the legend, as shown in Figure 11–34. Then, click **OK**.

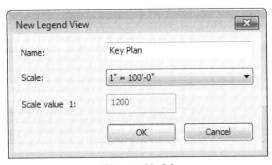

Figure 11–34

3. Place the components in the view first and then sketch the outline of the table when you know the sizes. Use alignment lines and temporary detail lines to line up the components.

How To: Use Legend Components

1. In the *Annotate* tab>Detail panel, expand ▱ (Component)

   and click ▤ (Legend Component).
2. In the Options Bar, select the *Family* type that you want to use, as shown in Figure 11–35.

   - This list contains all of the elements in a project that can be used in a legend. For example, you might want to display the floor plan view of each of planting types used in the project.

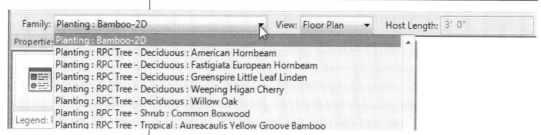

Figure 11–35

3. Select the *View* of the element that you want to use. For example, you might want to display the section of the floors or roofs, and the floor plan view of planting, as shown in Figure 11–36.

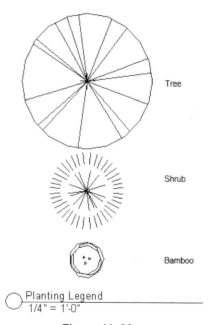

Tree

Shrub

Bamboo

Planting Legend
1/4" = 1'-0"

Figure 11–36

4. For section elements (such as walls, floors, and roofs), type a distance for the *Host Length*.

• Elements that are full size, such as planting components or doors, come in at their full size.

Hint: Using Thin Lines

The software automatically applies line weights to views, as shown for a section on the left in Figure 11–37. If a line weight seems heavy or obscures your work on the elements, toggle off the line weights. In the Quick Access Toolbar or in the *View* tab>Graphics panel, click ▉⊟ (Thin Lines) or type **TL**. The lines display with the same weight, as shown on the right in Figure 11–37.

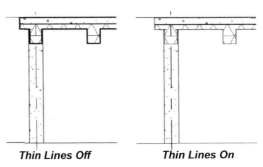

| Thin Lines Off | Thin Lines On |

Figure 11–37

- The **Thin Line** setting is remembered until you change it, even if you shut down and restart the software.

Practice 11b

Create Legends

Practice Objectives

- Create legends using legend components and text.
- Create a key plan using detail lines and text.

Estimated time for completion: 10 minutes

In this practice, you will create a Planting Legend and a Key Plan legend. You will create legend views, add legend components and a label with text. For the Key Plan, you will draw detail lines over the site plan and then cut them to the clipboard. You will paste them into a legend view and clean them up and add text. You will add both the Planting Legend and the Key Plan to sheets, as shown in Figure 11–38.

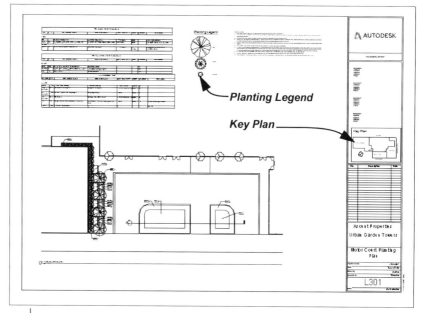

Figure 11–38

Task 1 - Create a planting legend.

1. Open the project **Urban-Garden-Legends.rvt** from the practice files folder.

2. In the *View* tab>Create panel, expand (Legends) and click (Legend) to create a new legend view.

3. Name it **Planting Legend** and set the *Scale* to **1/4"=1'-0"**.

This is the smallest tree in the group and doesn't take up as much room as the others.

4. In the *Annotate* tab>Detail panel, expand ⬜ (Component) and click ⊡ (Legend Component).

5. In the Options Bar, set *Family* to **Planting: RPC Tree - Deciduous: Weeping Higan Cherry** and *View* to **Floor Plan**. Place the component in the view.

6. Add **Planting: RPC Tree - Shrub: Common Boxwood** and **Planting: Bamboo-2D** below the tree.

7. In the *Annotate* tab>Text panel, click **A** (Text).

8. In the Type Selector, select **Text: 3/32" Arial** and add the text for **Tree**, **Shrub**, and **Bamboo**, as shown in Figure 11–39. Use alignment lines to help you place the text.

Planting Legend

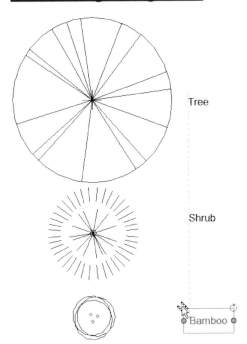

Figure 11–39

9. Continue in the **Text** command using the type **Text: 1/4" Arial** and add the text **Planting Legend**, as shown in Figure 11–39.

10. Save the project.

Task 2 - Create a Key Plan.

1. Create another legend view. Name it **Key Plan** and set the *Scale* to **1"=100'-0"**.

2. Open the **Floor Plans: Site** view.

3. In the Quick Access Toolbar, click 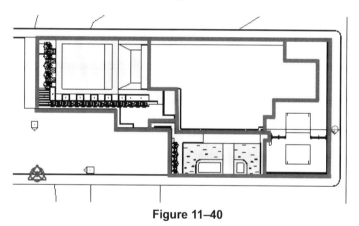 (Thin Lines). Ensure that you see the line width for the next steps.

4. In the *Annotate* tab>Detail panel, click (Detail Line).

5. In the *Modify | Place Detail Line* tab>Line Style panel, select **Outline**.

6. In the Draw panel, click (Line).

7. Trace over the outer edges of the building following the outline shown in Figure 11–40. It does not have to be exactly on the edges of the building.

Figure 11–40

8. Click **Modify**.

9. Window around the entire building.

10. In the *Modify | Multi-Select* tab>Selection Window, click (Filter).

11. In the Filter dialog box, click **Check None** and select **Lines (Outline)**, as shown in Figure 11–41.

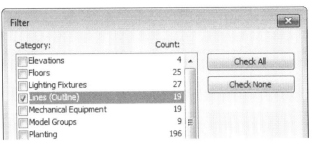

Figure 11–41

12. In the *Modify | Lines* tab>Clipboard panel, click ✂ (Cut to Clipboard).

13. Return to the Key Plan view and press <Ctrl>+<V> to paste from the clipboard. Click to place the elements and in the *Modify | Detail Groups* tab>Edit Pasted panel, click ✓ (Finish).

14. Select all of the lines (they will be very thick). In the *Modify | Lines* panel> Line Style panel, change the *Line Style* to **Wide Lines**.

15. Use the modify tools to cleanup the edges and add text, as shown in Figure 11–42.

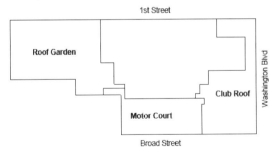

Figure 11–42

16. In the *Annotate* tab>Symbol panel, click ⊞ (Symbol).

17. In the *Modify | Place Symbol* tab>Mode panel, click ⬇ (Load Family).

18. Navigate to the *Revit Library>Annotations* folder and select **North Arrow 1.rfa** and click **Open**.

19. Place the North Arrow and rotate it 28 degrees, as shown in Figure 11–43.

Key Plan

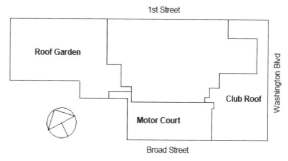

Figure 11–43

20. Save the project.

Task 3 - Add Legends to sheets.

1. Open the sheet **L301 - Motor Court Planting Plan**.

2. Drag and drop the Planting Legend from the Project Browser onto the sheet and place it next to the schedules, as shown in Figure 11–44.

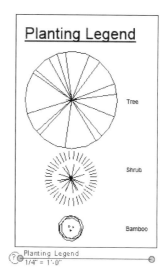

Figure 11–44

3. With the legend still selected, in the Type Selector, change the *Viewport* to **Viewport - No Title**.

4. Pan over to the edge of the title block and drag and drop the Key Plan above the revision table. Change the *Viewport* to **Viewport - No Title** so there is no title below the key plan, as shown in Figure 11–45.

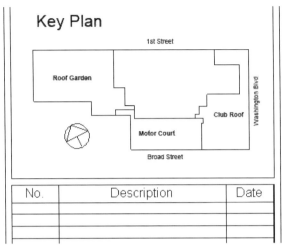

Figure 11–45

5. Zoom out to see the full sheet.

6. If time permits, add the Key Plan and Planting Legends to the other Planting Plan sheets.

7. Save the project.

Chapter Review Questions

1. What happens when you delete a plant in an Autodesk Revit model, as shown in Figure 11–46?

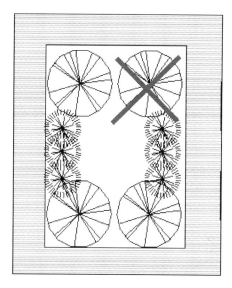

Figure 11–46

a. You must delete the plant on the sheet.

b. You must delete the plant from the schedule.

c. The plant is removed from the model, but not from the schedule.

d. The plant is removed from the model and the schedule.

2. In a schedule, if you change type information (such as a Type Mark), all instances of that type update with the new information.

a. True

b. False

3. What is the purpose of the upside down triangles shown in Figure 11–47 when adding schedules to a sheet?

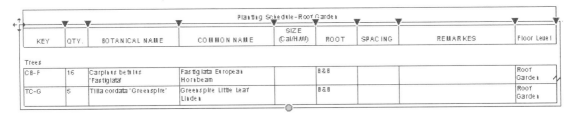

Figure 11–47

   a. Split the schedule at that column.

   b. Move the entire schedule.

   c. Control the width of the column.

   d. Recenter the column on the text.

4. Which of the following elements cannot be added when creating a Legend?

   a. Legend Components

   b. Tags

   c. Rooms

   d. Symbols

Command Summary

Button	Command	Location
Legends		
	Legend (View)	• **Ribbon:** *View* tab>Create panel> expand Legends
	Legend Component	• **Ribbon:** *Annotate* tab>Detail panel> expand Component

Creating Details

Creating details and specifying the exact information that is required to build a construction project are critical parts of the design process. The elements that you can add to a model include detail components, detail lines, text, tags, symbols, and filled regions for patterning. These details can be created from views in the model, or added as 2D details in separate views.

Learning Objectives in this Chapter

- Create drafting views where you can add 2D details.
- Add detail components that show the typical elements in a detail.
- Annotate details using detail lines, text, tags, symbols, and patterns that define materials.

12.1 Setting Up Detail Views

When developing projects in the Autodesk® Revit® software, most of the design is created using 3D model elements such as walls, floors, and stairs. However, the software does not automatically display how these elements should be built to fit together. For this, you need to create detail drawings, as shown in Figure 12–1.

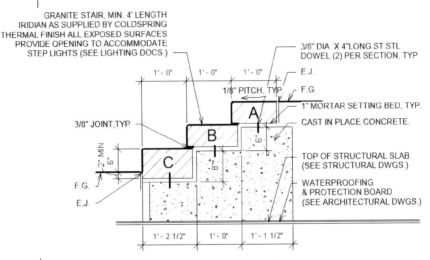

Figure 12–1

- Details are created either in 2D drafting views, or in callouts from plan, elevation, or section views.

How To: Create a Drafting View

1. In the *View* tab>Create panel, click ⬒ (Drafting View).
2. In the New Drafting View dialog box, enter a *Name* and set a *Scale*, as shown in Figure 12–2.

Drafting views are listed in their own section in the Project Browser.

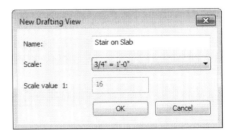

Figure 12–2

3. Click **OK**. A blank view is created with space in which you can sketch the detail.

How To: Create a Detail View from Model Elements

1. Start the **Section** or **Callout** command.
2. In the Type Selector, select the **Detail View: Detail** type.
   - The marker indicates that it is a detail, as shown for a section in Figure 12–3.

Callouts also have a Detail View Type that can be used in the same way.

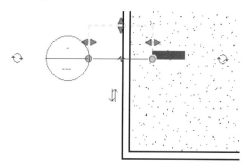

Figure 12–3

3. Place the section or a callout of the area that you want to use for the detail.
4. Open the new detail. Use the tools to sketch on top of or add to the building elements.

   - In this type of detail view, when the building elements change the detail changes as well, as shown in Figure 12–4.

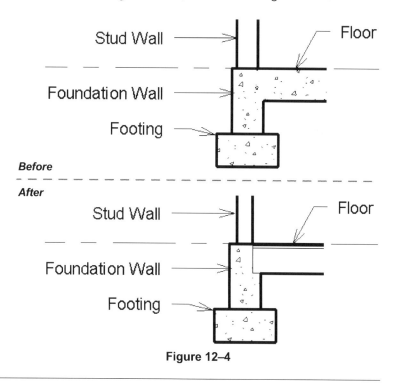

Figure 12–4

- You can create detail elements on top of the model and then toggle the model off so that it does not show in the detail view. In Properties, in the *Graphics* area, change *Display Model* to **Do not display**. You can also set the model to **Halftone**, as shown in Figure 12–5.

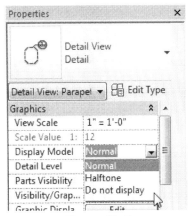

Figure 12–5

Referencing a Drafting View

Once you have created a drafting view, you can reference it in another view (such as a callout, elevation, or section view), as shown in Figure 12–6. For example, in a section view, you might want to reference an existing roof detail. You can reference drafting views, sections, elevations, and callouts.

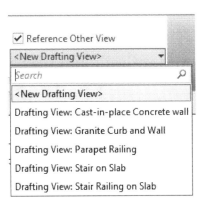

Figure 12–6

- You can use the search feature to limit the information displayed.

How To: Reference a Drafting View

1. Open the view in which you want to place the reference.
2. Start the **Section**, **Callout**, or **Elevation** command.
3. In the *Modify | <contextual>* tab>Reference panel, select **Reference Other View**.
4. In the drop-down list, select **<New Drafting View>** or an existing drafting view.
5. Place the view marker.
6. When you place the associated drafting view on a sheet, the marker in this view updates with the appropriate information.

- If you select **<New Drafting View>** from the drop-down list, a new view is created in the *Drafting Views (Detail)* area in the Project Browser. You can rename it as required. The new view does not include any model elements.

- When you create a detail based on a section, elevation, or callout, you do not need to link it to a drafting view.

- You can change a referenced view to a different referenced view. Select the view marker and in the ribbon, select the new view from the list.

Saving Drafting Views

To create a library of standard details, save the non-model specific drafting views to your server. They can then be imported into a project and modified to suit. They are saved as .RVT files.

Drafting views can be saved in two ways:
- Save an individual drafting view to a new file.
- Save all of the drafting views as a group in one new file.

How To: Save One Drafting View to a File

1. In the Project Browser, right-click on the drafting view that you want to save and select **Save to New File...**, as shown in Figure 12–7.

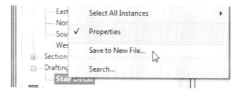

Figure 12–7

2. In the Save As dialog box, specify a name and location for the file and click **Save**.

You can save sheets, drafting views, model views (floor plans), schedules, and reports.

How To: Save a Group of Drafting Views to a File

1. In the Application Menu, expand ⊟ (Save As), expand 📖 (Library), and click ⬚ (View).
2. In the Save Views dialog box, in the *Views:* pane, expand the list and select **Show drafting views only**.
3. Select the drafting views that you want to save, as shown in Figure 12–8.

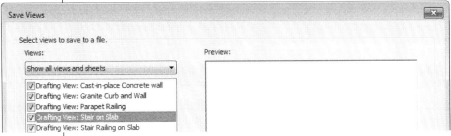

Figure 12–8

4. Click **OK**.
5. In the Save As dialog box, specify a name and location for the file and click **Save**.

How To: Use a Saved Drafting View in another Project

1. Open the project to which you want to add the drafting view.
2. In the *Insert* tab>Import panel, expand 📥 (Insert from File) and click 📄 (Insert Views from File).
3. In the Open dialog box, select the project in which you saved the detail and click **Open**.
4. In the Insert Views dialog box, limit the types of views to **Show drafting views only**, as shown in Figure 12–9.

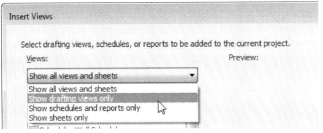

Figure 12–9

5. Select the view(s) that you want to insert and click **OK**.

Hint: Importing Details from Other CAD Software

You might already have a set of standard details created in a different CAD program, such as the AutoCAD® software. You can reuse the details in the Autodesk Revit software by importing them into a project. Once you have imported the detail, it helps to clean it up and save it as a view before bringing it into your project.

1. Create a drafting view and make it active.

2. In the *Insert* tab>Import panel, click (Import CAD).
3. In the Import CAD dialog box, select the file to import. Most of the default values are what you need. You might want to change the *Layer/Level colors* to **Black and White**.
4. Click **Open**.

• If you want to modify the detail, select the imported data. In the *Modify | [filename]* tab>Import Instance panel, expand (Explode) and click (Partial Explode) or (Full Explode). Click (Delete Layers) before you explode the detail. A full explode greatly increases the file size.

• Modify the detail using tools in the Modify panel. Change all the text and line styles to Autodesk Revit specific elements.

12.2 Adding Detail Components

Autodesk Revit elements, such as the bench section shown in Figure 12–10, typically require additional information to ensure that they are constructed correctly. To create details such as the one shown in Figure 12–11, you add detail components, detail lines, and various annotation elements.

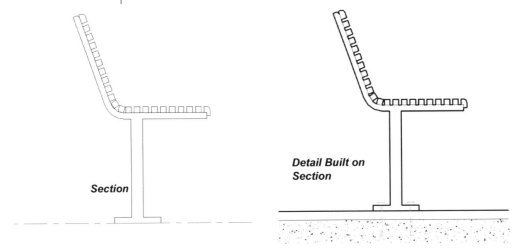

Section

Detail Built on Section

Figure 12–10   Figure 12–11

- Detail elements are not directly connected to the model, even if model elements display in the view.

Detail Components

Detail components are families made of 2D and annotation elements. Over 500 detail components organized by CSI format are found in the *Detail Items* folder of the library, as shown in Figure 12–12.

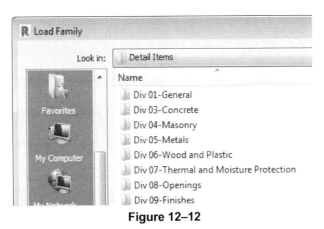

Figure 12–12

How To: Add a Detail Component

1. In the *Annotate* tab>Detail panel, expand 🗐 (Component) and click 🗐 (Detail Component).
2. In the Type Selector, select the detail component type. You can load additional types from the Library.
3. Many detail components can be rotated as you insert them by pressing <Spacebar>. Alternatively, select **Rotate after placement** in the Options Bar, as shown in Figure 12–13.

☐ Rotate after placement

Figure 12–13

4. Place the component in the view.

Adding Break Lines

The Break Line is a detail component found in the *Detail Items\ Div 01-General* folder. It consists of a rectangular area (shown highlighted in Figure 12–14) which is used to block out elements behind it. You can modify the size of the area that is covered and change the size of the cut line using the controls.

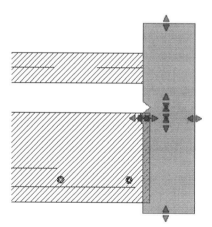

Figure 12–14

Hint: Working with the Draw Order of Details

When you select detail elements in a view, you can change the draw order of the elements in the *Modify* | *Detail Items* tab> Arrange panel. You can bring elements in front of other elements or place them behind elements, as shown in Figure 12–15.

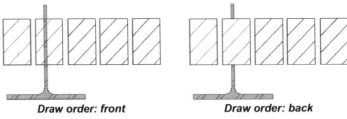

Draw order: front   Draw order: back

Figure 12–15

- (Bring to Front): Places element in front of all other elements.

- (Send to Back): Places element behind all other elements.

- (Bring Forward): Moves element one step to the front.

- (Send Backward): Moves element one step to the back.

- You can select multiple detail elements and change the draw order of all of them in one step. They keep the relative order of the original selection.

Repeating Details

Instead of inserting a component multiple times (such as with a brick or concrete block), you can use (Repeating Detail Component) and create a string of components, as shown in Figure 12–16.

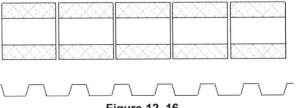

Figure 12–16

How To: Insert a Repeating Detail Component

1. In the *Annotate* tab>Detail panel, expand ⬜ (Component) and click 🔳 (Repeating Detail Component).
2. In the Type Selector, select the detail that you want to use.
3. In the Draw panel, click ✏ (Line) or ⬦ (Pick Lines).
4. In the Options Bar, type a value for the *Offset*, if required.
5. The components repeat as required to fit the length of the sketched or selected line, as shown in Figure 12–17. You can lock the components to the line.

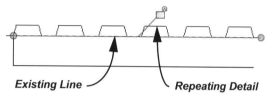

Existing Line ———   ——— *Repeating Detail*

Figure 12–17

Hint: ⧓ **(Insulation)**

Adding batt insulation is similar to adding a repeating detail component, but instead of a series of bricks or other elements, it creates the linear batting pattern, shown in Figure 12–18.

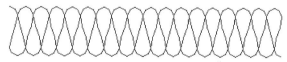

Figure 12–18

Before you place the insulation in the view, specify the *Width* and other options in the Options Bar, as shown in Figure 12–19.

Modify | Place Insulation   Width 0' 3 1/2   ☐ Chain   Offset 0' 0"   to center ▼

Figure 12–19

12.3 Annotating Details

After you have added components and sketched detail lines, you need to add annotations to the detail view. You can place text notes and dimensions (as shown in Figure 12–20), as well as symbols and tags. Filled regions are used to add hatching or poche.

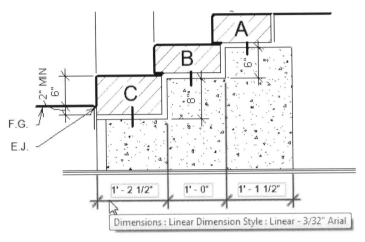

Figure 12–20

Creating Filled Regions

Many elements include material information that displays in plan and section views, while other elements need such details to be added. For example, the concrete wall shown in Figure 12–21 includes material information, while the earth to the left of the wall needs to be added using the **Filled Region** command.

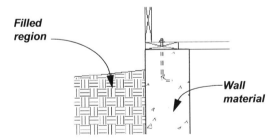

Figure 12–21

The patterns used in details are *drafting patterns*. They are scaled to the view scale and update if you modify it. You can also add full-size *model patterns*, such as a Flemish Bond brick pattern, to the surface of some elements.

How To: Add a Filled Region

1. In the *Annotate* tab>Detail panel, expand 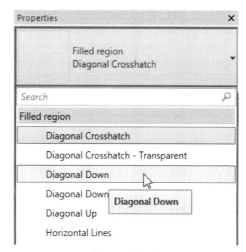 (Region) and click (Filled Region).
2. Create a closed boundary using the Draw tools.
3. In the Line Style panel, select the line style for the outside edge of the boundary. If you do not want the boundary to display, select the <Invisible lines> style.
4. In the Type Selector, select the fill type, as shown in Figure 12–22.

Figure 12–22

5. Click (Finish Edit Mode).

• You can modify a region by changing the fill type in the Type Selector or by editing the sketch.

• Double-click on the edge of the filled region to edit the sketch.

If you have the *Selection* option set to (Select elements by face), you can select the pattern.

Hint: Creating a Filled Region Pattern Type

You can create a custom pattern by duplicating and editing an existing pattern type.

1. Select an existing region or create a boundary.

2. In Properties, click 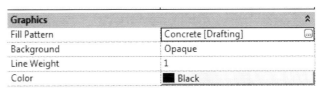 (Edit Type).
3. In the Type Properties dialog box, click **Duplicate** and name the new pattern.
4. Select a *Fill Pattern*, *Background*, *Line Weight*, and *Color*, as shown in Figure 12–23.

Graphics	⌃
Fill Pattern	Concrete [Drafting]
Background	Opaque
Line Weight	1
Color	■ Black

Figure 12–23

5. Click **OK**.

- You can select from two types of Fill Patterns: **Drafting** (as shown in Figure 12–24) and **Model**. Drafting fill patterns scale to the view scale factor. Model fill patterns display full scale on the model and are not impacted by the view scale factor.

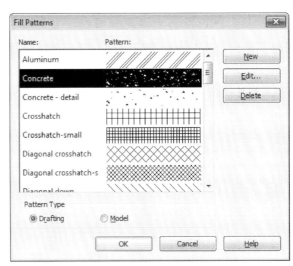

Figure 12–24

Adding Detail Tags

*The **Detail Item Tag.rfa** tag is located in the Annotations folder in the Library.*

Besides adding text to a detail, you can tag detail components using 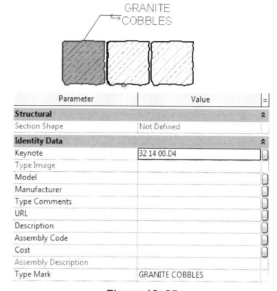 (Tag By Category). The tag name is set in the Type Parameters for that component, as shown in Figure 12–25. This means that if you have more than one copy of the component in your project, you do not have to rename it each time you place its tag.

Parameter	Value	=
Structural		☆
Section Shape	Not Defined	
Identity Data		☆
Keynote	32 14 00.D4	☐
Type Image		
Model		☐
Manufacturer		☐
Type Comments		☐
URL		☐
Description		☐
Assembly Code		☐
Cost		☐
Assembly Description		
Type Mark	GRANITE COBBLES	

Figure 12–25

Practice 12a | Create a Detail

Practice Objectives

- Create a drafting view.
- Add filled regions, detail components, and annotations.
- Place the detail on a sheet
- Add a detail marker on the referring plan.

Estimated time for completion: 15 minutes

In this practice, you will create a hardscape detail. You will add repeating running detail components, detail lines, and filled regions. You will then add annotation to complete the detail and place it on a sheet, as shown in Figure 12–26.

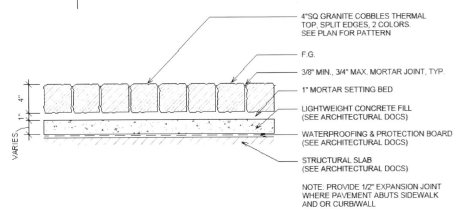

4"SQ GRANITE COBBLES THERMAL TOP, SPLIT EDGES, 2 COLORS. SEE PLAN FOR PATTERN

F.G.

3/8" MIN., 3/4" MAX. MORTAR JOINT, TYP.

1" MORTAR SETTING BED

LIGHTWEIGHT CONCRETE FILL (SEE ARCHITECTURAL DOCS)

WATERPROOFING & PROTECTION BOARD (SEE ARCHITECTURAL DOCS)

STRUCTURAL SLAB (SEE ARCHITECTURAL DOCS)

NOTE: PROVIDE 1/2" EXPANSION JOINT WHERE PAVEMENT ABUTS SIDEWALK AND OR CURB/WALL

4 — Cobble on Mortar
  1 1/2" = 1'-0"

Figure 12–26

Task 1 - Create a Detail.

1. Open the file **Urban-Garden-Details.rvt** from the practice files folder.

2. Create a drafting view named **Cobble on Mortar** at a scale of **1 1/2" = 1'-0"**.

3. In the *Annotate* tab>Detail panel, expand ⬛ (Component) and select ⬛ (Repeating Detail Component).

4. In the Type Selector, select **Repeating Detail: Cobblestone**.

5. Pick two points to define a line of eight cobblestones, as shown in Figure 12–27.

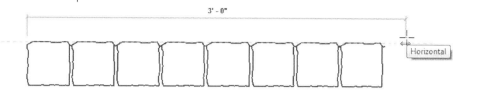

Figure 12–27

6. In the *Annotate* tab>Detail panel, expand ⬚ (Region) and click ⬚ (Filled Region).

7. In the *Modify | Create Filled Region Boundary* tab>Line Style panel, select the Line Style **Medium Lines.**

8. Sketch a rectangle, as shown in Figure 12–28. (You can sketch it and then come back and modify it using temporary dimensions.)

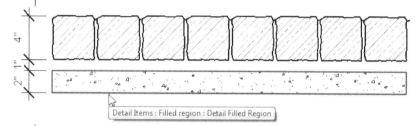

Figure 12–28

9. While still in the Edit Boundary process, in the Type Selector, select **Filled Region: Concrete**.

10. Click ✔ (Finish).

11. Using the **Detail Line** command, add two line below the concrete, as shown in Figure 12–29. The top one uses the *Line Style:* **Waterproofing** and the bottom one uses the *Line Style:* **Thin Lines.**

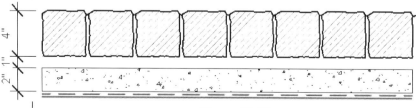

Figure 12–29

12. Start the **Filled Region** command again.

13. Set the *Line Style* to **<Invisible lines>**.

14. Draw a rectangle and assign it the type **Filled region: Diagonal Up**, as shown in Figure 12–30.

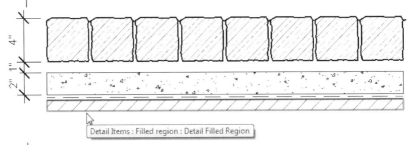

Figure 12–30

15. Save the project.

Task 2 - Add text.

---

1. Add the text shown in Figure 12–31.

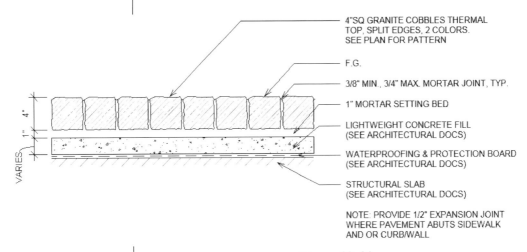

Figure 12–31

2. Save the project.

Task 3 - Place the detail on a sheet and add a detail callout.

---

1. Open the sheet **L400 - Site Details**.

2. Drag and drop the new **Cobble on Mortar** drafting view detail to this sheet.

3. Open the **Floor Plans:01 Motor Court-Paving and Grading Plan** view.

4. Select the two building sections that display, right-click and select **Hide in View>Elements**.

5. In the Quick Access Toolbar, click ⬙ (Section).

6. In the Type Selector, select **Detail View>Detail**.

7. In the M*odify | Section* tab>Reference panel, select **Reference Other View** and select **Drafting View: Cobble on Mortar**, as shown in Figure 12–32.

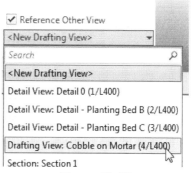

Figure 12–32

8. Pick two points to place the section marker, as shown in Figure 12–33. The number and sheet number are included in the marker.

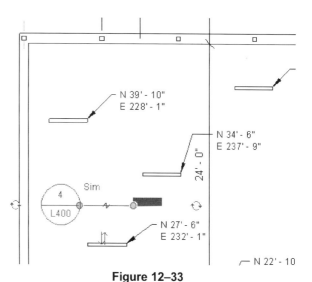

Figure 12–33

9. Save the project.

Practice 12b | Create an Additional Detail

Practice Objective

*   Create and annotate details.

In this practice, you will use detail lines, filled regions, text, and dimensions to create the detail, as shown in Figure 12–34.

Estimated time of completion: 15 minutes

*   Use the **Urban-Garden-Details.rvt** project as the base file for these tasks.

Task 1 - Create a stair detail.

In this task, you will create a stair on slab detail, as shown in Figure 12–34.

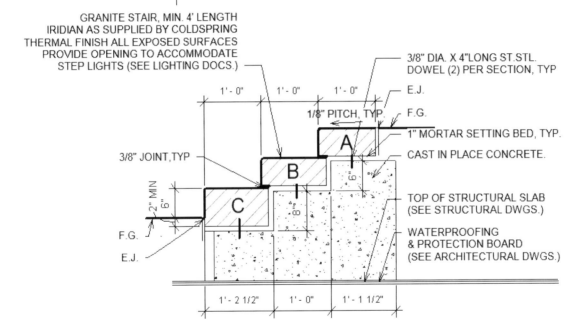

GRANITE STAIR, MIN. 4' LENGTH
IRIDIAN AS SUPPLIED BY COLDSPRING
THERMAL FINISH ALL EXPOSED SURFACES
PROVIDE OPENING TO ACCOMMODATE
STEP LIGHTS (SEE LIGHTING DOCS.)

3/8" DIA. X 4"LONG ST.STL.
DOWEL (2) PER SECTION, TYP

E.J.

1/8" PITCH, TYP.

F.G.

1" MORTAR SETTING BED, TYP.

CAST IN PLACE CONCRETE.

3/8" JOINT, TYP

TOP OF STRUCTURAL SLAB
(SEE STRUCTURAL DWGS.)

WATERPROOFING
& PROTECTION BOARD
(SEE ARCHITECTURAL DWGS.)

F.G.

E.J.

1' - 0"   1' - 0"   1' - 0"

1' - 2 1/2"   1' - 0"   1' - 1 1/2"

Figure 12–34

Practice 12c

Create a Detail Based on a CAD File

Practice Objectives

- Import a CAD file.
- Explode the CAD file and change all of the elements to Autodesk Revit specific elements.
- Save the new detail view and import it into a project.

Estimated time for completion: 10 minutes

In this practice, you will create a detail in a drafting view based on an existing detail created in the AutoCAD software, as shown in Figure 12–35. You will explode the imported file and change the text types and line styles of the elements to Autodesk Revit types. You will then create leaders for text and add patterning using filled regions. Finally, you will save the detail and import it into a project to create a clean Autodesk Revit detail without any CAD-based elements, as shown in Figure 12–36.

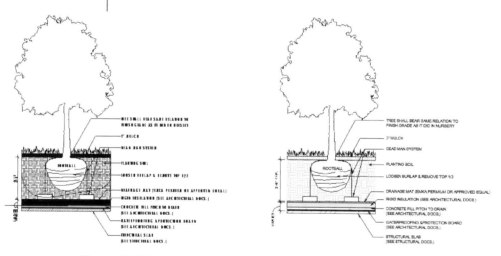

Figure 12–35   Figure 12–36

Task 1 - Create a detail based on a 2D CAD File.

1. Open the project **Detail Base.rvt** from the practice files folder. This file includes filled region types required in this practice.

2. Save the project as **Tree Planting Detail.rvt**.

3. In the *View* tab>Create panel, click ▭ (Drafting View).

4. In the New Drafting View dialog box, set the name and scale to the following:

   - *Name:* **Tree Planting**
   - *Scale:* **1 1/2" = 1'-0"**

5. In the *Insert* tab>Import panel, click ▭ (Import CAD).

6. In the Import CAD Formats dialog box, select the AutoCAD file **Tree Planting Block.dwg** from your practice files folder. Change the *Colors* to **Black and White** but keep the other default options, as shown in Figure 12–37.

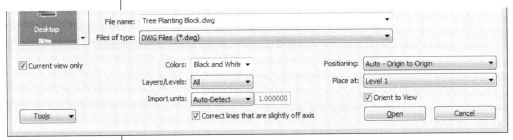

Figure 12–37

7. Click **Open** to place the detail.

8. Zoom out and select the imported detail, as shown in Figure 12–38.

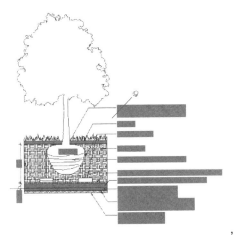

Figure 12–38

9. In the *Modify | Tree Planting Block.dwg* tab>Import Instance panel, expand ⬚ (Explode) and click ⬚ (Full Explode). You are now able to edit individual sections of the imported detail.

10. The filled region that shows the earth cannot be created. In the Error dialog box, click **Delete Element(s)**.

11. Select all of the text, as shown in Figure 12–39.

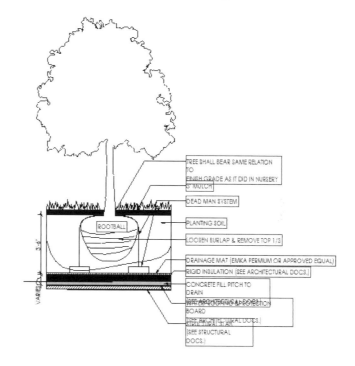

Figure 12–39

12. In the Type Selector, select **Text: 3/32" Arial**.

13. In the View Control Bar, change the *Scale* to **1/2"=1'-0"**, which fits the text size better.

14. Delete the dimension text and lines.

15. Click ⬚ (Modify) and select all of the individual elements. (**Hint:** use a crossing window.)

These lines are referenced to AutoCAD layers names rather than Autodesk Revit Line Type names.

16. In the *Modify | Multi-Select* tab>Selection panel, click (Filter).

17. In the Filter dialog box, click **Check None** and select **Lines (DEFPOINTS)**, as shown in Figure 12–40. Click **OK**.

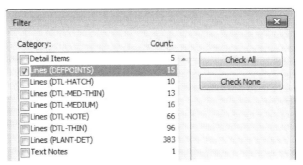

Figure 12–40

18. Press <Delete> to remove these elements from the view.

19. Select everything again. Then, in the Filter dialog box, select the following and click **OK**.

- **Lines (DTL-HATCH)**
- **Lines (DTL-THIN)**
- **Lines (PLANT-DET)**

20. In the *Modify | Lines* tab>Line Style panel, change the *Line Style* to **Thin Lines**.

21. Repeat the process with the other line types changing:

- *Lines (DTL-MED-THIN)* to **Medium Lines**
- *Lines (DTL-MEDIUM)* to **Wide Lines**

22. Save the project.

Task 2 - Modify text leaders and add dimensions.

---

1. Select the top text element. In the *Modify | Text Notes* tab> Format panel, click ⌐A (Add Left Side Straight Leader). Modify the leader to point to the correct element, as shown in the example in Figure 12–41.

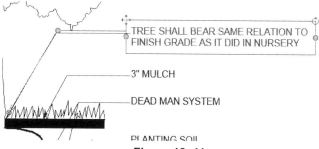

Figure 12–41

2. Repeat the process of adding leaders to the text, pointing to the appropriate parts of the detail using the existing leader lines as a guide.

3. Select everything again and use the **Filter** command to select **Lines (DTL-NOTE)**. Delete these lines as they are not used.

4. Add two separate dimensions as shown in Figure 12–42.

5. Modify the dimension text as shown in Figure 12–43.

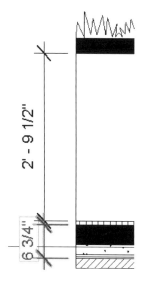

Figure 12–42   **Figure 12–43**

6. Save the project.

This area was hatched in the AutoCAD file. The hatching was automatically converted to a filled region when the file was imported into the project, but was not assigned an Autodesk Revit based pattern.

Task 3 - Update and add filled regions.

1. Select the Filled Region shown in Figure 12–44.

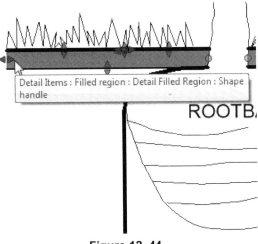

Figure 12–44

2. In the Type Selector, select **Filled region: Mulch**.

3. Select each of the other filled regions and update them with the related Autodesk Revit pattern type.

4. Make a window selection around the bottom of the rootball. You will see that there are a lot of separate lines, as shown in Figure 12–45. Delete these and add new detail arc using the *Line Type* **Thin Lines**.

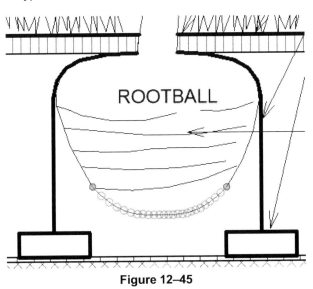

Figure 12–45

5. Select the heavy lines that make up ropes of the Dead Man System and temporarily hide them.

6. In the *Annotate* tab>Detail panel, click ▨ (Region).

Use the <Invisible lines> type because the boundary does not need to display.

7. In the *Modify | Create Filled Region Boundary* tab>Line Style panel, set the line style to **<Invisible lines>**.

8. In the Draw panel, use Pick Lines and Line to draw the boundary shown in Figure 12–46. Zoom in close to where the trunk meets the rootball and add short lines to close the boundary.

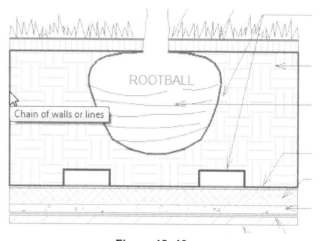

Figure 12–46

9. In the Type Selector, select **Filled region: Earth**.

10. Click ✓ (Finish Edit Mode).

11. In the View Control Bar, expand ☝ (Temporary Hide/Isolate) and select **Reset Temporary Hide/Isolate**.

12. The detail view now consists of only Autodesk Revit elements and is safe to use in another project.

Task 4 - Create a View and Import it in to a Project.

1. In the Application Menu, expand 💾 (Save As), expand ⬚ (Library), and select **View**.

2. In the Save Views dialog box, verify that **Drafting View: Tree Planting** is selected, as shown in Figure 12–47. Then, click **OK**.

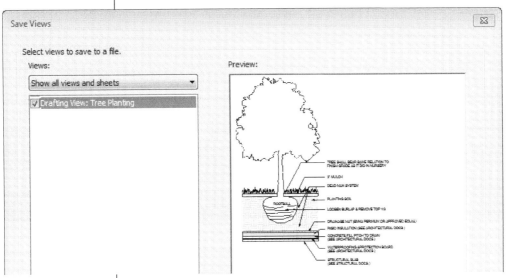

Figure 12–47

3. In the Save As dialog box, navigate to your practice files folder and click **Save**.

4. Open **Urban-Garden-Details.rvt**.

5. In the *Insert* tab>Import panel, expand (Insert from File) and click (Insert Views from File).

6. In the Open dialog box, navigate to your practice files folder and open **Tree Planting.rvt**.

7. In the Insert Views dialog box only this view is available. Click **OK**.

8. Accept any warnings that might display about duplicate types. They do not impact the project.

9. Open the sheet **L301 - Motor Court Planting Plan** and drag and drop the new detail on the sheet.

10. Save the project.

Chapter Review Questions

1. What are the different ways in which you can create a detail? (Select all that apply.)

    a. Make a callout of a section and sketch over it.

    b. Draw all of the elements from scratch.

    c. Import a CAD detail and modify or sketch over it.

    d. Insert an existing drafting view from another file.

2. In which type of view (access shown in Figure 12–48) can you add detail lines? (Select all that apply.)

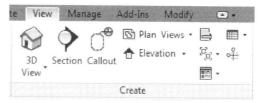

Figure 12–48

    a. Plans

    b. Elevations

    c. 3D views

    d. Legends

3. How are detail components different from building components?

    a. There is no difference.

    b. Detail components are made of 2D lines and annotation only.

    c. Detail components are made of building elements, but only display in detail views.

    d. Detail components are made of 2D and 3D elements.

4. When you sketch detail lines, they ...

    a. Are always the same width.

    b. Vary in width according to the view.

    c. Display in all views associated with the detail.

    d. Display only in the view in which they were created.

5. Which command do you use to add a pattern (such as concrete or earth as shown in Figure 12–49) to a part of a detail?

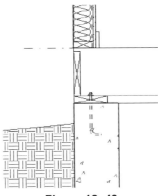

Figure 12–49

a. Region

b. Filled Region

c. Masking Region

d. Pattern Region

Command Summary

Button	Command	Location
CAD Import Tools		
	Delete Layers	• **Ribbon:** *Modify	<imported filename>* tab>Import Instance panel
	Full Explode	• **Ribbon:** *Modify	<imported filename>* tab>Import Instance panel> expand Explode
	Import CAD	• **Ribbon:** *Insert* tab>Import panel
	Partial Explode	• **Ribbon:** *Modify	<imported filename>* tab>Import Instance panel> expand Explode
Detail Tools		
	Detail Component	• **Ribbon:** *Annotate* tab>Detail panel> expand Component
	Detail Line	• **Ribbon:** *Annotate* tab>Detail panel
	Insulation	• **Ribbon:** *Annotate* tab>Detail panel
	Filled Region	• **Ribbon:** *Annotate* tab>Detail panel
	Repeating Detail Component	• **Ribbon:** *Annotate* tab>Detail panel> expand Component
View Tools		
	Bring Forward	• **Ribbon:** *Modify	Detail Items* tab> Arrange panel
	Bring to Front	• **Ribbon:** *Modify	Detail Items* tab> Arrange panel
	Drafting View	• **Ribbon:** *View* tab>Create panel
	Insert from File: Insert Views from File	• **Ribbon:** *Insert* tab>Import panel> expand Insert from File
	Send Backward	• **Ribbon:** *Modify	Detail Items* tab> Arrange panel
	Send to Back	• **Ribbon:** *Modify	Detail Items* tab> Arrange panel

Additional Tools

There are many other tools available in the Autodesk® Revit® software that you can use when creating and using models. This appendix provides details about several tools and commands that are related to those covered in this learning guide.

Learning Objectives in this Appendix

- Add site elements to toposurfaces, including property lines, building pads, and sub-regions.
- Add slab edges to floor elements.
- Create text types.
- Add revision clouds, tags, and information.
- Annotate dependent views with matchlines and view references.
- Import and export schedules.
- Create basic building component schedules.

A.1 Additional Site Tools

Several additional site tools can be used with toposurfaces. You can add property lines and building pads (the cutout for the building location), as shown in Figure A–1. You can also create sub-regions of a toposurface and modify the materials as a preliminary step before you start modifying the contours.

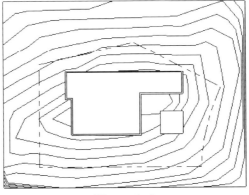

Figure A–1

Creating Property Lines

Property lines can be created by sketching lines or inputting information into a table of distances and bearings.

*   Property lines can, but do not need to be, drawn on a toposurface.

How To: Add a Property Line

1. In the *Massing & Site* tab>Modify Site panel, click (Property Line).
2. In the Create Property Line dialog box, select how you want to create the property line, as shown in Figure A–2.

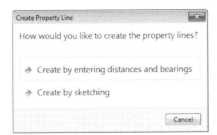

Figure A–2

3. If you selected **Create by sketching**, use the Draw tools to create the property line, and click 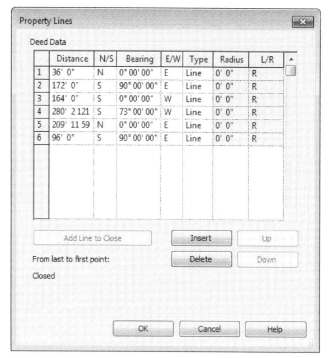 (Finish Edit Mode). If you selected **Create by entering distances and bearings**, fill out the appropriate information, as shown in Figure A–3. Then, click **OK** to finish.

	Distance	N/S	Bearing	E/W	Type	Radius	L/R
1	36' 0"	N	0° 00' 00"	E	Line	0' 0"	R
2	172' 0"	S	90° 00' 00"	E	Line	0' 0"	R
3	164' 0"	S	0° 00' 00"	W	Line	0' 0"	R
4	280' 2 121	S	73° 00' 00"	W	Line	0' 0"	R
5	209' 11 59	N	0° 00' 00"	E	Line	0' 0"	R
6	96' 0"	S	90° 00' 00"	E	Line	0' 0"	R

Figure A–3

- When typing the bearings, you do not need to insert the symbols after the numbers, just separate them with a space. For example, 54 23 47 displays as 54° 23' 47".

- Property lines do not need to close to be inserted into the drawing. Not all of the information you receive for a deed or survey adds up to a closed property line. Click **Add Line to Close**, as required.

- A sketched property line can be converted into a table. Select the property line and in the *Modify | Property Lines* tab> Property Lines panel, click (Edit Table). When it has been converted, it cannot go back to a sketch.

Creating Building Pads

Building pads are not compatible with Site Designer elements.

A building pad on a toposurface cuts or fills the surface around the area of the pad. You can create the pad from existing walls or sketch it with lines. The example in Figure A–4 shows the site with a building pad in section.

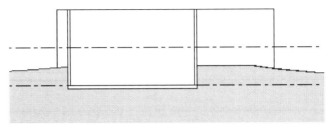

Figure A–4

- A pad is an element in the project that might be in the same plane as a floor.

- A pad affects the surrounding surface and a floor element does not.

- Pads can be toggled off in the Visibility/Graphic Overrides dialog box.

How To: Create a Building Pad

1. Open the site plan view with an existing toposurface. Building pads must be drawn on a toposurface.
2. In the *Massing & Site* tab>Model Site panel, click

   (Building Pad).
3. In the *Modify | Create Pad Boundary* tab>Draw panel, click

   (Boundary Line). You can use any of the Draw tools or

   click (Pick Walls) to establish the outline of the building pad.
4. In Properties, specify a *Level* and a *Height Offset from Level* for the depth of the pad and set any phasing, as required.

5. Click (Finish Edit Mode).

- The sketch of a pad must form a closed loop, but can contain additional loops inside to display openings (such as a courtyard). If you have several buildings, create a pad for each one.

- You can slope pads in one direction for drainage using

   (Slope Arrow).

Creating Subregions

Subregions are not compatible with Site Designer elements.

When you submit a preliminary proposal, you might want to display different materials on parts of the toposurface without changing the contours. You can quickly create subregions of the surface and apply different materials to them, as shown in Figure A–5.

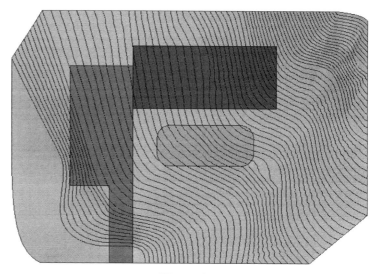

Figure A–5

The subregions display with a boundary, but are still part of the main toposurface. Set the Visual Style to Shaded, Consistent Colors, or Realistic to display the colors of the materials.

How To: Create a Subregion

1. In the *Massing & Site* tab>Modify Site panel, click 🔲 (Subregion).
2. In the *Modify | Create Subregion Boundary* tab>Draw panel, use the Draw tools to outline the subregion.
3. In Properties, modify the *Material* for the subregion as required.
4. Click ✔ (Finish Edit Mode).
5. With the subregion still selected, specify a material in Properties, if you did not do it before.

• To modify a subregion, in the *Modify Topography* tab> Subregion panel, click 🖉 (Edit Boundary).

• To remove a subregion, select it but do not edit the boundary. Press <Delete>.

A.2 Slab Edges

You can add slab edge elements to floors, such as the curb shown in Figure A–6.

The curb is created using a 2D profile sketch.

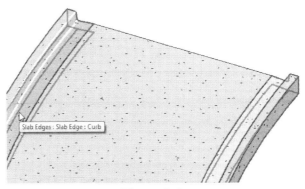

Figure A–6

Once the slab edge is in place it needs to be joined to the floor, as shown in Figure A–7.

Cutting a section through the objects you want to join helps to display them more clearly.

Figure A–7

- Slab edges work with floors, structural floors, and structural slabs, but cannot be applied to roof elements.

How To: Place a Slab Edge

1. Open a 3D view that displays the slab.
2. In the *Architectural* tab>Structure panel, expand (Floor) and click (Floor: Slab Edge).
3. In the Type Selector, select the slab edge type.
4. Select the edges of the slab or floor where you want to apply the slab edge, as shown in Figure A–8. You can press <Tab> to highlight and select all sides of the slab, as required.

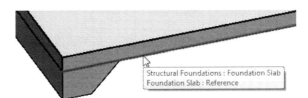

Figure A–8

A.3 Creating Text Types

If you need new text types with a different text size or font (such as for a title or hand-lettering), you can create new ones, as shown in Figure A–9. It is recommended that you create these in a project template so they are available in future projects.

General Notes

1. This project consists of
   furnishing and installing...

Figure A–9

- You can copy and paste text types from one project to another or use **Transfer Project Standards**.

How To: Create Text Types

1. In the *Annotate* tab>Text panel, click ⌄ (Text Types).
2. In the Type Properties dialog box, click **Duplicate**.
3. In the Name dialog box, type a new name and click **OK**.
4. Modify the text parameters, as required. The parameters are shown in Figure A–10.

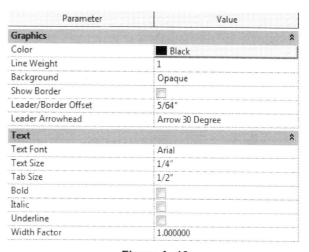

Parameter	Value
Graphics	⌄
Color	■ Black
Line Weight	1
Background	Opaque
Show Border	☐
Leader/Border Offset	5/64"
Leader Arrowhead	Arrow 30 Degree
Text	⌄
Text Font	Arial
Text Size	1/4"
Tab Size	1/2"
Bold	☐
Italic	☐
Underline	☐
Width Factor	1.000000

Figure A–10

- The **Background** parameter can be set to **Opaque** or **Transparent**. An opaque background includes a masking region that hides lines or elements beneath the text.

- In the *Text* area, the **Width Factor** parameter controls the width of the lettering, but does not affect the height. A width factor greater than **1** spreads the text out and a width factor less than **1** compresses it.

- The **Show Border** parameter, when selected, includes a rectangle around the text.

5. Click **OK** to close the Type Properties dialog box.

A.4 Revision Tracking

When a set of working drawings has been put into production, you need to show where changes are made. Typically, these are shown on sheets using revision clouds and tags along with a revision schedule in the title block, as shown in Figure A–11. The revision information is setup in the Sheet Issues/Revisions dialog box.

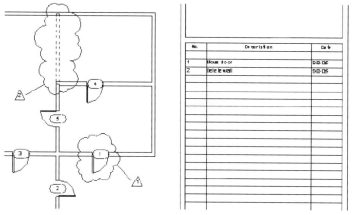

Figure A–11

- More than one revision cloud can be associated with a revision number.

- The title blocks that come with the Autodesk Revit software already have a revision schedule inserted into the title area. It is recommended that you also add a revision schedule to your company title block.

How To: Add Revision Information to the Project

1. In the *View* tab>Sheet Composition panel, click 🌀 (Sheet Issues/Revisions).
2. In the Sheet Issues/Revisions dialog box, set the type of *Numbering* you want to use.
3. Click **Add** to add a new revision.

4. Specify the *Date* and *Description* for the revision, as shown in Figure A–12.

Figure A–12

- Do not modify the *Issued*, *Issued by*, or *Issued to* columns. You should wait to issue revisions until you are ready to print the sheets.

5. Click **OK** when you have finished adding revisions.
   - To remove a revision, select its *Sequence* number and click **Delete**.

Revision Options

- *Numbering:* specify **Per Project** (the numbering sequence is used throughout the project) or **Per Sheet** (the number sequence is per sheet).

- *Row:* To reorganize the revisions, select a row and click **Move Up** and **Move Down**, or use **Merge Up** and **Merge Down** to combine the revisions into one.

- *Numbering Options:* Click **Numeric...** or **Alphanumeric...** to bring up the Customize Numbering Options dialog box where you can specify the numbers or letters used in the sequence as well as any prefix or suffix, as shown for the *Alphanumeric* tab in Figure A–13.

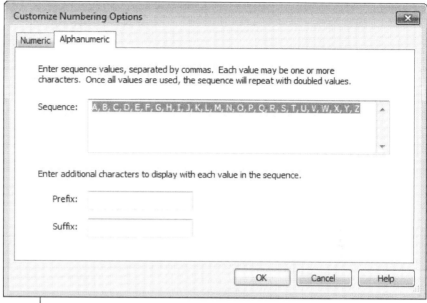

Figure A–13

- *Arc length:* Specify the length of the arcs that form the revision cloud. It is an annotation element and is scaled according to the view scale.

How To: Add Revision Clouds and Tag

1. In the *Annotate* tab>Detail panel, click ⬡ (Revision Cloud).
2. In the *Modify | Create Revision Cloud Sketch* tab>Draw panel, use the draw tools to create the cloud.
3. Click ✓ (Finish Edit Mode).

4. In the Options Bar or Properties, expand the Revision drop-down list and select from the Revision list, as shown in Figure A–14.

If the revision table has not be set up, you can do this at a later date.

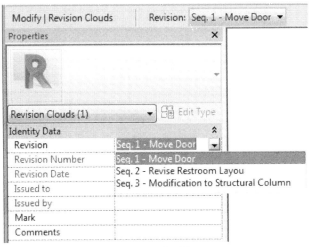

Figure A–14

5. In the *Annotate* tab>Tag panel, click 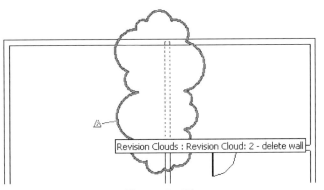 (Tag By Category).
6. Select the revision cloud to tag. A tooltip containing the revision number and revision from the cloud properties displays when you hover the cursor over the revision cloud, as shown in Figure A–15.

Figure A–15

- If the revision cloud tag is not loaded, load **Revision Tag.rfa** from the *Annotations* folder in the Library.

- The *Revision Number* and *Date* are automatically assigned according to the specifications in the revision table.

- Double-click on the edge of revision cloud to switch to the Edit Sketch mode and modify the size or location of the revision cloud arcs.

- You can create an open cloud (e.g., as a tree line), as shown in Figure A–16.

Figure A–16

Issuing Revisions

When you have completed the revisions and are ready to submit new documents to the field, you should first lock the revision for the record. This is called issuing the revision. An issued revision is noted in the tooltip of a revision cloud, as shown in Figure A–17.

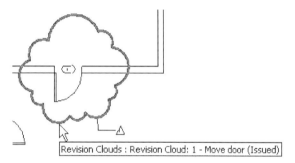

Revision Clouds : Revision Cloud: 1 - Move door (Issued)

Figure A–17

How To: Issue Revisions

1. In the Sheet Issues/Revisions dialog box, in the row for the revision that you are issuing, type a name in the *Issued to* and *Issued by* fields, as required.
2. In the same row, select **Issued**.
3. Continue issuing any other revisions, as required.
4. Click **OK** to finish.

- Once **Issued** is selected, you cannot modify that revision in the Revisions dialog box or by moving the revision cloud(s). The tooltip on the cloud(s) note that it is **Issued**.

- You can unlock the revision by clearing the **Issued** option. Unlocking enables you to modify the revision after it has been locked.

A.5 Annotating Dependent Views

The **Duplicate as a Dependent** command creates a copy of the view and links it to the selected view. Changes made to the original view are also made in the dependent view and vice-versa. Use dependent views when the building model is so large you need to split the building up on separate sheets, as shown in Figure A–18.

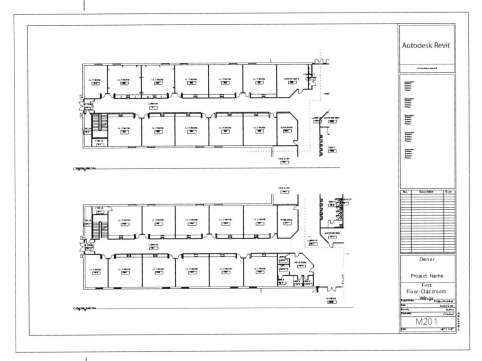

Figure A–18

- Using one overall view with several dependent views makes it easier to see changes, such as *to the scale* or *detail level*.

- Dependent views display in the Project Browser under the top-level view, as shown in Figure A–19.

Figure A–19

How To: Duplicate Dependent Views

1. Select the view you want to use as the top-level view.
2. Right-click and select **Duplicate View>Duplicate as a Dependent**.
3. Rename the dependent views as required.
4. Modify the crop region of the dependent view to show the specified portion of the model.

- If you want to separate a dependent view from the original view, right-click on the dependent view and select **Convert to independent view**.

Annotating Views

To clarify and annotate dependent views, use **Matchlines** and **View References**, as shown in Figure A–20.

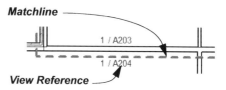

Figure A–20

- Sketch Matchlines in the primary view to specify where dependent views separate. They display in all related views and extend through all levels of the project by default.

- View References are special tags that display the sheet location of the dependent views.

How To: Add Matchlines

1. In the *View* tab>Sheet Composition panel, click (Matchline).

2. In the Draw panel, click (Line) and sketch the location of the matchline.

3. In the Matchline panel, click (Finish Edit Mode) when you are finished.

- To modify an existing matchline, select it and click (Edit Sketch) in the *Modify | Matchline* tab>Mode panel.

- To modify the color and linetype of Matchlines, in the *Manage* tab>Settings panel, click ⬚ (Object Styles). In the Object Styles dialog box that opens, in the *Annotation Objects* tab, you can make changes to Matchline properties.

How To: Add View References

1. In the *View* tab>Sheet Composition panel or *Annotate* tab> Tag panel, click ⬚ (View Reference).
2. In the *Modify | View Reference* tab>View Reference panel specify the *View Type* and *Target View*, as shown in Figure A–21.

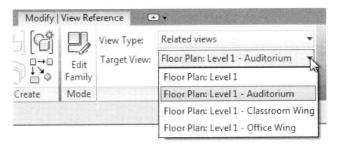

Figure A–21

3. Place the tag on the side of the matchline that corresponds to the target view.
4. Select another target view from the list and place the tag on the other side of the matchline.
5. The tags display as empty dashes until the views are placed onto sheets. They then update to include the detail and sheet number, as shown in Figure A–22.

Figure A–22

- Double-click on the view reference to open the associated view.

- If only a label named **REF** displays when you place a view reference, it means you need to load and update the tag. The **View Reference.rfa** tag is located in the *Annotations* folder. Once you have the tag loaded, in the Type Selector, select one of the view references and, in Properties, click 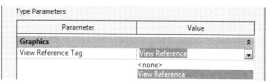 (Edit Type). Select the **View Reference** tag in the drop-down list, as shown in Figure A–23, and click **OK** to close the dialog box. The new tag displays.

Figure A–23

A.6 Importing and Exporting Schedules

Schedules are views and can be copied into your project from other projects. Only the formatting information is copied; the information about individually scheduled items is not included. That information is automatically added by the project the schedule is copied into. You can also export the schedule information to be used in spreadsheets.

How To: Import Schedules

1. In the *Insert* tab>Import panel, expand (Insert from File) and click (Insert Views from File).
2. In the Open dialog box, locate the project file containing the schedule you want to use.
3. Select the schedules you want to import, as shown in Figure A–24.

*If the referenced project contains many types of views, change Views: to **Show schedules and reports only**.*

Figure A–24

4. Click **OK**.

How To: Export Schedule Information

1. Switch to the schedule view that you want to export.

2. In the Application Menu, click 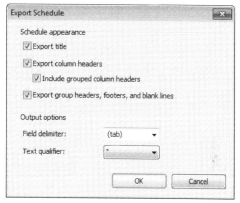 (Export)> (Reports)> (Schedule).

3. Select a location and name for the text file in the Export Schedule dialog box and click **Save**.

4. In the Export Schedule dialog box, set the options in the *Schedule appearance* and *Output options* areas that best suit your spreadsheet software, as shown in Figure A–25.

Figure A–25

5. Click **OK**. A new text file is created that you can open in a spreadsheet, as shown in Figure A–26.

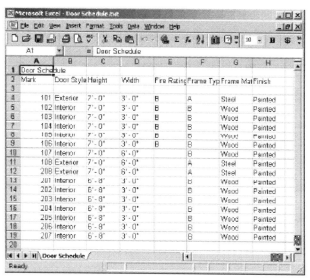

Figure A–26

A.7 Creating Basic Schedules

A Building Component schedule is a table view of the type and instance parameters of a specific element. You can specify the parameters (fields) you want to include in the schedule. All of the parameters found in the type of element you are scheduling are available to use. For example, a door schedule (as shown in Figure A–27) can include instance parameters that are automatically filled in (such as the **Height** and **Width**) and type parameters that might need to have the information assigned in the schedule or element type (such as the **Fire Rating** and **Frame**).

\<Door Schedule\>							

A	B	C	D	E	F	G	H
Mark	Height	Width	Fire Rating	Frame Type	Frame Material	Finish	Function
2	7' - 0"	10' - 0"	A	A	Steel	Brushed	Exterior
3	6' - 8"	3' - 0"	B	B	Wood	Paint	Interior
4	6' - 8"	3' - 0"	B	B	Wood	Paint	Interior
5	6' - 8"	3' - 0"	B	B	Wood	Paint	Interior
6	6' - 8"	3' - 0"	B	B	Wood	Paint	Interior

Figure A–27

How To: Create a Building Component Schedule

1. In the *View* tab>Create panel, expand ▦ (Schedules) and click ▦ (Schedule/Quantities) or in the Project Browser, right-click on the Schedule/Quantities node and select **New Schedule/Quantities**.

2. In the New Schedule dialog box, select the type of schedule you want to create (e.g., Doors) from the *Category* list, as shown in Figure A–28.

In the Filter list drop-down list, you can specify the discipline(s) to show only the categories that you want to display.

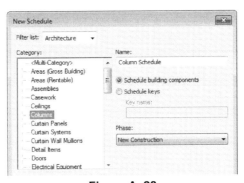

Figure A–28

3. Type a new *Name*, if the default does not suit.

4. Select **Schedule building components.**
5. Specify the *Phase* as required.
6. Click **OK**.
7. Fill out the information in the Schedule Properties dialog box. This includes the information in the *Fields*, *Filter*, *Sorting/Grouping*, *Formatting*, and *Appearance* tabs.
8. Once you have entering the schedule properties, click **OK**. A schedule report is created in its own view.

Schedule Properties – Fields Tab

In the *Fields* tab, you can select from a list of available fields and organize them in the order in which you want them to display in the schedule, as shown in Figure A–29.

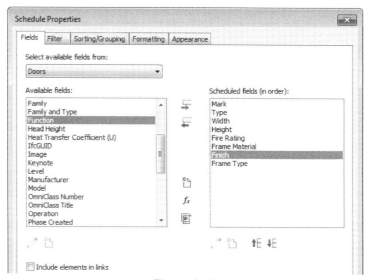

Figure A–29

How To: Fill out the Fields Tab

You can also double-click on a field to move it from the Available fields to the Scheduled fields area.

1. In the *Available fields* area, select one or more fields you want to add to the schedule and click ⯮ (Add parameter(s)). The field(s) are placed in the *Scheduled fields (in order)* area.
2. Continue adding fields, as required.

  • Click ⯬ (Remove parameter(s)) to move a field from the *Scheduled fields* area back to the *Available fields* area.

  • Use ↑E (Move parameter up) and ↓E (Move parameter down) to change the order of the scheduled fields.

Other Fields Tab Options

Select available fields from	Enables you to select additional category fields for the specified schedule. The available list of fields depends on the original category of the schedule. Typically, they include room information.
Include elements in links	Includes elements that are in files linked to the current project, so that their elements can be included in the schedule.
(New parameter)	Adds a new field according to your specification. New fields can be placed by instance or by type.
fx **(Add Calculated parameter)**	Enables you to create a field that uses a formula based on other fields.
(Combine parameters)	Enables you to combine two or more parameters in one column. You can put any fields together even if they are used in another column.
(Edit parameter)	Enables you to edit custom fields. This is grayed out if you select a standard field.
(Delete parameter)	Deletes selected custom fields. This is grayed out if you select a standard field.

Schedule Properties – Filter Tab

In the *Filter* tab, you can set up filters so that only elements meeting specific criteria are included in the schedule. For example, you might only want to show information for one level, as shown in Figure A–30. You can create filters for up to eight values. All values must be satisfied for the elements to display.

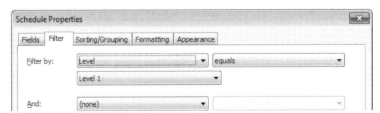

Figure A–30

- The parameter you want to use as a filter must be included in the schedule. You can hide the parameter once you have completed the schedule, if required.

Filter by	Specifies the field to filter. Not all fields are available to be filtered.
Condition	Specifies the condition that must be met. This includes options such as **equal**, **not equal**, **greater than**, and **less than**.
Value	Specifies the value of the element to be filtered. You can select from a drop-down list of appropriate values. For example, if you set *Filter By* to **Level**, it displays the list of levels in the project.

Schedule Properties – Sorting/Grouping Tab

In the *Sorting/Grouping* tab, you can set how you want the information to be sorted, as shown in Figure A–31. For example, you can sort by **Mark** (number) and then **Type**.

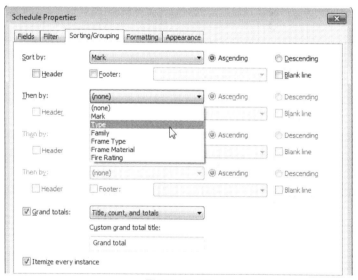

Figure A–31

Sort by	Enables you to select the field(s) you want to sort by. You can select up to four levels of sorting.
Ascending/ Descending	Sorts fields in **Ascending** or **Descending** order.
Header/ Footer	Enables you to group similar information and separate it by a **Header** with a title and/or a **Footer** with quantity information.
Blank line	Adds a blank line between groups.
Grand totals	Selects which totals to display for the entire schedule. You can specify a name to display in the schedule for the Grand total.
Itemize every instance	If selected, displays each instance of the element in the schedule. If not selected, displays only one instance of each type, as shown below.

<Window Schedule>						
A	B	C	D	E	F	G
Type	Count	Height	Width	Manufacturer	Model	Comments
36 x 36	6	3' 0"	3' - 0"	Anderson	FX3636	
36" x 48"	7	4' - 0"	3' - 0"	Anderson	FX3648	
Grand total: 13						

Schedule Properties – Formatting Tab

In the *Formatting* tab, you can control how the headers of each field display, as shown in Figure A–32.

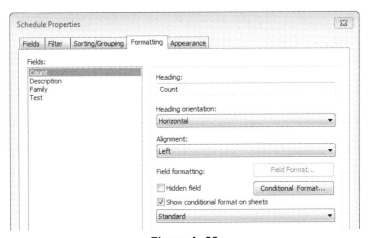

Figure A–32

Fields	Enables you to select the field for which you want to modify the formatting.
Heading	Enables you to change the heading of the field if you want it to be different from the field name. For example, you might want to replace **Mark** (a generic name) with the more specific **Door Number** in a door schedule.
Heading orientation	Enables you to set the heading on sheets to **Horizontal** or **Vertical**. This does not impact the schedule view.
Alignment	Aligns the text in rows under the heading to be **Left**, **Right**, or **Center**.
Field Format...	Sets the units format for the length, area, volume, angle, or number field. By default, this is set to use the project settings.
Conditional Format...	Sets up the schedule to display visual feedback based on the conditions listed.
Hidden field	Enables you to hide a field. For example, you might want to use a field for sorting purposes, but not have it display in the schedule. You can also modify this option in the schedule view later.
Show conditional format on sheets	Select if you want the color code set up in the Conditional Format dialog box to display on sheets.
Calculation options	Select the type of calculation you want to use. All values in a field are: • **Standard** - Calculated separately. • **Calculate totals** - Added together. • **Calculate minimum** - Reviewed and only the smallest amount is displayed. • **Calculate maximum** - Reviewed and only the largest amount is displayed. • **Calculate minimum and maximum** - Reviewed and both the smallest and largest amounts are displayed. • This is often used with rebar sets.

Schedule Properties – Appearance Tab

In the *Appearance* tab, you can set the text style and grid options for a schedule, as shown in Figure A–33.

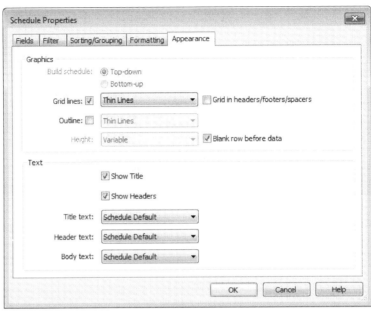

Figure A–33

Grid lines	Displays lines between each instance listed and around the outside of the schedule. Select the style of lines from the drop-down list; this controls all lines for the schedule, unless modified.
Grid in headers/ footers/spacers	Extends the vertical grid lines between the columns.
Outline	Specify a different line type for the outline of the schedule.
Blank row before data	Select this option if you want a blank row to be displayed before the data begins in the schedule.
Show Title/Show Headers	Select these options to include the text in the schedule.
Title text/Header text/Body Text	Select the text style for the title, header, and body text.

Schedule Properties

Schedule views have properties including the *View Name*, *Phases* and methods of returning to the Schedule Properties dialog box as shown in Figure A–34. In the *Other* area, select the button next to the tab that you want to open in the Schedule Properties dialog box. In the dialog box, you can switch from tab to tab and make any required changes to the overall schedule.

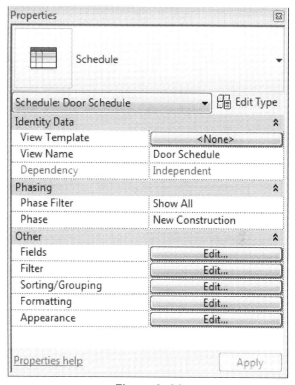

Figure A–34

A.8 Creating a Repeating Detail

Repeating detail components are very useful when working on complex details, such as those that include a brick wall. You can also create a repeating detail using any detail component, such as the glass block shown in Figure A–35.

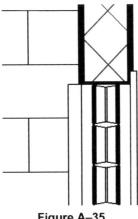

Figure A–35

How To: Create a Repeating Detail

1. Load the detail component you want to use.

2. In the *Annotate* tab>Detail panel, expand (Component) and click (Repeating Detail Component).

3. In Properties, click (Edit Type).
4. In the Type Properties dialog box, click **Duplicate...**. Enter a name.
5. Set the *Detail* parameter. This is the component name.
6. Fill out the rest of the parameters, as shown in Figure A–36.

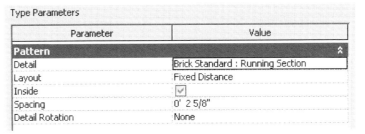

Parameter	Value
Pattern	
Detail	Brick Standard : Running Section
Layout	Fixed Distance
Inside	☑
Spacing	0' 2 5/8"
Detail Rotation	None

Figure A–36

7. Set the *Layout* to **Fill Available Space**, **Fixed Distance**, **Fixed Number**, or **Maximum Spacing**. Select **Inside** if you want all components to be within the specified distance or line. Leaving this option clear causes the first component to start before the first point.
8. Set the *Spacing* between components if you are using **Fixed Distance** or **Maximum Spacing**.
9. Set the *Detail Rotation* as required, and close the dialog box.

Command Summary

Button	Command	Location
Annotations		
	Matchline	• **Ribbon:** *View* tab>Sheet Composition panel
	View Reference	• **Ribbon:** *View* tab>Sheet Composition panel or *Annotate* tab>Tag panel
Details		
	Edit Type	• **Properties** (with a Repeating Detail element selected)
Revisions		
	Revision Cloud	• **Ribbon:** *Annotate* tab>Detail panel
	Sheet Issues/ Revisions	• **Ribbon:** *Manage* tab>Settings panel> expand Additional Settings
Schedules		
	Insert Views from File	• **Ribbon:** *Insert* tab>expand **Insert from File**
n/a	**Schedule (Export)**	• **Application Menu:** expand Export> Reports>Schedule
	Schedule/ Quantities	• **Ribbon:** *View* tab>Create panel> expand Schedules • **Project Browser:** right-click on Schedule/Quantities node> New Schedule/Quantities...
Site Tools		
	Building Pad	• **Ribbon:** *Massing & Site* tab>Model Site panel
	Property Line	• **Ribbon:** *Massing & Site* tab>Modify Site panel
	Subregion	• **Ribbon:** *Massing & Site* tab>Modify Site panel
Slabs		
	Slab Edges	• **Ribbon:** *Architecture tab*> Build panel> expand Floor

Index